About the Author

Romeo Richards is the founder of the Business Education Centre, an institute that shows professional entrepreneurs such as doctors, lawyers, dentists, consultants, trainers, coaches, and security firm owners how to make "7 Figure" in twelve months. He is also the creator of the Business Success Quadrangle Framework and The Blue Ocean Strategy Canvas for: doctors, lawyers, dentists, consultants, retailers, coaches, trainers and security firms.

He has authored eight books on retail profit improvement and is currently writing four additional books on retail store design, visual merchandising, how to market a retail store and how to make profit in retail and the "How to effectively market and manage a professional firm" series for doctors, lawyers, dentists, consultants, trainers, coaches and security firms.

He has authored several White Papers and regularly writes articles on entrepreneur development, retail profit improvement and speak on the same.

Mr Gamble of Proctor and Gamble once said "Any fool can make soap. It takes a genius to sell soap."

This statement is so fitting for the current retail environment where retail stores are springing up left and right both online and offline. Currently, anyone, even without a single penny can open a fully functional online retail store within minutes.

This phenomenon is frustrating many brick and mortar retailers who have to spend a fortune to drive footfall to their stores. Books and entertainment retailers are all but wiped out.

The likes of Amazon and eBay have devastated the entire retail sector. Ghost town after ghost town continues to appear in many city centres across the UK, as one retailer after the other ceases to exist.

Powerful retail brands that were once considered permanent fixtures on the High Street to the absolute shock of most people have disappeared overnight.

The situation became so bad in the UK in late 2011, the British government was forced to set up a commission to investigate reasons behind the failures. The Australian and other Western governments were also forced to step in to protect their retail industry to avert mass unemployment.

Did government intervention change the fortune of the retail industry?

Like most governments band aid programs, it provided the industry temporary reprieve. However, because the fundamental issues bedevilling the industry remained unaddressed, therefore, the industry continues to struggle.

So what can the retailers do to breathe new life into their dying industry?

The answer to this and other questions are in this book.

The aim of this book is to teach retailers how to navigate the changing retail environment. There is no doubt online shopping has changed consumers' buying behaviour.

In the coming years, more consumers are going to be doing their shopping online. This is going to further affect brick and mortar retailers.

Despite what might seem a gloomy picture, people still prefer doing business with other people.

A vast majority of information in books can be found online for free, yet millions of books are still sold each year.

Why are people still buying books when the information in books can be found online for free?
Answer: people still trust information from traditional publishers than free unregulated information.

This is the same reason the majority of people will continue to shop in brick and mortar retail stores despite the fact that they can do all of their shopping from the comfort of their homes.

The only question you need to answer is; would they buy from your store or from that of your competitor?

You will be able to answer this question after reading this book. It will teach you how to ensure your store becomes their store of choice.

How to Make Profit in Retail

Romeo Richards

www.theprofitexperts.co.uk
+44(0)78 650 49508
romeo@theprofitexperts.co.uk

© Copyright Protected; 2013. The Business Education Center. All Rights Reserved.

Dedication

I wrote about vision as your reason for doing anything. I do what I do first and foremost to be an example to my son.

Secondly, to have the ability to help my people shed the curse of poverty.

Alex this book is for you!

Africa this book is in your honour!

Table of Contents

About the Book i
About the Author iii
Dedication vii
Acknowledgements xi
Why You Should Read This Book xv
Introduction xix

Part One – Store Design Blueprint 1
The Psychology of A Beautiful Store Design 3
How To Increase Retail Sales With Attractive Store Design 17
How to Increase Retail Sales With Brand Image Selling 41
Designing Store For Increase Customer Flow 53
How To Choose Your Store Colour And Layout 63
The Best Retail Store Lighting System 71
How To Wow Customers With Creative Storefront Design 83
How To Choose The Right Materials For Store Design 93
How To Design A Profitably Retail Store 107
The Best Store Design Technologies 115

Part Two – Visual Merchandising Display 119
The Psychology Of Visual Merchandising Display 121
How To Use Visual Merchandising To Increase Sales 133
Challenges Facing Visual Merchandisers 149
How To Burst The Price Myth With Creative Merchandise Display 161
The Best Merchandise Display Strategy 177
How To Maximise Display Space Allocation With Creative Display 191
The Benefits Planogram Software 205
How To Profitably Display Merchandise 219

Part Three – The Most Effective Retail Loss Prevention Strategies.... 229

The Culture of Loss Prevention 231

Employee Theft 267

Retail Employee Error 295

An Efficient Receiving Process 319

Shrinkage the Profit Killer 333

Perishable Shrinkage 335

Non-Perishable Shrinkage 347

Shoplifting 359

The Most Effective Retail Loss Prevention Technologies 393

Summary 421

Great Books by Romeo 422

Book Romeo 431

Acknowledgements

My sincere gratitude to Mr. White, John and Michael for editing the book.

Thanks Jen for formatting it and Joseph for managing the entire project.

How to Make Profit in Retail

Romeo Richards

www.theprofitexperts.co.uk
+44(0)78 650 49508
romeo@theprofitexperts.co.uk

Why You Should Read This Book

During my research for this book, I visited Harrods. I have heard a lot about Harrods, but had not actually visited it. When my sister visited me from the States, Harrods was on her list of places to visit; however, by the time we arrived it was already closed.

You can imagine my anticipation and apprehension at visiting one of the most famous retail stores where royalties, Hollywood A-list stars and the "who is who" from around the world go shopping.

In my mind, everything in Harrods was made of gold. I even bought a special outfit for the occasion to ensure I was in sync with the royalties and A-list stars.

I was hoping I will catch a glimpse of Roman Abramovich and some of his billionaire friends or some Saudi prince.

However, instead of Russian oligarch or Middle East Sheikh; what caught my attention was a bus.

I had bought the identical bus for my son from ASDA. It was the same bus in the same packaging.

An odd question popped into my mind when I noticed the bus: why is it that the same bus, in the same packaging, probably made in the same factory in China, by the same people, was being sold in Harrods for almost three times the price it was sold for in ASDA?

At first it was a mystery to me. But as I walked around Harrods the answer came to me.

ASDA sells toy bus. Harrods sells classy toy bus; even if it is made in the same factory in China.

There is a distinction and that distinction is what this book is about.

The price of a product is not determined by the cost of bringing that product to the marketplace as we are taught in business school, rather by *who is buying; how much they are willing to pay and how the product is sold.*

The reason the same bus, made in the same factory in China is sold in Harrods for almost three times the price it is sold for in ASDA comes down to *who shops at Harrods and how the bus is sold to them.*

For a start, cheapskates like me are not Harrods target market. Harrods know their target market is oil Sheikhs and Russian oligarchs whose focus is not on the products but on *the manner in which the product is sold to them.*

This is a very important point I will like you to take from this book. Most retailers fail because they ignore this simple but fundamental marketing principle. The majority of retailers do not even know their target market.

They open their stores, stock them with goods and hope that customers will show up simply because they are open for business.

This is a very big mistake!

You first need to decide who you want to sell to and then create a selling environment to attract those types of people.

Harrods have obviously decided who they want to sell to, so they created a selling environment that appeals to only those types of people.

Harrods is one of the most successful retailers in the world. Their success stems from three things:

- Beautiful store design
- Attractive visual merchandise displays
- Effective loss prevention

Harrods have one of the best store design and visual merchandise display in the retail industry…Period.

I mean that literally because in my research for this and my other retail books, I researched the best retail stores across the globe.

Most retailers underestimate the relevance of store design and visual merchandise display to their success.

Your selling environment determines the customers you attract and the price you can charge.

The retail business is 'showbiz.' The extent to which you are willing to put up a great performance for your customers is the extent to which you are going to succeed.

Harrods also have one of the most effective loss prevention strategies in the retail business.

To shoplift from Harrods you have to be:

- A member of a retail crime gang syndicate
- Really brave
- Really stupid

The goal of this book is to teach you the psychology of designing a beautiful store and attractive visual merchandise displays as well as how to devise an effective loss prevention strategy.

This book is not about changing or improving upon what you are already doing; it is about hidden opportunities in your retail business that you have not paid attention to.

I guarantee you, you will easily triple or even quadruple your profit margin in less than 90 days by implementing a third of the information in this book.

Introduction

In his book: "The One Thing You Need to Know" author Marcus Buckingham said when he interviewed Sir Terry Leahy who transformed Tesco into an international powerhouse: he asked him; what was the key to Tesco's transformation.

Sir Terry Leahy said the key to Tesco's transformation was asking and answering the question: Who do we serve. After answering the question, the next step in the process was putting in place mechanism to ensure they serve their target market better.

This is a very critical point which many retailers ignore hence the reason they continue to struggle or cease to exist.

We now live in a world in which consumers are faced with what author Barry Schwartz calls the 'paradox of choice'. Consumers are overwhelmed with choices.

The average person is exposed to over three thousand adverts every single day. This excludes online ads from social media and email marketing. If we add the fact that consumers can now do their shopping online, you see that the brick and mortar retail sector is on the brink.

The High Street in many Western cities will undergo complete transformation five years from now. Many of the brands that have graced the High Street for decades will cease to exist.

Despite the rise in online shopping, consumers are still going to shop at their favourite shopping malls and High Street. However, the reasons consumers visit a shopping mall or High Street has changed.

I for one have not visited a book store for the last five years. Yet I do buy a lot of books. When I want to buy a book, I just flip open my laptop or phone and order my book on Amazon.

There are millions upon millions of shoppers like me who are increasingly turning to the internet. How can retailers get someone like me back into their stores?

However, the key question is: why do I prefer to shop online instead of going to a physical brick and mortar retail store?

Let me answer this question with a story.

Every time I visit my local PC World and I ask staff for help, they will just point to the direction of the product. If I needed explanation as to which model will be suitable for me, at best they will have no clue, at worst they will lie to me.

Everything that is sold at PC World can be found on Amazon. On Amazon, there are even reviews and forums for people to help me choose the right products for my situation.

So why should I drive all the way to PC World to by an item when I can get it on Amazon?

The only reason I will want to go to PC World is to be able to speak to another human being. But it those people will stand from afar and just point and if they have no clue about the product, I might as well take my chances online.

The situation is not unique to PC World; it is the norm in the retail industry. In my local Staples for example, there is only a single staff member there capable of cutting stamps and doing most of the admin works.

When she is off, there is no other staff in the store capable of doing anything. That type of customer service was acceptable ten or twenty years ago. In this connected age, it is the wrong type of customer service.

Retailers spend millions on marketing in an effort to drive footfall to their stores without understanding that marketing strategies of yester year will not work in the new retail environment.

The only form of marketing that will work in this paradox of choice age is permission and relationship marketing. Most importantly it is about building the marketing into the product and service.

What this means for the retail industry is having well-trained staff capable of answering customers questions.

It is about designing your store in such a way that it attracts shoppers as they walk pass it.

It is about creating an attractive visual merchandise display that tells the story of your brand and speaks directly to your target market.

It is about having a loss prevention strategy that is fit for the current retail environment.

This is what this book is about, to help you develop a retail growth blueprint that results in rapid profit increase.

Part one deals with retail store design. It teaches how to create a store design that both attract shoppers as they walk pass and retain them for longer in the store.

Part two addresses visual merchandise display. The focus is how to create an attractive yet secure display.

The third part focuses on how to create an effective loss prevention strategy.

The retail environment is changing. Strategies and tactics of the past will not work in the new retail environment. This book provides you the type of strategies that will help you to not only survive the current fierce competitive retail landscape but to be profitable in the process.

Part One
Store Design Blueprint

Chapter One

The Psychology of A Beautiful Store Design

Harrods is one of the more successful retailers in the world. In 2011, in the thick of the global financial crisis; the London based retailer's annual sales were in the region of a billion pounds. When thousands of well-known retail brands were struggling to survive and some forced to close shop.

What is it that makes Harrods more successful than most retail organisations?

Harrods success can be attributed to the following three factors:

- Good store design
- Attractive visual merchandise displays
- Effective loss prevention strategy

The ability to design their store or create visual merchandise displays that incorporate all these elements is one of the determining factors for the success of Harrods and many of the world's most successful retailers.

Harrods' store design is in a class of its own. It is unique, innovative and clever. One important element of their store design is the concept of the stores inside. The store is designed in such a way that as customers move from one department to the next, they get the feeling of moving from one store to another in a shopping centre. Whoever conceived that design concept provided Harrods with a huge competitive advantage over its competitors.

Harrods's visual merchandise displays are as attractive and inviting as displays can get. As customers move from one designer outlet to another; they are met by a completely different display that is indicative of that designer. It is as if the designers themselves went into Harrods to arrange the displays.

Store design and visual merchandise displays need to serve four objectives:

- Attract potential customers as they pass by the store
- Entice those potential customers to enter into the store
- Maintain their interest whilst they are in the store
- Persuade them to buy.

Harrods' ability to effectively utilise these four principles in its store design and visual merchandise displays has been responsible for its phenomenal success.

In his book "Blink", author Malcolm Gladwell introduced the concept of thinking without thinking. "Blink" "the power of thin slicing" and "rapid cognition" is the type of thinking process that occurs in the blink of an eye.

As shoppers walk through a shopping mall of two three hundred stores or a busy high street, they are thin slicing each and every store.

What entices them to choose one store over the other is what Mr. Gladwell alluded to in his first book "Tipping Point"…the little things that make a huge difference. Some of the little things determine whether someone enters your store as opposed to that of your competitor is your store design.

As one walks around Harrods, it is evident that their success does not stem from 'Made in China' products that can be found in stores all over the UK. Their success comes from their ability to apply the principles from "Blink" and the "Tipping Point" to their store design and visual merchandise displays.

Harrods success can be linked to its belief that little things make a big difference:

> Little things like having store associates within easy reach of every customer
>
> Little things like the extraordinary use of mannequins

Harrods success also results from having one of the best store designs and visual merchandising display in the retail industry.

What is Store Design Psychology?

All retailers strive to satisfy every customer that enters their store and give them the kind of service they desire. Offering good customer service and fine quality products are a given in the retail business. But a core element that attracts customers into a retail store is the aesthetics of the store.

The majority of shoppers are more likely to enter a store and purchase when the store has an attractive layout and is convenient for shopping. The key in persuading more shoppers to visit a store lies in it having an attractive store design.

Every retail store has a unique design which entices shoppers into the store. Retail stores are designed to generate an easy and delightful shopping experience. A very important element in retail store design is the psychology that augments the design.

The large windows endowed with eye-catching designs; aisle widths and rack heights are carefully detailed to create a positive feeling which lures shoppers into a store.

All four corners of the store must be viewed and evaluated accurately. The wall colours, signage, checkout counters, racking schemes, displays, and other areas form part of the store layout.

The interior design of a retail store plays a key role in attracting shopper and increasing sales. Proper placement of props such as mannequins and racks help the store to appear more attractive. Creating a theme also helps develop vibes that entice shoppers.

A well designed store makes it convenient and easy for customers to shop. When a shop creates a design concept that matches with the products they are selling, it makes it easier and appealing for the customers to buy.

Furthermore, having a colour scheme that matches the products adds more pleasure for customers to shop. The right colour scheme creates a positive mood for the customer when shopping. For example, a baby clothing store that uses light pastel colours reflects the target market.

The majority of people derive pleasure from shopping in a light and spacious environment. A spacious and clutter-free store is also an advantage for you and your employees.

It becomes easy for your store associates to watch over products and reduce shoplifting. Tables in the central areas, cabinets and shelves towards the back walls create the illusion of a more spacious store.

Apple stores are always packed as customers just love hanging out in their stores. The Early Learning Centre is a children's toy store in the UK. I have been to a few of them and noticed there is not enough space for children to sample toys. You cannot have a toy store that is compact; you lose the potential for sale.

Some retail store designs tend to be excessive. Excessive and unnecessary use of colour and other design elements results in the opposite effect. Instead of enticing shoppers into the store, it repels them.

Therefore, striking the balance between an attractive store that serves as a magnet for shoppers and one that repels them needs an understanding of store design psychology.

Most retailers forget that retailing is about sales and marketing. The most effective marketing strategy a retailer has at his disposal is a well-designed store and attractive merchandise displays.

When there are two or three hundred stores in a shopping centre, the difference between deciding to enter in or pass by a store rests on the design of the store front.

When customers are in a store there needs to be a reason for them to stay longer. The longer they stay, the higher the chances of them buying.

The three main aspects of a store design that keep customers engaged for longer are:

- Designs that enables good customer flow
- An attractive and good lighting system
- Overall atmosphere of the store

Why do people buy?

Why do people buy? We all buy for diverse reasons. The human thought process is complex and irrational. Even though we try to rationalise our actions based upon artificial environmental factors; the reality is, we all do things for the same three reasons:

- Status

- Survival
- Sex

What does everyone want?

In marketing we are taught to believe that individual's wants are different.

This statement is true to an extent but not exactly true. Human psychology has not changed since the dawn of time. The same desire humans had when we lived in caves; we still hold those desires today.

Every prospect, client or customer wants the following three things:

- Result
- Solution
- Relief from something

How these three things manifest themselves in our brain takes the form of the products and services we choose to buy. However, the fundamental principle is this: in the final analysis when customers take out their credit card to buy a product or service, no matter what that product or service is, they are doing so to satisfy all or at least one of the above.

Being aware of that, as you prepare to design your store, here are some questions that should be going through your mind:

1) Which one of the above three are you marketing to satisfy with your store design?
2) Which one of the three are you marketing to satisfy with your shop window display?
3) What emotion are you aiming to trigger?

4) What result should they imagine your store is going to produce for them?

5) What solution should they think your store design would provide?

6) Finally, what pain is the store design going to relieve?

This is not to say that when someone enters your store they will achieve all of those results, your store design just needs to plant the perception of those results in their minds.

But there is a catch. The store designer needs to know the benefit and hidden benefit. It is only when the store designer knows the benefit behind the benefit that they will be able to create a beautiful and attractive store design that captivates your target market.

Figure 1: Think of the benefit behind the benefit in your display

I will use Victoria's Secret as an example. A woman passing by a Victoria Secret store spots sexy lingerie in the shop window; her first thought is: I will look sexy in that or that bra would prop up my cleavage.

But here is the catch, that bra would prop up her cleavage not because she just wants her cleavage propped up but to attract the opposite sex. (I must add a disclaimer that here I am not trying to be sexist I am just using this as an example.)

Therefore as you design your store, your aim should be to match the thinking of the shopper with your store design. Do not design your store to appeal to the beauty of the breast but the outcome that the beautiful breast will result in – the opposite sex!

A major part of store design is being able to analyse shoppers thought process. As was alluded to previously, the human thought process is complex and irrational. The human brain is set up with areas for various functions.

There are three brain types:

- Retile
- Mammal
- Thinker

The problem is these three brains are not integrated. They work separately. The thinking brain is the least dominant of three, which is why our thinking process is in most cases irrational. In the majority of cases, our decisions are based upon triggers from the unconscious.

Remember "Blink"? The power of "thin slices" and "rapid cognition"; this is our predominant thought pattern.

Thin-slicing is a psychological term for the ability to find patterns in events based upon minimal information. It means making rapid decisions with the least amount of information.

When an individual walks through a mall of three hundred stores or on a High Street on Saturday afternoon; his mind races and he thinks at a fast rate. The decision as to which store he enters is made in a blink of an eye.

The merchandise display and store design that catches his attention will win his patronage. Except if he had pre-planned a visit to a particular store; his decisions are based purely upon thin slicing each store as he walks.

Many of our actions, behaviour and thinking originate from the adaptive unconscious, which the majority of us are unaware of.

However, the good news for the retail industry is…other humans are capable of altering those unconscious biases just by tinkering with the little details.

In "The Tipping Point" as I pointed out earlier, Malcolm Gladwell demonstrated how to tinker or social engineer humans to get them to behave in ways we would like them to.

The retail landscape is changing rapidly. Too many choices; disruptions and hoards of information from all directions, either confuse or overwhelm customers.

As the customer walks through a shopping mall, there are gazillion things going through his head. Yours is not the only store in the shopping mall neither is it the only stores design he had seen on that day.

Figure 2: Your window display has to be attractive enough to capture shoppers as they walk pass your shop

There is a cluster of information and stores all around him. Therefore, in order to ensure that your store stands tall above the rest, you need to design it to match his thinking process. That can only be done when you understand store design psychology and use it as a framework for designing your store.

People don't like to be sold but they love to buy, so your store design should sell to them without peddling to them.

The most effective store designs are those that speak directly to the customer's desire for:

- Result
- Solution
- Relief from something

Remember! It is all about:

- Status
- Survival
- Sex

To achieve the above effectively requires you do the following:

- Identify your target market
- Find out what appeals to them
- Incorporate it into your store design

How to apply the principle of store design psychology?

To influence shoppers buying behaviour and design a store that appeals to them demands an in-depth research into your target market's buying habits. This can be done in-house or through an external research agency.

The following steps would assist you implement the psychology of store design effectively:

Step 1:
Conduct, or hire an outside research firm to research into your target market. Using the aims and objectives of your business as a guide...the age, gender, or income group you intend to serve.

Step 2:

Create a store design blueprint tailored to your target market. Focus on colours; types of material; flooring; lighting and fixture arrangement.

Step 3:

Focus the store design on customer flow. This means the aisle width, height and size as well as the location of check-out counters.

Step 4:

Incorporate security and loss prevention into the store design. Pay attention to the location of your entrance and exit, staff areas and warehouse.

A good store design leads to: increased sales, improved staff productivity, reduced shrinkages and increased profit. However, this cannot be done without taking into consideration the psychology of the process.

Things to consider in your store design blueprint:

Display fixtures:

Figure 3: Ensure you consider the types of fixtures you will eventually use when designing your store

Display fixtures are essential components of a retail store design. Consequently, it is essential they are added to the original blueprint.

Lighting system:

Figure 4: Good lighting system enhances the appearance of your store

Lighting plays a crucial role in a retail environment. Lighting has to be a part of the store design blueprint. There needs to be adequate lighting to enhance product appearance.

The placement of the lights should be considered as lights need to be adjusted to accommodate the store layout and climatic conditions.

Fittings:

Figure 5: Fittings need to complement not confuse shoppers

Fittings such as hanging chandelier in the middle of the store, large clock at the rear of the counter and other designs that complement the store's overall appearance need to be also taken into consideration.

Fittings need to be kept to a minimum to avoid confusing the customer. The objective of a store design is to enhance merchandise, not to be points of focus.

Maintaining the ideal design of your store would result in increased sales and brand awareness. Always ensure that you create a lighter aura and a clutter-free store design.

Chapter Two

How To Increase Retail Sales With Attractive Store Design

I have received internet marketing training from the best internet marketers in the world. These are guys who together make billions on the internet each year. Therefore, when attending their training, one would expect them to teach techniques and tricks for making money on the internet.

But whether their training is for a day or a weekend, they spend very little time teaching techniques for using the internet effectively. Instead they focus exclusively on marketing fundamentals. I remember asking one of them during a training section why is it that they do not teach techniques for using the internet effectively. He responded that participants will not be able to effectively use the internet to market their products or services if they do not know basic marketing fundamentals.

Come to think of what he said as I write this book, I believe he was absolutely right. The most successful businesses are not successful because of the industry they are in or because of the product or services they provide; they are successful because they apply simple business and marketing fundamentals.

Apple is a typical example of a business that is not successful because it sells the best products in the world. Its success is based upon the fact that its products function.

Apple's product design is based on three principles:

- Functionality

- Simplicity
- Elegance

Prior to the release of a new Apple product there is the usual hype and buzz around about how good the product is going to be. However, when the product is released the recurrent question that always pops up is what was all the fuss about? There is nothing extraordinary about the product design yet it outsells its competitors. So the question that comes to mind is why is Apple able to outsell its competitors all the time?

Answer: Apple products are functional.

When Apple is about to release a product, its focus is not on how cool the product is going to look but how would it make the life of users easier or even how could it change their lives.

Apple designers go into the head of the average buyer of an Apple product and ask the questions:

Who is the person we are producing this product for?
What work does he do?
Where does he live?
How would this product make his work or home life easy?
What else would he be able to do with this product?
How can this product change his life for the better?

It is only when Apple designers are able to provide answers to the above questions would they embark on the process of designing the product.

Similar thought process goes into the design of cars, whether it is Mercedes-Benz, BMW or Ferrari, their designers ask themselves those question prior to designing their cars.

Mercedes-Benz appeals to a completely different market from BMW or Ferrari. While the average Mercedes-Benz owner might be focused on comfort or luxury, the BMW or Ferrari owner might be focused on speed. Therefore as the designers of these automobile manufacturers sit to design their cars, they concentrate on fulfilling the desires of their target market.

Google arguably one of the most successful businesses of our time has the same web page that it had when it started. Even though it 'Googelise' its logo every day, the design of the webpage remains the same. Which is one of the main reasons it over took other search engines and it continues to dominate the search engine market.

What does the information regarding Apple, Google and automobile manufacturers have to do with retail store design?

Everything!

Retail store design like any other design is subject to similar design principles. In order for a retail store to achieve similar phenomenal success as any other successful business, retail stores have to conform to the same fundamental business principles that make other businesses successful.

For most of this book I am going to use Harrods as an example of a good retail model. The reason for this is that Harrods is one of the most successful retailers in the world.

Therefore, there is no better example to use than one of the most successful retailers in the retail industry. As I searched for the secret behind Harrods' success, I came to the conclusion that the key is its application of the five fundamental business principles:

- Visionary leadership

- Great people
- Good system
- Good marketing system
- Good business model

Take its marketing strategy in its children section for example. When you enter Harrods children, you will first notice play consultants playing with the toys and asking parents and their children to join in the game.

This is basically moving further from just having the children seeing and touching the toys to actually having to play with them to get them emotionally invested in the toys.

Figure 6: Harrods creates the atmosphere for children to sample their toys

After playing with the toy, how many kids will not automatically want to take the toy home with them to continue playing.

In contrast to Harrods, when children and parents enter the Early Learning Centre, it is like a dental suite. The stores is crammed one can hardly breathe. There is nowhere for the children to sample the toys.

Figure 7: Early learning centre stores are like soviet dental suite

Do you see the difference?

Do you see now why it is critical to learn marketing fundamentals before you consider designing your retail store?

One thing you need to learn from the onset is this: the fundamentals of business never change. They remain the same whether it is for the HSBC bank in the city of London or a cleaning business in a dusty New Delhi ghetto. The fundamentals of business are similar to the fundamentals of science or engineering.

The formulas that were used in chemistry since the times of the Roman Empire or the civilization of Egyptian apply to today's chemistry. There might be slight modifications and advancements but the fundamentals remain the same.

The same applies to business. Every successful business has the same five components that make it successful:

- Visionary leadership
- Great people
- Good system
- Good marketing system
- Good business model

The absence of any of the above will cause any business to fail. These are core principles. They are not just something that might be good for a business, they are elements that businesses cannot survive without.

The aim of this chapter is to outline the process of increasing retail sales with attractive store design using those five business success fundaments.

In a book on store design, you will expect techniques and strategies on ways of designing your store to increase sale. However, the best strategies will not work if the person implementing the strategy does not know the reason they are implementing them.

This chapter and the next one would specifically answer the question: why it is important for a retail stores to be designed in a specific way.

I am of the belief that it is only after you have grasped this concept would you be able to derive the maximum benefit from the technique and strategy I will be outlining in subsequent chapters.

However, my aim in this book is not to address the five business fundamentals, I will be dealing with the forth component: a good marketing system. It is my belief that marketing is the most essential of the five business fundamentals.

Conventional wisdom holds that a business cannot make a profit until its third year of operation and we have all bought into that lie. I am here to tell you that, this belief is completely false.

A retail store can begin to make profit from its first month of operation if it applied the principles written in this book. The application of those five core elements is a insurance against any retail business failure.

Understanding how to increase retail sales is very crucial for the success of any retail business and more so now with the increasing failure of many retail businesses.

Background

Lingerie specialist La Senza went into administration in the first week of 2012. It is amongst some 183 UK retailers including: Barratts, Clinton Cards, Habitat, HMV, Focus DIY, JJB Sports, Jane Norman, Mothercare, Oddbins, TJ Hughes and Thorntons that got into trouble in 2011. This is in addition to the thousands of retailers that went bust without making the headlines.

The British Prime Minister alarmed by the prospects of many UK town centres turning into ghost towns, appointed a committee headed by UK retail guru, Mary Portas, to look into why the UK High Street was at risk of extinction.

Her report concluded that the main reason for the demise of the High Street was:

"High Streets have reached 'crisis point' with the rise of super-malls, out-of-town supermarkets and internet shopping".

This follows another report by Colliers CRE which highlighted the "downward spiral and degenerating or failing" of the UK High Street.

As I write this book, the Australian government has also commissioned a report into the future of the Australian retail industry.

So why is the retail industry facing such difficulty even though literally no one can survive without visiting a retail store?

The answer to this question is simple:

The retail industry is the only industry where increased sales area is the key performance indicator.

A large part of this chapter was written as a White Paper on Boxing Day (2011), which is the day when most retailers start their biggest sales of the year. The irony is even though they make their biggest sales on that day, the large majority of retail stores did not make a single red penny in profit.

How can a business expect to make a profit from discounting products at 50% or 70%? Retail profit is an average of 3%. Even the most profitable retailers make between 3 and 5% profit.

The large majority of retailers make a profit margin of between 1.5–3%. Therefore, if a retailer is making a 3% profit margin and is discounting his merchandise by 50%, how much profit will he be making?

I am aware that it might sound contradictory that I am writing a chapter on how to increase retail sales with attractive store design yet seem to be criticising the concept of increasing sales.

I would like to clarify the fact that I am not critical of the concept of increasing sales, increased sales must also simultaneously result in increased profit.

> *To increase sales without simultaneously increasing profit is a wasted opportunity.*

Therefore, my aim in this chapter is to show you how to increase sales while increasing profit.

How to increase retail sale and profit simultaneously

The 18th century business environment was about speed. The 19th century business environment was about quality. The 21st century business environment is about two things:

- Value
- Total customer experience

What is value?

Value is a quantifiable benefit between both parties involved in a transaction. The key phrase here is: quantifiable benefit. Value has to be sensory specific.

I will further nail down the definition of value with quotes from renowned business experts starting with the Oracle of Omaha, Warren Buffett:

> *"Price is what you pay. Value is what you get."*

Value according to Ron Baker is the amount a customer is willing to pay for a product or service.

> *"Too many people think only of their own profit. But a business opportunity seldom knocks on the door of self-centred people. No customer ever goes to a store merely to please the storekeeper."* Kazuo Inamori, founder of KYOCERA Corp.

> *"The successful producer of an article sells it for more than it cost him to make, and that's his profit. But the customer buys it only because it is worth more to him than he pays for it, and that's his profit. No one can long make a profit producing anything unless the customer makes a profit using it."* Samuel B. Pettengill.

The above quotations by prominent business thinkers were introduced to emphasise the point that for a product or service to be considered valuable, it has to benefit both you and your customers.

What is total customer experience?

Marcus Buckingham in his book "The One Thing You Need to know" wrote that when he interviewed Sir Terry Leahy the man who propelled Tesco into a global brand, he asked him: how he turned Tesco from a UK retailer to the fourth biggest retailer in the world.

Sir Terry told him that when he took over Tesco, the first thing he did was to ask and answer the question: who do we serve?

This question is classic marketing 101: know thy customer.

When they established who they were going to serve, he put in place mechanisms for ensuring they serve their preferred customer. One of those mechanisms they put in place was to increase the numbers of checkout counters in each Tesco store.

When asked why he focused on the checkout counters, he replied with something to the tune of; part of good customer service was to show respect for your customer and what better way of showing respect for someone than showing respect for their time.

21st century retail success therefore, would not be just about the quality of the products you sell or the price you sell them for, but the total customer experience when they visit your store. Total customer experience is your entire package:

- The quality of your products
- The price of your products
- The way your staff interact with the customers

- The way the merchandises are displayed
- Your store design

Below is a list of good customer service quotes that I hope will help you in your journey towards providing total customer experience.

"Do what you do so well that they will want to see it again and bring their friends". Walt Disney.

"It's our job every day to make every important aspect of the customer experience a little bit better." Jeff Bezos, founder of Amazon.

"Your most unhappy customers are your greatest source of learning." Bill Gates, founder of Microsoft.

"There is only one boss. The customer and he can fire everybody in the company from the chairman on down, simply by spending his money somewhere else". Sam Walton, founder of Wal-Mart, the world's largest retailer.

"Customers do you a favour by choosing to do business with you. You aren't doing them a favour by serving them." Mark Sanborn

"If you're not serving the Customer, you'd better be serving someone who is." Jan Carlzon, former president of SAS Airlines

"People will forget what you said. People will forget what you did. But people will never forget how you made them feel." Maya Angelou

*"If your business cannot pledge 100% Satisfaction Guaranteed or your money back something is broken. Fix it...No customer walks into your business, gives you money and then says, Dissatisfy me, please. Aim for 100% customer satisfaction...Delivering good cus-

tomer service is business common sense. Your job is to make it common practice". Bill Quiseng

Retail success fundamentals

In addition to "Level five" leadership and good loss prevention strategy, the key components that have been responsible for the success of a few retail organisations are the following:

- Understanding of their target market
- Trained staff
- Skilled sales staff
- Product knowledge
- Great customer service provision
- Understanding of Their Target Market

I visited Harrods for research about this book and my book on visual merchandise display, Harrods, as previously stated is the Mecca of retailing. Royalty, A-list celebrities and the 'who's who' from around the world fly into London just to shop at Harrods.

You can now imagine my anticipation when I visited Harrods. In my mind everything in Harrods was made of gold. I was disappointed, when I noticed a toy bus I had purchased for my son from ASDA, was also being sold in Harrods.

It was exactly the same toy bus, in exactly the same packaging as the toy in ASDA.

A question popped into my mind, why is it that exactly the same bus, probably manufactured in exactly the same factory in China, is sold in Harrods for twice the price that it is sold for in ASDA?

The answer is decisively simple – ASDA sells a 'toy bus', however, Harrods sells a 'classy toy bus'.

There is a difference.

> *This is marketing 101: people buy emotionally but justify their decision logically.*

Customers who shop at Harrods do not shop there to buy Harrods' products; they shop at Harrods to buy elegance and class. Harrods sells them class even if it is 'Made in China'.

How does Harrods pull this off?

They achieve it with the combination of an elegant store design and attractive visual merchandising displays.

When you move from one department to the next in Harrods, it is like moving from one store to another. Their ability to use their store design to create the illusion of differentiation is one of the keys to Harrods' success.

Harrods understand their customers; they know what their customers desire so they design their store and display their products to satisfy the desire of their customers.

> Tesco serves the ordinary Joe Bloke.
> Wal-Mart serves the person who lives: pay check to pay check.
> The Body Shop serves the ethical consumer.
> Waitrose and Holland & Barrett serve the consumer who wants to live longer.

Ann Summers took merchandise once hidden in secret 'adult' shops; made them chic and took them to the High Street. They made a taboo subject acceptable to the mainstream.

If I was to take my partner shopping at John Lewis, she would probably phone my mother to inform her that I was having a nervous breakdown. She would not want to be caught dead in a

John Lewis' outfit. She describes John Lewis' clothing department as a Bridget Jones museum where they store a collection of Bridget Jones costumes.

However, John Lewis continues to increase profits year on year because John Lewis understands their target market.

Someone like my significant other might not want to be caught dead in John Lewis' outfit, but there are people in the UK, who love Bridget Jones' memorabilia, these people are John Lewis' target market, so John Lewis caters to them.

The most successful retailers understand their target market and show their understanding of their target market through their store design and visual merchandising displays.

On Christmas Eve, I had not done my grocery shopping and was dreading the prospect of entering a supermarket, knowing how packed they were going to be. But as I drove past my local Lidl store, I noticed it was empty. I rushed in and completed my shopping.

As I drove back home a question came to my mind; why is it that even on this day when most supermarkets are typically jam packed was Lidl empty?

The answer is: Lidl does not have a target market. One of their biggest sins was making the decision to force customers to pay for carrier bags. Marks & Spencer can afford to do that because they appeal to a different class of customers.

In Tesco and ASDA, customers who are environmentally conscious have the option of paying for carrier bags. However, those who do not want to pay for carrier bags also have the option of getting free bags.

This is because Tesco and ASDA understand their customers. Lidl's senior management, on the other hand, believed that having implemented a similar strategy in Europe, they could do the same in the UK. If the Brits do not like it, tough! Well, the Brits had shown their displeasure with their feet.

I have used the above examples to demonstrate that success or failure in retail is the result of the strategies every retailer adopts. Those retailers who understand their target market and cater to them will continue to move from success to greater success. Those who roll the dice and hope that customers show up are the ones who will struggle or go into administration.

I hate to be the one breaking this type of news to the retail industry but I guess someone will have to do it: the internet is not going away. This means that retailers are not only competing with one another, they are also competing with factory owners in China whose names they have never heard. Shoppers are now ordering directly from warehouses and distributors, for example an individual can log on to eBay and order a pallet load of goods.

Here is the good news: the majority of people still prefer to shop from physical retail outlets. The question for you is this: how do you ensure that shoppers are attracted to your store?

It can be done by designing your store to take into account their buying habits.

Trained Staff

A friend of mine is a manager at Tesco. He knows the profit margin on each and every product in his store. Why does knowing the profit margins matter for his products?

There are numbers of reasons. Firstly business is about making profit and secondly it highlights the significance of "training" to retail success.

As a manager at Tesco, my friend receives periodic training on every aspect of running a retail business. Little wonder Tesco is the second most profitable retailer in the world and the third most profitable business in the UK.

Tesco, like most successful retailers, understand the significance of staff training to the success of their business. Subsequently, they ensure their staff are constantly trained.

> *It never ceases to amaze me how an individual will open a retail store worth millions of pounds only to have the store managed by someone they are unwilling to spend a few hundred pounds to train.*

The two common excuses retailers give for not training their staff are:

- It is expensive
- Absentee cover

I'm probably the only person who doesn't get it, just imagine this scenario:

Someone, somewhere, is leaving his multi-million pound retail store in the hands of an individual and he says it is too expensive to spend a few hundred pounds to provide that person with the requisite training to manage his store well; can you imagine that?

What am I missing?!

Sales Training

According to a survey commissioned by Blue Martini Software; retailers could be losing up to 85 billion pounds per year as a result of inadequate staff training. The survey revealed that 84% of potential customers who left stores without buying said they were going to buy from another retailer.

This means that the store they entered was unable to sell them on yes, so they sold them on no.

As many as 95% of retail employees have never received any form of sales and marketing training. As a result of their inability to sell, most retail staff just stand by as shoppers examine merchandise and cross their fingers hoping they will decide to buy.

Worst of all are the ones who keep asking the same stupid question for which they know exactly the answer they are going to get: "can I help you?"

"No I am just looking"

Retailing is about selling. This means that anyone in retail should at the very least be given basic sales training.

If retailing is about selling and 95% of retail staff have never received any form of sales training, surely there is a linear relationship between sales training and retail success.

It is like a medical doctor who has never been to medical school, how many people in this world would want an untrained doctor to treat them?

Product Knowledge

Covert sting operations, conducted by 'Which?' the consumer organisation, in 2011, revealed that many retail employees lacked knowledge of the products they sold. Just 8 out of the 154 stores investigated, scored an excellent mark. No well-known High Street brand was amongst those eight.

Surprised?

Maybe not.

In this information age where consumers have access to vast amounts of information one would expect retailers to realise the importance of product knowledge for their staff.

Nowadays, many shoppers search on the internet for products prior to stepping foot in a shop. They read information such as product specification, where to get the best deal and customer reviews. They visit shops to basically clarify what they have already read. If the store staff are unable to answer their questions, there is no chance that they will be able to sell to them.

> Here is the secret, despite the fact that people conduct research on the internet, the large majority still don't trust information found on the internet. That is why books are still highly rated even though the information in most books can be found online.

People still trust other people and prefer to interact with people. This is one reason why despite the internet, bricks and mortar retailing will survive. However, there is a new dynamic and retailers need to understand this.

The consumer of today is better informed than the consumer of ten or twenty years ago. Consequently, today's retail staff need to be better informed than the retail staff of ten or twenty years ago.

> *One cannot navigate the 21st century with a 19th century skill set; it will not work.*

Richer Sounds has been featured in the Guinness Book of Records for the past 20 years as having the highest sales per square foot of any retailer in the world.

Coincidentally, they continue to top the 'Which?' survey for excellent customer service and product knowledge.

Good Customer Service Provision

These days, the only reason I visit my local PC World store is to buy ink for my printer. This is due to the fact that it is the only retailer in my locality that sells the type of ink cartridge suitable for my printer.

Every time I enter a PC World store, I encounter a similar level of service. I am always forced to queue up for a long time at the checkout, waiting for staff to serve me. Even when the store is empty I have to wait to be served, whilst there will be a group of staff chatting a few metres away from the vacant checkout.

PC World and her sister company Curry's are struggling and their management wonder why?

I am sure if they were to go bust the CEO would blame harsh trading conditions. The fact that his store ranks at the bottom of many customer satisfaction surveys would not be seen as a factor in their demise.

In this "Long Tail" retail environment where consumers are constantly presented with endless choices, one would think that retailers, especially High Street retailers would realise the importance of excellent customer service and try to instil it as a fundamental part of their business strategy.

Thirty to 40% of people will buy solely on price. The majority 70% of people will buy on quality and convenience. Even though the retail industry is in crisis, the luxury sector of the industry is still growing strong. This is because no matter what the economic situation is people still shop. The only question is where will they shop.

Luxury retailers understand this fact and train their staff in excellent customer service.

I have noticed in my local ASDA that when staff are asked for information, they do not just point; they take customers to the location and ask them what else they can do for them.

People go to restaurants where the food is terrible but never complain because of the attitude of the staff. However, if it was the other way around, the food tasted great but the service sucked, they are highly unlikely to return to that restaurant.

Good customer service is a key component to the success of many of the most successful retailers whilst bad customer service has been one of the major contributing factors for the failure of many retail ventures.

This is a book about store design, I am sure you would expect me to provide you with tips about designing the physical aspect of your store. So why does it seem as though I am going on about subjects that do not seem related to store design?

The answer is this: store design is about marketing. Remember a business needs five components to succeed:

- Visionary leadership
- Great people
- Good system
- Good marketing system
- Good business model

The life blood of any retail business is its ability to acquire and retain customers. Your success as a retailer will depend on your ability to acquire and retain customers. Your store design is a critical part of your marketing process. Your ability to design your store making use of fundamental business principles will determine your level of success.

One thing you need to understand is, the store design itself is not going to attract customers or increase your sales, your ability to use your store design as a vehicle for the achievement of customer acquisition will be the determining factor.

As stated previously, the likes of Google, Facebook and all of the successful internet entrepreneurs are not successful because of their ability to use the internet better than the rest of us. They are successful because of their ability to effectively use the internet as a tool through which they can apply fundamental business principles.

> In Value Migration, Adrian Slywotzky stated that *"A business (model) design is the totality of how a company selects its customers, defines and differentiates its offerings (or responses), defines the tasks it will perform itself and those it will outsource; configures its resources; goes to market; creates utility for customers and captures profits. It is the entire system for delivering utility to customers and earning a profit from that activity"*.

In their paper *"while the term 'business model' is often used these days, it is seldom defined explicitly."* Chesbrough and Rosenbloom point out that there are six specific functions of a business model:

- Articulate the value proposition – the value created to users by using the product.

- Identify the market segment – to whom and for what purpose is the product useful; specify how revenue is generated by the firm.
- Define the value chain – the sequence of activities and information required to allow a company to design, produce, market, deliver and support its product or service.
- Estimate the cost structure and profit potential – using the value chain and value proposition identified.
- Describe the position of the firm with the value network – link suppliers, customers, counterparts and competitors.
- Formulate the competitive strategy – how will you gain and hold your competitive advantage over competitors or potential new entrants.

Joan Magretta wrote in the Harvard Business Review in May 2002: *"A good business model answers Peter Drucker's age-old questions: "Who is the customer?" And "what does the customer value?" It also answers the fundamental questions every manager must ask: How do we make money in this business? What is the underlying economic logic that explains how we can deliver value to customers at an appropriate cost"?*

Your retail store is first and foremost a business and like any business it is dependent on your marketing process – your ability to acquire and retain customers; the extent to which you are capable of marketing your retail store with an attractive store design that is focused on providing value and total customer experience, will be the extent to which you are going to succeed.

Incidentally while writing this chapter; I took a break to relax. I switched on the television. BBC Click was on. The program was about new types of buildings that respond to the movement of people.

Just like the new great buildings that are being constructed to generate energy automatically, the building will be capable of changing in relation to the movement of people. Even a chair will adjust itself to suit the shape of the person sitting on it.

In short, buildings of the future are going to be designed on functionality. The question that this brings to mind is: How functional is your retail store?

Is your store designed for the customers of two decades ago or is it designed for customers of the next two decades?

Let me provide you a few tips on how to design a retail store that results in increased sales:

Step 1:
Identify your target market.

Step 2:
Find out what factors influence their buying behaviour.

Step 3:
Focus your store design exclusively on satisfying the desires and buying behaviours of your target market.

Step 4:
Choose colour schemes, fixtures, fittings, display space, location of cashier counter, location of customer services desk, shelf height, in accordance with the findings made in your target market research.

Step 5:
Incorporate the security of your merchandise into your store design. This is the most important aspect of the store design as stores need to be designed in such a way that they design-out crime. (Whether it is employee theft or shoplifting; a well-designed store can effectively design out crime.)

Step 6:

Take the effective use of technology into account when designing your store. Whether it is a POS, CCTV or EBR system they all need to be included in the design blueprint. A good POS system can rapidly increase sales by reducing queues. CCTV and EBR systems reduce crime whether shoplifting or employee theft.

Chapter Three

How to Increase Retail Sales With Brand Image Selling

There is more to retailing than merchandise and selling. It is also about your customers' perception of your brand and what it represents. Their perception and the connection they make with your brand and what it represents is the most important component of your marketing strategy.

Retail business is like showbiz. It is all about image, brand and style. Many people choose to work in a particular business, not because of the financial reward they hope to gain, but the value the business represents.

> Most people associate The Body Shop with ethics.
> Harrods is perceived as elegant and classy.
> Victoria's Secret is the lovers' choice for lingerie.

Customers who shop at The Body Shop do so largely because their products are not tested on animals. They also feel that by purchasing The Body Shop products they are swaying their conscience.

Harrods markets itself as an elegant store that attracts classy people. Royalties the world over, Hollywood 'A' list stars and the 'who is who' in the world go to London specifically to shop at Harrods, all because it has created an image of elegance.

Victoria's Secret is the preferred choice for ladies shopping for lingerie for that special occasion. In the minds of most of them, Victoria's Secret has come to represent love. When women want to go on a special date or when they want to surprise their significant other, they shop for their special bedroom lingerie at Victoria's Secret. Wearing lingerie from Victoria's Secret gives them confidence.

These retailers have carved a place in the hearts of shoppers by getting them to link their brand with their image. The image cultivated by those brands has been responsible for their phenomenal success in the retail industry.

Image selling is vital for the success of any retail venture, without it most retail businesses struggle. Image selling is a very effective sales strategy and used properly, it can make the selling process very easy.

The crux of image selling is twofold:

- The image that the customer wants to portray by purchasing your merchandise
- The image that the customer already knows that your store represents

A person willing to spend a quarter of a million pounds to buy a Ferrari is not doing so simply because he wants to drive a fast car. He chose to buy a Ferrari because of the prestige associated with owning a Ferrari.

Every person deep down wants recognition and the appreciation of others. Shrewd marketers tap into the human desire for recognition and craft their marketing messages to fulfil that desire.

In his book "Breakthrough Advertising" Eugene Schwartz describes this human behaviour as identification. He defined identification as:

> *"the desire of a person to act a certain role in their lives and to define himself to the world around him—to express the qualities within himself that he values and the position he has attained. All products may benefit from the power to define. But in particular, when you have a product that does the same job as competing products, and is so priced that price is no longer a factor then expect choice will almost overwhelmingly depend on the difference in role that your product offers him".*

I once watched an interview with a Ferrari executive. He let it be known that when you drive a Ferrari, you drive a dream.

This statement is so true.

Most men who are into cars view Ferrari as the ultimate driving machine. Although it is not the most expensive car in the world, driving a Ferrari is like a dream come true for many people.

As you design your store you need to be considering the roles and characteristics you want your customers to associate it with. Whatever role and characteristic you choose must be one they already possess in their head. You cannot invent a role or characteristic from thin air.

> *Remember? Driving a Ferrari is driving a dream.*
>
> *Going into your retail store is what…Complete the sentence.*

I attended a business start-up event in London and met a few retail businesses. When I interviewed the retailers at the stands about what made their products different from those of the other retailers in the arena, not a single one could tell me any differentiating factor. They all said their products were made specifically for the consumer et cetera, et cetera.

I kept priming them to see if at least one could come up with anything that was closely relate to the benefit the customer will derive from purchasing their products. Not a single one was able to come up with the benefit of their products to their customers.

A prerequisite for success in the retail industry or in any business for that matter is the ability to differentiate your business from that of the competition.

The second aspect of image selling is the association you want your customers to have with your brand.

Image selling is the ability to market an idea that people cling to, that which in the end creates a positive perception in their mind about your brand.

Certain brands are associated with ethics, healthy lifestyle, elegance, class, low quality, safety, innocence or quality.

However, to sell an image effectively, the image has to be implanted in the minds of your customers from the start of your business.

Certain retail organisations have been trying to flaunt their Green credentials by selling carrier bags. Although they might be honestly doing it for environmental reasons, the fact that they had not done it from their formative stages leads most people to think they are just doing it as an excuse to increase their profit margin.

Europe based supermarkets such as ALDI and LiDL operating in the UK and US charge for carrier bags. However, they have been doing so from the start of their operations in those countries, even though other retailers give carrier bags for free. Therefore, no one will accuse them of charging for carrier bags to increase profit.

The image your retail organisation projects could be that of the philosophy of the founder. Your organisation could represent *fun, love or passion for life*.

It really does not matter what image you choose to project. What is important is your brand is associated with something. To maintain that image, your store and entire work environment should reflect that image.

For example, if the image you want to project is that of a fun-loving organisation, your store colours should be bright and it should be designed to be cheery.

If you want to project the image of an environmentally conscious organisation; then your store colour should be green and it should be designed so that all of your fixtures are made from recyclable materials.

However, your brand image is not just your logo, colour or store design. It is also your brand promise. It is what customers can expect when they interact with your brand. A good brand image is part and parcel of the retail success secret of successful retailers and is a very effective marketing tool utilised with laser accuracy by those retailers.

Although image is intangible; it is more valuable than the products in your store.

Just the Logo of multinational corporations such as Coca Cola, Nike, Google and Apple carry a value many times that of some developing countries. Those multinationals spare no effort because they know that brand sells the products not the other way round.

    Nike represents hero
    Timberland represents adventure

Rolex represents luxury

Why is image and branding so important for store design?

Branding and image is important because they are the information upon which the store design blueprint is based. When customers enter your store, they need to be able to connect to your brand image inside the store.

Your brand image is an implicit promise to your customers about who you are and what you represent, consequently it is essential that you jealously protect and promote your image.

Store design fundamentals

> *"So with any other mail order ad which has long continued. Every feature, every word and picture teaches advertising at its best. You may not like them. You may say they are unattractive, crowded, hard to read — anything you will. But the test of results has proved those ads the best salesman those lines have yet discovered. And they certainly pay"* (Claude C. Hopkins – Scientific Advertising).

The above summarises the concept of creating a marketing design. Most retailers have not connected their store design with their marketing strategies so they leave the design of the store to store fitters with no knowledge about marketing or advertising.

As I previously pointed out the difference between someone passing by your store in a busy shopping centre and entering your store, rests upon your store design.

Most designers equate beauty with good design. The aim of a marketing design is not to impress customers with beauty. It is to enhance your marketing message. Some marketing designs don't work because those creating the design do not understand the fundamentals of marketing design.

Most designers think that it is about adding fancy images to a design to make it look fanciful. Fanciful designs are good for comics and children's' books. In the marketing world it is about the message. Every component of the design has to serve the purpose of enhancing the core marketing message, not distract from it.

The one thing that should be uppermost in your mind when it comes to marketing design is simplicity. Most Apple products are not the best designed products in the world. However, they outsell all products in their niche.

Why, because Apple focuses on *simplicity, elegance and functionality.*

Their products are functional and elegant.

Google website is one of the top five high traffic websites in the world. Yet the Google home page is just the Google logo, and a few tabs at the top.

Look at ads in the top selling newspapers and magazines. You will notice that they are mostly in black and white and most of them have no images, only essential information relating to the product or service.

When the London 2012 logo was unveiled, no one except the designers seemed to know what they had designed. Some people described it as a child's drawing. Some say it symbolised an angry reaction.

It was call various things, but a reference to the Olympics. The chairman of the London organising Olympic committee had to go on television to explain to the British public what the logo meant.

When a logo is designed for an event as popular as the Olympics and no one understands the design, there is a serious design fault.

Figure 8: London 2012 Olympic logo confused everyone

This is a lesson for you. Pay attention. As you create your store design you need to ensure that the design is clearly understood by your target market and that it appeals to them.

The goal of your store design has to be:

- Simplicity
- Functionality
- Clarity

Why do most advertising fail?

"Some ads are planned and written with some utterly wrong conception. They are written to please the seller. The interests of the buyer are forgotten. But one can never sell goods profitably, in person or in print, when that attitude exists" (Claude C. Hopkins – Scientific Advertising).

Although store design is advertisement, many store designs fail to attract customers for the same reasons that many advertisements fail to attract customers' attention.

Look at your current store design and ask yourself the following questions:

- Was it designed with the customer in mind?
- Does your store fit with your customer avatar?
- Did you take into account your competition?
- Is your store design simple, functional and clear?
- Does your store design represent your core message?

If you cannot answer all the above questions in the affirmative, you will want to reconsider your current store design.

How to design a store that represents your brand image

The following steps are effective for creating your image:

Step 1:
Identify the image you want to be associated with. It can either be the philosophy of the founder or the organisation as a whole. It first needs to be identified along with the story of why you want to be associated with that particular image.

Step 2:
Communicate that image to your store designer in order for it to be incorporated into the store design blueprint.

Step 3:
Design your store to reflect that image. Every fixture, lighting and decor in the store needs to be congruent with that image.

Step 4:
Ensure all store assistants are well briefed and up to speed on your brand image. Their uniforms, actions and interaction with customers need to reflect your projected image.

The main point to remember here is that as powerful as image selling is, it is a process. It is not an event. It is a process that needs to be consciously built into your marketing strategy and plan from your formative stages.

What is Brand Image?

The most successful retailers have carved out an image that the buying public can easily associate them with.

How to Market Your Brand Image?

Steps for Marketing Your Brand Image

The following steps will help you to effectively market your image:

Step 1:
Identify your desired brand image. You need to have a mission and value statement that articulates what you stand for. It must also contain information about why you stand for that.

Step 2:
Ensure your store designers fully understand the image you want to project to your customers in order for every aspect of it to be incorporated into your store design blueprint.

Step 3:
Ensure your store is designed in congruence with your desired image.

Step 4:
Ensure all employees within your organisation are aware of your brand image and adhere to it in every aspect of their job.

Your brand image is the most valuable asset in your retail organisation, it is an intangible asset. A good image can make you successful. A negative image will cause you to fail, so build and guard your image and ensure that the message of your image is communicated to your store designers.

Chapter Four

Designing Store For Increase Customer Flow

In chapter one, I mentioned two retailers from different spectrum of the retail success continuum: Harrods one of the most successful retailers in the world and Early Learning Centre a struggling UK retailer.

They both sell children's toys.

In Harrods children are able to play with the toys in the store strategically stimulating an attachment to the toys that results in them pressurising their parents to buy it for them.

While the Early Learning Centre has a Soviet style dental suite store where children cannot even breathe or walk around without stepping on each other's toes and parents have to stay outside of the store when their children are inside.

Increasing retail sales requires four core elements

- Attracting customers as they pass by the store
- Enticing them to enter the store
- Retaining them longer in the store
- Persuading them to buy

There is not a single one of these four core elements that one would stand out as a single factor that on its own can result in increased sales. However, if it is a case of being forced to choose one from four, I will say retaining customers in the store would be the most important of the four. This is because the longer customers stay in the store, more likely they are to buy.

To hold customers in your store for a long time, they need to be able to move freely within the store without any form of hindrance. A retail store has three basic design components:

1) Selling area
2) Services area
3) Circulation area

The extent to which these areas are effectively utilised, especially the selling area will have an effect on the success of the retailer.

Shopping is a favoured pastime for many people. For a great many people shopping is a necessity. However, in a majority of the cases, recreational shopping is more prevalent than shopping out of necessity. Visit any city centre at the weekend and you will notice the High Street jam packed with shoppers. Despite the hoard of people in the city centre, as you walk around, you will notice some packed and empty stores.

Have you ever wondered why this is the case?

The reason for this is that for most people the act of going to shopping is an event. Those who buy for recreational purposes do not go shopping just to buy things. They love the experience. There might be ten thousand people in the city centre on a particular day, but each one of them has a personal reason for being in the city.

The stores that attract the most customers are those that appeal to the reasons for those people being in the city centre. 21st century retailing is not about buying and selling, it is also about the experience that customers have in the process; it is about the atmosphere in the store and how comfortable customers feel in it.

Starbucks sells coffee like many other coffee shops, yet people prefer Starbucks to other coffee shops. Starbucks does not sell some types of technologically advanced coffee that is proven to give long life, yet customers prefer Starbucks over other Cafes.

This is due to the fact that Starbucks creates an environment in which customers feel relaxed and comfortable. When customers feel this way they are more inclined to purchase more coffee. A similar principle applies to your retail store. It must be a place where customers will not only come to buy what they need but also somewhere that they like to relax.

An Apple store in a shopping centre is always full of people. Even in the middle of the day when most retail stores are empty, Apple stores are buzzing with people. The reason for that, Apple stores are cool places to be.

Many people make buying decisions in the store after they have had the time to browse the merchandises. You want your customers spending their time buying, and not waste time navigating clutter.

The goal of any retail store is to attract customers and then persuade them to buy. Good advertising and promotion works to bring customers into the store. But when they are in the store, their decision to buy could be down to the layout and design. Both play a huge role in how customers rate their experiences, whether they buy and if they return or recommend the store to others.

Think about the experience you want to create for customers who enter your store. Picture the type of store design that would make it possible for customers to move from the front to the rear of the store browsing products and how they will go to the checkout counter without encountering obstacles.

Another important element in customer flow is the interaction of your store's sales assistants with customers:

> When customers enter your store, how are they greeted?
>
> When they need help, are store associates ready to assist them?
>
> Are they trained to provide answers to the costumers' questions?

I know a sports retailer in the UK that spends millions advertising in prime locations all around the country. However, when customers visit their stores, there are never enough store associates to serve them and when they have a question; the store associates haven't a clue.

> *How do you display high-value and impulse items?*
>
> *Do you strategically locate high-value and impulse products?*

Take some time to strategically locate high ticket items. It will determine your level of sales of those items. One objective of your store design should be to create a space where customers and sales associates can move freely, maximize space and make the most of your product exposure.

What is customer flow?

Customer flow in a retail environment refers to the manner in which customers move from the point of entry into the store until they leave the store. Customer flow refers to the ease with which customers walk through the aisles; many ways in which they gain access to products, sample products, have their questions answered and ease with which they pay for products and exit the store.

A good customer flow system should respond to customer's choice. The customer should have visible options. These ought to include easy access to products and customer service that results in positive impression of your store.

In a retail environment where the entire operation depends on various actors and factors, customer flow doesn't just happen. It must be purposely created as a part of your store design blueprint; managed and continuously improved to take into account the changing retail environment.

Store design plays a key part in relation to customer flow because the design of the store facilitates easy movement of your customers from end to end.

Your store is a stage for your brand; a display case for your products and an exceptional three-dimensional experience for your customers. The design, style and finish of your store will have a powerful, lasting impact on customer loyalty and purchasing decisions.

Aisle signage and shelf labelling form another part of your customer flow plan. Throughout the store signage and labelling should be set to enable customers locate products easily and familiarise themselves with the store layout.

You might want to consider seasonal themes. In summer you can create tropical scenery to lure customers to an area in the store where they can view related products and so on.

What are the various types of store design?

Listed below are the three basic types of store designs that encourage customer flow:

Free flow design

The Free flow design system allows products to be arranged throughout the store. Use racks and shelves that enable customers to browse freely with store associates on hand and ready to provide assistance when necessary.

A free flow store design is mainly used in boutiques, clothing, jewellery, and specialty stores. The cons of this design is: if display racks and products are not well arranged the store can appear cluttered and difficult for customers to navigate.

Grid pattern design

The Grid pattern design is usually used by drugstores, supermarkets and superstores. Mostly used in a rigid retail environment that offers less flexibility and encourages customers to search for items on their own.

But a grid pattern layout requires multiple rows filled with a variety of products throughout the store. High ticket items are displayed in high traffic locations and end caps so the customer can't help but notice them.

Such locations also support impulse buying. With a Grid pattern design customers are only able to familiarise themselves with the store layout and location of products after repeated visits.

Spine design

The spine design contains elements of the free flow and grid pattern store design. It is the third most commonly used retail store design strategy. It has a single long main aisle that goes from the entrance of the store to the back of the store. With the spine design, products can be displayed on both sides of the aisle using either the free flow or grid layout or a combination of the two. This design is mostly favoured by department stores because of the different range of products they display.

How to use store design to increase customer flow

A research into customer flow in the UK revealed that 75% of customers only saw a maximum of 25% of products on display in a retail store.

Just pause and think for a moment!

What will happen to your sales if your customers saw at a glance, all of the products on display in your store.

Your objective should be to design your store in such a way that it leads customers around the store. Furthermore, the aim has to be to create a design that ensures they are purposefully directed around the store instead of walking aimlessly around.

To use this analogy, you are designing a racetrack and not a runway. A racetrack design encourages customers to go around the store and be exposed to all the products in the store, whilst a runway encourages customer to move up and down the store in high speed.

Here now are some tips on designing your store to increase customer flow:

Positioning your checkout counters

The position of checkout counters is critical for controlling the movement of customers in your store. Generally customers walk away from checkout counters because checkout counters remind them that they are going to spend money.

Therefore, it is crucial that you position the checkout counter in such a way that it is not the first thing customers see when they enter the store. After they are relaxed, they will naturally gravitate towards it. The right positioning of your checkout counter can result in increased sales.

Control customer movement

You are designing to encourage customer movement around the store. To achieve this; products need to be strategically displayed to persuade shoppers to move from one end to the next and in the process view other products. The way to ensure this is to place essential products in different locations of the store.

Especially essential products such as:

- Milk
- Bread
- Sugar
- Toilet paper
- Detergent
- Coffee
- Beverages

Strategically locate these products around your store in order to force customers to walk around in search of them.

Make adequate use of sightlines

Sightlines are a very critical component for encouraging customer flow. They attract customer's attention as they move around the store and they generate curiosity. Strategically locating sightlines in your store would encourage customers to move around and get to know what products are on display.

Create destination departments

There needs to be destination departments in key locations of your store and ensure customers are aware of them. They need to be strategically located close to the entrance and exit points and in high traffic areas of the store.

Examples of such departments may be:

- The Power Tool Department
- The Seedling or Bedding Plants department
- The Ski Department
- The In-house Deli
- Lighting
- Shoe
- Electronics
- Technology

Use the right lighting system

At all times your customers need to be able to easily see as they walk around the store. Product areas need to be properly lit to attract their attention. When customers feel trapped or lost in your store they will leave immediately.

Create narrow aisles

Create narrow aisle space that would slow down customers as they walk around your store and get them to look at more products. However, the aisles have to be wide enough for the comfort of the customer. Wide aisle space encourages customers to move fast through them without actually browsing the products especially if they already know what they want to buy.

Strategically locate high demand products

High demand merchandise needs to be located at the end of the aisles. This encourages customers to walk pass other products before getting to them.

Display impulse items strategically

Display impulse buys, small and constantly in need and regularly purchased products close to checkout counter and in high traffic areas.

Strategically locate promotional products

Feature or promotional products should never be placed at the entrance to your store. When customers enter your store, they need time to adjust to the environment. They are less likely to pay careful attention to products that they see as they enter.

Do not neglect disabled customers

When designing your store, consideration has to be made for customers with disabilities and special needs. Aisles need to be wide enough to accommodate wheelchairs or mother with prams.

A successful retail store design strategy creates a store that leaves your customers with a happy experience. However it is essential that you regularly refresh your design to take into account and reflect changing trends.

Your store associates can play an important role in increasing customer flow and enhancing your customer experience. The quality of service and experience your customers receive will result in return customers.

Chapter Five

How To Choose Your Store Colour And Layout

Design is the most important aspect of a store layout. When the design is poor, the shopping experience of the customer can be ruined resulting in complaints and eventually loss of customers. The key to a workable design that attracts customers to your store is to determine the total customer experience you wish to achieve.

The appearance of a store is often fundamental to the success of that store. The most successful retailers maintain a consistent layout, colour scheme and other thematic elements that help customers recognise the organisation.

The colour and layout of a retail store can be the difference between a great shopping experience and one that results in a shopper exiting your store empty-handed.

In many stores, customers are unable to touch products that are in packaging. As a part of your store strategy, you need to think of ways of creating an interactive layout that provides customers an opportunity to have a feel of the products.

One way would be to display models of the products as was discussed in the case of Harrods' children section, to allow customers the opportunity of sampling products. An example will be to place batteries in electronic devices so that customers are able to sample them. This strategy alone can dramatically increase your sales.

A good store layout will not only help you influence customer's behaviour by properly designing customer flow, merchandise placement and the entire ambiance; it also provides you with an understanding of sale per square foot. This can help you properly determine the extent to which you are utilising your selling space.

Below is a breakdown of the benefits of having good store layout.

Layout your image

Your store is not only the theatre for the physical display of your products. It is also an outline of the image of your store. Like any business, image sells and your store image is more valuable than your merchandise. Having the right layout can enhance your overall image.

Predict customer buying behaviour

The strategic arrangement of fixtures, strategic placement of staircases, escalators and departments affect store traffic and the amount of time customers spend in your store. The longer customers stay in your store, the more likely is it that they will buy. Therefore, the goal of your store layout needs to be to keep customers as long as possible in your store.

A good example of strategically laying out a retail store to retain customers for longer in the store is the display strategy used by supermarkets and grocery retailers. They display essential products such as bread, milk and egg at the end of the store.

It forces customers to walk pass other products before reaching them. Department stores also use this strategy. By placing children department on the top floor of their store, they encourage customers to walk through other departments thus increasing the possibility of them buying other things as they walk.

Maximize selling space

You can measure the productivity of your sales space per square foot by monitoring the sales figure of each area in your store. Based on your assessment of the outcome of your measurement, if you notice that a specific area of the store is not meeting its sales goals, you can rearrange the fixtures and merchandises to improve the situation.

The objective of an effective store layout is to display as much merchandise as possible per square foot and ensure the merchandise is displayed to attract sales.

Ensure high value items are given priority when designing your store layout. Low ticket items can be displayed in such a way as to ensure they occupy minimum space.

Implement contextual display

The implementation of a contextual display is another way of making effective use of your display space. Products that are somewhat related to one another can be displayed in the same location. This is likely to trigger impulse buying and maximise the use of your selling space.

Also placing similar brands in the same section or displaying complementary products such as shirts and ties increases the possibility of sales and is a good use of display space.

Use layout to instigate positive emotions

Your store layout can determine the customer's emotion and sentiment they display while they are in your store. The emotions your store layout triggers in customers as they walk around would determine whether they buy or not.

If you intend to trigger a positive and relaxed feeling, your choice of colour, the arrangement of the merchandise and fixtures would determine whether you trigger your desired emotion in the customer.

Loss prevention

In the final analysis, your ultimate desire is to make a profit. The best way of making profit is to increase sales and reduce shrinkage. Creative arrangement of your merchandises, fixtures and layout can reduce the possibility of crime in your store.

The manner, in which your store is laid out, sends a signal to criminals, dishonest employees or shoplifters that you will not tolerate any form of criminal activity. It is very critical that you involve loss prevention in the preparation of your store design blueprint. By including loss prevention in the process you can benefit from expert advice on how to use your store layout to design out crime.

The importance of colour in store design

Colour is a very critical aspect of your store design. Colour is a very powerful intangible aspect of a design that if used properly can result in enormous benefit for the store.

On the other hand executed poorly, it can result in loss sales. Colour has a huge effect on the mood of people. Colour can stimulate happiness, relaxation, a feeling of comfort or it can result in anxiety and restlessness.

Consequently, as you make the decision on the colour of your store, the deciding factor has to be what emotion you want to trigger in your customers. Choosing a colour scheme to distinguish your store from the competition is somewhat of an art and a science, and it depends on your type of retail store and the image you wish to convey.

There are a lot of guidelines regarding colour application. For instance dark colour is inappropriate for small spaces or painting a space white makes it appear larger and grander.

Imagine how inviting your store would look with professionally painted signs, texture effects and the latest paint finishes. Or a super-modern digital print hangings, stencilled designs and murals that create a striking feature that will attract new customers to your store.

Colours such as blue, purple, white and green are believed to encourage a feeling of calm and relaxation. It is believed that stores decorated with these colours stimulate a feeling of rationalisation and positive thoughts in the minds of customers, resulting in them spending more in those stores.

Customers in stores with those colours are generally calmer, go about their shopping slowly and stay longer in the store.

On the other hand, stores with red or orange considered hot colours generate a feeling of anxiety and claustrophobia in their customers. Customers in those stores do not stay long because they feel uneasy, restless and impatient.

However, all colours have their pros and cons. Bright colours such as red and orange are excellent colours for attracting attention to your store. In most instances, the first thing a customer notices when on a shopping spree is not the name of the retailer or its brand logo but its colour.

How to determine a good colour and store layout?

Listed below are steps for determining your store's colour and layout:

Step One

It is very critical that every aspect of your store layout is taken into consideration during the planning stage of your store design. The essence of the layout is to reflect your store's image; therefore it has to be part and parcel of your store design blueprint.

Step Two

Decide on the type of atmosphere you want to have in your store. You might prefer your store to look feminine, sophisticated, masculine, child friendly, gothic or unisex.

Step Three

Choose the appropriate colour scheme for your target market. If your store is a lingerie store, you might want to go for a sultry, sensual feel. This would demand using colours such as black, cream, gold, deep pink and red, as opposed to blue, green or yellow.

When choosing walls and flooring colours, it is very important to keep the goal of the space usage in mind. If you intend on selling children products, warm and exhilarating colours would be appropriate.

Step Four

Offer multiple buying opportunities when customers are in your store. Create your design blueprint in a way that popular items are placed at the back of the store to ensure customers walk through the entire store. Display inexpensive and impulse items at the front of the store or close to the checkout counter.

Step Five

Make your store as easy as possible to navigate by placing clear signs in each section. Ensure products are accessible by using fixtures that are easy for customers to reach. When customers are unable to reach products, they might just leave without buying.

Step Four

Ensure you have adequate space for customers to walk freely across aisles. Narrow aisles create a feeling of entrapment. The front of the store should be more spacious than other areas because that is the where the highest level of traffic is located.

Step Five

Ensure high ticket items are displayed in secured cabinets to reduce the risk of theft. When customers want to see those items, a staff member should be available to open the cabinet for them.

Step Six

Select the appropriate lighting system. Store lighting systems would be dealt with in another chapter. However, it is important that you include the lighting system in your store design layout because light plays a crucial role in product presentation. A good lighting system can make a product appear more valuable than it actually is.

The layout and design you chose for your store needs to be based on the overall vision of your store. You first and foremost need to take into account your target market. It is the selection of your target market that would determine the type of layout and colour that would suit your store.

Chapter Six

The Best Retail Store Lighting System

Retailers tend to focus on ample lighting while paying scant attention to the quality of the light in their store. But the quality of light in your store is a very significant determinant of the success of your store. Good lighting is important for:

- Attracting customers into your store
- Guiding them through the store
- Helping them evaluate the products
- Helping your store associates complete sale swiftly and accurately

More than the above light is closely linked to:

- Increasing store sales
- Providing customers with a good impression of your type of store
- Increasing the perceived value of your products
- Creating a conducive shopping environment for your customers

The most common things taken into consideration whenever retailers think of ways of increasing sales are:

a) Increased advertising

b) Intensive promotion

c) New product line

d) Changing store fixtures

e) Relocating products

The lighting scheme of their store is never taken into consideration. A good quality lighting system in your store enhances the look of both the store and the display.

When your store appearance is enhanced because of good lighting customers are more likely to believe that the products in your store are of high quality. The core of marketing is perception…what the customer thinks about your store.

I am not suggesting you deceive your customers with lighting technology. What I am trying to point out is that good lighting increases the chances of customers wanting to enter your store.

Listed below are the most commonly used retail lighting systems:

Ambient Lighting

Figure 9: Ambient lighting aid shoppers movement around the store

Ambient lighting is the basic lighting system in a retail store that aids customers' movement around the store and helps them to evaluate products. Ambient lighting is just a basic lighting system;

light that enables people to see clearly when they get on with mundane activity in a slightly dark area.

Accent Lighting

Figure 10: Accent Lighting is used to highlight a specific item in a displace

Accent lighting commonly known as "focus" lighting is used to draw attention to a few products in a retail store. This is particularly useful for highlighting high ticket or promotional products.

Accent lighting is the favoured lighting system of luxury retailers. That's because it allows them to highlight individual products in the store. Except for promotion accent lighting is not very useful in a low end store.

High Activity Lighting

Figure 11: High Activity Lighting focuses attention on a specific department

High Activity Lighting schemes are used to focus attention on a particular area of the store. Whilst accent light focuses on a specific product, High Activity Lights focus on specific areas. There might be areas of the store that are darker because of location or fixtures. High Activity Lights can be used to brighten up such areas.

High Activity Lights can also be used to promote a certain department or section of the store. If there is less traffic in certain areas of the store, High Activity Lights can be used to increase traffic to those areas by highlighting them.

Shelf and Case Lighting

Figure 12: Shelf and Case Lighting is used to illuminate display cabinet

Shelf and Case Lightings are used in display cabinets and shelves where certain high ticket or exclusive items are displayed. Shelf and Case Lighting serves two purposes: to ensure that the product is properly seen in the display case and to enhance the appearance of the product.

Perimeter and Valance Lighting

Figure 13: Perimeter and Valance Lighting is used for towers and tall shelves

The Perimeter lighting scheme is used for tall vertical shelving and displays. While a valance lighting scheme conceals the source of light on merchandise. Perimeter lights are often positioned in a way that they illuminate the vertical surfaces of the area.

Architectural Lighting

Figure 14: Architectural lighting highlights the design of a building

The Architectural lighting scheme is used to light up and highlight the architectural design of a building. Architectural lighting can be used on the inside or outside of a building. Luxury retailers use Architectural lighting to show up the shape of their retail design.

Task Lighting

Figure 15: Task Lighting is used to conduct specific task

Task lights are installed specifically for use by staff assigned to specific tasks. They can be installed at the checkout counter, customer services counter or in specific areas of the store where store associates are expected to perform specific tasks.

Your lighting scheme needs to help customers to see what you sell and your store associates perform their duties well.

Be aware that Illumination of your store is a major factor in your customer's buying decision. In most instances shoppers will not buy a product if they have not had the opportunity to properly evaluate it and establish its specific attributes such as colour, texture and quality.

Your store lighting must also be good enough for customers to be able to read the price tag and labels of products.

Generally, a good lighting level in a store is about 75 foot candle and a bit higher level if your target market is older people.

The decision as to which lighting system you choose for your store should be guided by the primary objectives of any retail lighting system:

Attracting customers into your store

The style of lighting you have in your store should signal to your customers that your store is open for business. Your lighting system needs to breed curiosity in shoppers as they pass by your store.

Guide them through the store

You lighting needs to guide customers around the store and to specific areas you would like them to see. When you make effective use of accent lighting, you can control customers' movement within the store and persuade them to go from one section to the next to see what's on display.

Helping the customers evaluate the products

An adequately lit area makes it easier for customers to weigh up products and make buying decisions. When customers have the opportunity to checkout products without any form of hindrance, they are more likely to make a buying decision.

Helping your store associates complete sale swiftly and accurately

The point-of-sale, customer service desk, changing rooms and all other points of the store where store associates are expected to serve customers, need to be well lit so they could perform their duties easily.

Below are some important factors to consider when installing lighting system in your store:

- Colour rendering index/colour temperature

- Contrast/accent/highlight
- Daylight Integration/regulator
- Direct glare/reflected glare
- Image/style
- Modelling of objects/shadows
- Visual priority/organization
- Quantity of light on vertical displays
- Quantity of light on horizontal surfaces
- Use high colour rendering lights

When selecting your lighting system, you need to ensure that the types of bulbs you choose are those that make product colours appear as natural as possible.

What to look for when selecting your light system?

The specification on the packaging that indicates it renders colours accurately.

Colour rendering index (CRI) is specified on bulb packaging or on manufacturer's catalogues.

CRI of lights ranges from one to as high as a hundred. For your store, you need to select lights with a CRI of 80 or above. Some standard halogen incandescent, fluorescent and metal halide lights meet the 80 and above CRI value.

Lighting fixtures should limit glare

Ensure that the type of lighting system you choose limit the customer's view of the light louvers, baffles, and lenses. When light shines in the eyes of the customer, it creates discomfort and reduces the customer's desire to stay in your store.

Lighting system such as accent Lighting should be aimed directly at the products. Spot lights with small beams should be selected as well as fixtures in which the light is dipped into the fixture's opening. Ensure that lights are not aimed directly toward the aisles or doorways to prevent it shining into the eyes on customers.

Properly distribute light

Light has to be evenly distributed throughout your store. The entrance, areas between aisles and display have to be well lit to ensure customers are able to see products properly as they move around the store.

Since most products are displayed vertically, it is essential that the lighting system you select can properly light vertical surfaces. This is possible by using adjustable fixtures that can be directed toward shelves and vertical displays or by selecting ceiling-mounted fixtures that are designed for all round coverage.

Attract customers to products with light

Figure 16: A good lighting system makes products appear more attractive and valuable

A good lighting system can be an effective way of attracting customer's attention to specific areas of your store you would like them to go.

It is a mistake to use spot or accent Light such as halogen reflector lamps all over your store. They make the store appear cluttered and can sometimes confuse the customers. Light should be effectively used to attract customers and adequate in specific areas such as checkout or customer service counters.

Below is a further guide for choosing and implementing an effective lighting system:

> Place the lighting source as close as possible to the merchandise.
>
> For ambient lighting, use efficient diffusers such as fluorescents.
>
> For accent lighting, use narrow beam spotlights such as Halogen PARs or Low-Voltage MR-16s.
>
> Brighten up your store aisles with spill light from the accented merchandising areas or displays.
>
> Use the lightest colours on the interior surfaces of shelving.
>
> Ensure you use organized patterns of lighting fixtures. Chaotic patterns may confuse, agitate or fatigue the customers.
>
> Ensure you use high colour rendering lamps for both ambient and task lighting

In clothing stores the lights must be adequate in sales areas and dressing rooms so that customers can see how the items look prior to purchasing.

While lighting must attract customers to your store, the objective needs to be to enable customers to read signage and move unhindered throughout the store. The level and quality of the illumination in your store will create a lasting impression on your customers and will be the key to whether they will return to your store.

Be aware that the lighting system is as dynamic as the products you display; therefore you cannot be rigid about it. You need to understand that certain displays and seasons might require a different lighting system.

Consequently, it is extremely important that you ensure that your store designers make provisions for such events.

Chapter Seven

How To Wow Customers With Creative Storefront Design

As a part of my research for this book, I stopped in at shopping centres around the UK. That was in January, one of the most important months in the sales calendar for the retail industry. The January sales come in the wake of Christmas and more particularly the Boxing Day sales.

Retailers sell and conjure massive discounts as they bid to unload excess end of year stock before they restock and update lines for the New Year. So shoppers are wooed with discounts of up to 70%.

What happens during these sales is every business rule is broken. Instead of focusing on profit, retailers focus entirely on sales. I couldn't help but observe that there was total disregard for the security of the merchandises and storefronts ceased to function as instruments of marketing.

However, the first two points are not the topics of discussion in this chapter, therefore, I will limit my discussion to the third aspect which is the storefront.

A retail storefront serves three main purposes:

1) It is the image of the store and all that it represents
2) It serves as an effective marketing tool to attract customers into the store
3) It is the point of transition between the outside world and your store

Despite the significance of the storefront in retailing, too many retailers pay scant attention to this area. They spend most of their time getting the inside of their store design right and completely ignore the storefront.

For a start, the storefront window is the most expensive part of a retail space. It is considered to be equal to one third of the entire cost of the store rental. In his book: "Window and Interior Display – The Principles of Visual Merchandising", Robert Kretschmer reveals that *"A small store out of the high-rent district, with a rental of $100 a month, would put a yearly rental value of $400 on its window. Windows of the higher-class stores are often considered to be worth £20,000 a year or more. In New York City stores such as Macy's value their window space at more than $100,000 a year".*

Kretschmer feels that the value of the store window is based on the number of people who pass by it each day. "So" he explains *"in towns with populations ranging from 2500 to 25,000, window passers-by number between 372 per hour and 4,464 per day."*

To calculate the current value of your storefront, try *Kretschmer's* formula:

> *"The value of a window space is the basis upon which a charge against the merchandise department is determined. Two factors must be taken into consideration: (1) the comparative importance of the space and (2) the actual rental cost of the window. For example a store with 16 windows, 4 of them on a main thoroughfare and the remaining 12 on a side street carrying less traffic, would of course, place a higher rating on its 4 front windows.*
>
> *Windows one through four, on the main thoroughfare, would be rated highest in importance and value. Then, starting with win-*

dow 5 and down the side street to window 16; each window would diminish in value.

Assuming that each of the 4 front windows had an equal rental and budget cost of $18,200 a year, each department using one of them would be charged at that rate, or $60.66 a day (on the basis of 300 working days a year). Window number 16, with a rental and budget cost of only $4800 a year, would draw only $16.00 a day from the departments using it".

Based upon the above formula, calculate the value of your own storefront. You will grasp the importance of maximising its value.

In the beginning of the chapter, I outlined the result of my own research into storefront usage in the UK.

Figure 17: Even though the store front is the most valuable space in a retail store, most retailers do not make good use of the space

Figure 18: Successful retailers know the value of their storefront

When I took a trip around shopping centres in the UK, one observation I made which Kretschmer confirms in his book was that tier one retailers made proper use of their store windows. While tier two and independent retailers not knowing the value of their storefront, covered their entire storefront with discount signs.

> To quote Kretschmer again: *"the modern high-class store shows a few carefully chosen articles in a single unit of a display to create an atmosphere of quality and exclusivity of style. A store of this type may devote forty weeks a year to these simple, exclusive showings.*
>
> *Yet the same store can cram a window full of merchandise for its January white sale or its August housewares clearance or for its Christmas toy displays, without sacrificing any of its dignity.*
>
> *The character of the store is so firmly established by its regular display policy that these sporadic outbursts of high-powered sales promotions only accentuate the high-class rating of the store. The so called middle-class store has a tendency to crowd its display just a little.*
>
> *This store puts more merchandise in its windows than the high-class store, yet at the same time it strives to imitate the style of the quality store. Its aim then must be to attract some of the cream of the trade while still catering to the very profitable middle class."*

The lower-class store directs its attention mainly to the purchaser of low-priced goods. The windows of such a store are often crowded up to the hilt, more like the old-time general store. You can further identify this type of store by its inferior price tickets and gaudy show cards and banners.

Figures (1-5) show images of a tier one retailer. Figures (6-7) show images of tier two and three retailers during the January sales period. As you can see while tier one retailers only have a few sales signs in their windows, tier two and independent retailers cover their entire storefront with sale signs.

> *One of the most important elements of a storefront display is to tell the story of the display. Having a sign that says 70% as the only storefront display of a retail store tells customers that particular retailer has no story to tell.*

The general consensus in marketing is that people buy emotionally but justify their decisions rationally. To appeal to their emotions, you should have more than your price displayed at your storefront. Price is a single factor for which people buy and in most cases it's the least of the reasons why people buy.

Thirty up to 40% of customers will buy on price alone. However, up to 70% will buy on the basis of convenience, good customer experience and quality. Therefore, in order to persuade the large majority of people to enter your store, you need more than 70% discount stickers displayed at your storefront.

First and foremost you need to have a storefront display that triggers all of their buying emotions.

How to design an attractive storefront

The storefront needs to convey a clear message about your brand and products. The message must be simple, unambiguous and to the point that shoppers get it as they walk by. The decision to take a closer look at your display or enter your store depends on how attractive he (she) finds your storefront display.

There is a direct correlation between your storefront design and customer traffic. Traffic will increase if your storefront is designed to catch the eyes and get in to the psyche of shoppers as they pass by your store.

The power of your storefront is as much in its signage, as it is in its lighting; interactive window displays and visual merchandise displays.

Storefronts vary from one store to another. Depending on the type of retailer it can include wholesale stores, kiosks, barrows, market stalls and internet based retail stores. However, all retail storefronts must meet the following three objectives:

    a) Attract shoppers attention
    b) Entice shoppers to enter the store
    c) Persuade them to buy

To meet the above objectives your storefront design must above all else, *represent your store image.*

Your storefronts should be an expression of your store's image. Your storefront has to be design in such a way that it expresses your store's individual identity.

Storefront entrance

Your door location and design are essential components of your storefront. They are the customer's transition from the outside world to your store. Your doors should place customers in the frame of mind of the type of experience they are about to receive. Consequently, it is advisable that doors provide direct link from the sidewalks or streets and should create a unique experience that distinguishes your store from other stores.

Storefront materials

Every component of your storefront needs to be purposefully designed to achieve your objective of attracting customer's attention. All materials used in the design need to be well thought through and of the highest quality. Your window needs to be designed in such a way that it creates a visual connection between the inside and outside of your store. Your entire storefront needs to be well glassed.

The most appropriate materials for a storefront are:

- Wood
- Metal
- Brick
- Stone
- Glass
- Concrete

Your storefront lighting system

A well-lit storefront is a must for the right store image. Effective lighting is good for merchandise displays as well as the safety of your customer and the general public. Sign lighting, including flat-mounted signs, blade and banner signs ought to be lit with covered or down lighting.

Lighting fixtures need to be positioned in such a way that they focus on the products on display not the window or street. When lighting fixtures are not positioned well, they either distract from the display or allow shadows that interfere with the display.

Your awnings

If your store has awnings ensure it is periodically cleaned to maintain the veracity of fabrics; seam and colour. Periodic cleaner also avoids the unnecessary expense of replacement. The awnings can be used as an effective marketing and image building tool. By placing information about your store on it you add feel to the streets cape and variety to the building façade.

It also saves the storefront displays from sun. Design and position should balance the scale of the store facade design.

The best types of awnings are retractable or open side as opposed to vinyl or internally lit awnings.

Signage

Your storefront signage illuminates the outside of your store and attracts customers like moths to a flame. Here the lighting also builds a sense of branding and brand engagement. The signage peeps into the souls of customers and creates a connection between them and your storefront signage.

This helps in the creation of brand awareness and brand loyalty. Your storefront signage needs to be incorporated into your entire storefront design and the store design itself.

Strategies for designing an attractive store

Display your finest products in your storefront window

Display your best and newest collection of products in your storefront window. However, avoid the temptation of cluttering the display with too many items. This would only confuse your customers. Displaying a few items with adequate space around them will allow each product to stand out. Ensure that the theme of the season is clearly visible in the display. Changing the theme of your displays on a constant basis will bring an aura of newness to the display.

Maintain a clean storefront

Your storefront ought to be clean and tidy at all times. You need to ensure that glass windows are sparkling clean to increase visibility; bricks and mortar buildings are pressure washed, wooden buildings are treated with vanish with a gloss finish and litter, leaves or any types of dirt is constantly removed from your store entrance.

Encourage curiosity with sidewalk sales

Extending your display to outside of your store, for example in the centre of the shopping centre, stirs curiosity. For loss prevention reasons, ensure the products displayed outside of your store are in inexpensive. Where ever possible display dummies. Remember the goal is to stimulate curiosity not to facilitate theft.

Make promotion and discount visible

This might seem to run contrary to what I said in an earlier chapter about displaying huge sales signs on your storefront. I am not suggesting that you display large signs that prevent shoppers from seeing your displays. There needs to be a balance between advertising and display. You need to ensure that customers are able to see the products on display while at the same time in a distinct yet visible manner make them aware of promotions and special offers.

Decorate storefront with plants

If possible enhance your storefront with plants. Placing plants at the entrance of your store sends very warm message of welcome to your customer and make them feel at home in your store.

There is almost a mystical or magical connection between humans and plants. Plants stimulate our natural senses especially in towns and cities, people want to have the opportunity to get closer to nature. Therefore, just having plants at the entrance of your store is enough to attract customers to your store.

Steps for designing an attractive store

Step One
Ensure your storefront is made entirely of glass with focal points, wooden cubes and shelves for merchandise.

Step Two
Fit awnings to protect shoppers viewing your displays, from rain, sun or snow.

Step Three
Install attractive and informative signage that is visible from the other side of the road and is easy to read. Signs should be hung on the outside of the building, front door and windows.

Step Four
Decorate the pavement of the door front with attractive tiles and ensure that door frames are big enough for all sizes of customers.

Step Five
Install an adequate lighting system at your storefront. Ensure proper lighting on display and the entrance as a whole.

Step Six
Paint your storefront with a vibrant colour; hang seasonal banners; flags or holiday decoration. Just do anything that would make your storefront standout.

Remember your storefront is the best and most inexpensive marketing tool at your disposal. Make full use of it and make sure that every decision you make about your storefront design is based on sound marketing principles.

Chapter Eight

How To Choose The Right Materials For Store Design

Design of a building starts with the concept or reason the building is to be designed. The next step is the development of the blueprint followed by the purchasing of the materials to construct the building.

Each of these aspects of a building is equally important because without the concept, the blueprint would not be created and without the materials the building would not be built.

In the last few chapters, we have dealt with the concept and the blueprint. This chapter is about showing you the best materials to use in the creation of a magnificent store design and why they are the best.

Retailing like any other business is very competitive. To compete in a crowded field, victory is possible once you have the ability to stand out from the crowd. Like most things in life, the difference between success and failure depends on doing the little things better than the rest of the field. In retailing one of those little things is to ensure that you acquire the right materials for your store design.

The three areas of your store design you really need to focus on are:

- Ceiling
- Walls
- Floor

In the rest of this chapter, I will introduce the most commonly used ceilings, walls and floors in retail store design and explain the benefits of using them.

Ceiling

I am quite aware that not a lot of people entering retail store raise their head to see how the ceiling looks. I promise you, there are a lot of people who will notice if your ceiling is not impressive. It is curious how thing like this works. When things are right, it is taken for granted. However, when things go wrong everyone notice them.

I introduce the concept because as I dive into the most commonly used types of ceilings, there is the tendency for many retailers especially tier two and three retailers to belief that people would not notice their ceiling.

> *When your ceiling looks good, hardly anyone will pay attention to it. That is a fact. However, if it is not presentable everyone will notice it, remember that.*

Ceilings are classified in accordance with their appearance or construction:

- Cathedral ceiling
- Cathedral ceiling is a tall ceiling area similar to that used in churches
- Dropped ceiling

Dropped ceilings are specifically used for aesthetic or practical purposes either to achieve a certain ceiling height or to provide space for piping.

Listed below are suggestions on what to consider as a good ceiling design:

Flat white ceiling

Figure 19: Flat white ceiling give the illusion of height

A flat white ceiling is necessary in a retail store with low ceiling. It gives the perception of height in a store with low ceiling.

Tin ceiling

Figure 20: Tin ceiling gives the store an elegant appearance

Tin ceilings can give your store an elegance appearance and draw customers' attention as they shop. The name tin ceilings originated from the material used for the ceiling during the Victorian era.

They are now available in different metallic finishes. Aluminium is the most commonly used type because unlike some other metals, aluminium does not corrode and is very light, flexible and reasonably priced.

Wooded ceiling

Figure 21: Wooded ceiling adds warmth and charm to the store

Using wooden panelling would add warmth and charm to your store and provide a subtle finish. Matching a wooden surface with other wooden surfaces such as wooden curtain poles or ornaments can result in a cohesive and stylish finish.

Acoustic Ceiling

Figure 22: Acoustic Ceiling are sound-absorbing ceiling

Acoustic ceiling tiles are sound-absorbing ceiling tiles dropped into grid metal strips suspended from the actual original ceiling of the store. They were originally developed by interior designers as a way of lowering ceilings and reducing the level of noise in a room.

In addition to reducing noise, acoustic ceilings can also conceal unattractive fixtures, wires and pipes that may be running along the ceiling of older buildings.

The following are the pros and cons of using acoustic ceilings:

Pros:

- Acoustic ceiling reduces sound between floors of building and inside the store making it comfortable for customers to carry on their shopping.
- Acoustic ceiling tiles are simple to maintain or replace and can be painted.

Cons:

- Panels can be easily damaged by moisture causing the panel to drop from the ceiling unexpectedly in extreme cases.

- Moisture damage show and dries leaving an unpleasant stain on the ceiling.

Gypsum board ceilings

Figure 23 & 24: Gypsum board ceilings are commonly used products

Gypsum board is a common product currently used for walls and ceilings in homes and stores. It is easy to install however, the installation of suspension system requires a professional installer.

Gypsum can be found in sedimentary rocks all around the world. A layer of gypsum sandwiched between two sheets of thick paper is known as Dry wall.

The pros and cons of gypsum board ceilings:

Pros:

- Gypsum board ceilings are relatively simple to install and are reasonably priced
- Gypsum ceiling tile provides variety of designs, acoustical and aesthetic qualities.

Cons:

- Gypsum board ceilings do not absorb sound very well.
- Gypsum board ceilings can be easily damaged. It is recommended you use chemically treated gypsum wallboard that is moisture resistant in a store that has high moisturised contents.

Plastic Ceiling

Figure 25: Plastic Ceiling are alternative to wood and tile

Plastic ceiling tiles are an alternative to wood or plaster tiles that are commonly used by a majority of retailers. Plastic ceilings are reasonably priced, strong and long lasting. They are very light in comparison to wood making it easier to work with them. They do not appear as elegant or presentable as acoustic tiles or gypsum board ceilings.

Aluminium Ceiling

Figure 26: Aluminium Ceiling will not rut or crack

Aluminium ceilings are very durable ceiling that would not rust or crack because they are made from a non-porous material. They are easy to install because they consist of different panels. They can be installed like acoustic ceiling and fitted to the main ceiling.

Walls

The decision of wall covering in your store should be based upon: style, ambience, theme, image and the practicality of maintenance. If you choose to paint your store, it is advisable to use washable paints.

The most commonly used materials for walls in a retail store are gypsum board (dry wall). Their surface has slots which allow pipes, cables and conduits to run through them. Retail walls are either full height or partial height.

Plaster walls can also be used in place of gypsum board. They can be moulded into different shapes enabling them to form curve or soffit walls which cannot be done with gypsum board walls. Plaster walls are more durable than gypsum board walls and can be used in other areas of the shopping centre.

Wall Covering

The most commonly used wall covering in retail space is painting. In addition to heavy-textured paints, the three main types of wall finishing are gloss, semi-gloss and flat.

Flat paints are suitable for walls, while gloss and semi-gloss are suitable for doors, trims and high contact areas.

Wall paper is another type of covering used in some retail stores. Wall papers need to be located in less contact areas; probably close to the ceilings.

Wood

Figure 27: A combination of soft and hard wooden walls are commonly used

Oak, red or white wood are the most common types of wooden wall finishing in retail stores. Combinations of hard and soft woods are constantly used depending on the preference of the retailer. Hard wood include walnut, rosewood, mahogany, ash, oak and teak, while softwoods are pine, birch, cedar and redwood.

Hardboard, metal and plastic wall panelling

Figure 28: Hardboard panelling is an inexpensive thin particle board

Hardboard panelling is an inexpensive thin particle board about a quarter inch thick, composing materials that simulate solid wood. They can also be found in laminated tambour created to achieve batter effect.

Panelling or laminated plastic made from three quarter inch particle board layers of plastics which can be custom designed for individual retail stores. Plastic laminates are very durable and available in different colours, finishes and patterns and easy to clean but susceptible to chipping at the corners.

Metal laminates are also very durable especially when laminated to particle board. They are available in different types and finishes, stainless steel, aluminium, copper and brass.

Glass Walls

Figure 29: Glass is not easy to work with

Mirrors are used to create the illusion of extra space or reflect images. Mirrors are available in clear, grey and bronze finishes and are about a quarter thick. Glass is not particularly easy to work with, therefore the design needs to be uncomplicated.

Tile Walls

Figure 30: Tile Walls is durable and offers great degree of flexibility

Ceramic tiles can also be used as a wall finishing and are available in different sizes, shapes and colours. Terrazo is also very durable wall finishing that offers great degree of flexibility.

Flooring

Flooring is another very important component of retail store design. Unlike the ceiling, customers actually look at the flooring when they enter the store, therefore, it is imperative that you lay good flooring in your store.

Carpeting is the most widely used flooring type in the retail industry for the obvious reason that it is reasonably priced and comes in a variety of colours and textures and it has significant sound absorbing properties.

Other flooring materials used are:

- Resilient floors
- Wooded floors
- Non-resilient floors

Ceramic tile flooring

Figure 31: Ceramic tile is a very durable surface used for any type of application

Ceramic tile is a very durable surface that is recommended for basically any type of application. Ceramic is water resistant and there are porcelain tiles which are frost resistant and frost proof in some cases.

Ceramic tiles are so far the favourite retail flooring because they are highly resistant to moisture, stain and wear. They are generally produced in larger sizes and are suitable for large retail areas.

Vinyl composition flooring

Figure 32: Vinyl composition tiles are also widely used because they are very durable

Vinyl composition tiles are also widely used because they are very durable and the tiles bump flush together.

There are two types of vinyl floors:

Printed vinyl containing fillers of durability are made by imprinting a design on a film over a vinyl base.

Solid vinyl is widely preferred in high-traffic retail stores as the colour and pattern go through the entire thickness.

Eco tile flooring

Figure 33: Eco tile is an attractive and hardwearing interlocking floor tile

Eco tile is an attractive and hardwearing interlocking floor tile. It is designed to allow quick and simple glue less installation. They are thick and durable and are popular amongst retailers. Eco tile floor finishes are also low maintenance and last significantly longer than conventional vinyl or any other carpet alternative.

Listed below are tips for choosing your store materials:

- Select materials that are modern
- Select materials that are extremely durable
- Select materials that are quick and easy to install

- Select materials with good anti-slip properties
- Select materials that are easy to clean and maintain
- Select materials that are dynamic can be easily changed if the situation demands
- Select materials that are ideal for oily substrates

Chapter Nine

How To Design A Profitably Retail Store

In chapter two, I outlined the three factors responsible for Harrods phenomenal success as:

- Good store design
- Attractive visual merchandise display
- Effective loss prevention strategy

The subject of loss prevention is something that has never been taken seriously by the retail industry even though the industry spends billions each year on loss prevention. In fact in the last ten years, loss prevention spending has increased tremendously. In 2011 retail spending on loss prevention rose to $128 billion, however, in the same period retail shrinkage rose to $119 billion.

So why is it that despite the huge amount spent on loss prevention, retail shrinkage continues to rise?

To answer this question, let's take a peek into Harrods loss prevention strategy.

Harrods store design and visual merchandising displays are definitely factors in its success. However, the key factor responsible for Harrods' success is its ability to remain profitable. And in business, profit is king.

In retail the formula for making profit is to increase sales and reduce shrinkage.

Increasing sales requires good store design and attractive visual merchandising. Reducing shrinkage requires an effective loss prevention strategy.

So what do Harrods and most successful retailers have over the rest in the retail industry? It is their ability to simultaneously increase sales and reduce shrinkage. Most retailers know how to increase sales, but when it comes to reducing their shrinkage, they are challenged.

Getting these two right is the fundamental principle of retail success. No retailer can succeed without simultaneously increasing sales and reducing shrinkage.

Why does shrinkage reduction or loss prevention measures fail in most retail organisations?

Loss prevention measures fail as a result of the following:

- Lack of understanding of the subject
- Senior management's failure to prioritise
- Outsourcing loss prevention without a mechanism for accountability
- Inexperienced loss prevention managers
- Ineffective use of loss prevention technology

Harrods is the first retail store that I have ever entered that has no visible blind spots. I am not suggesting that there are absolutely no blind spots as I managed to spot a few.

> *However, the difference with other stores is that Harrods' blind spots are invisible to the untrained eyes.*

Anyone deciding to shoplift in Harrods would have to be:

- A professional shoplifter or part of an organised retail crime syndicate
- Really brave
- Really stupid

Products are displayed in such a manner that each department seems wide open. Store employees standing at one end of a department have a clear view of the entire department.

There is CCTV in every corner of the store. In addition to electronic surveillance store assistants buzz around like bees and make it difficult for anyone who might be intending on shoplift.

I am not saying that it is impossible to shoplift from Harrods. Far from that, shoplifting prevention requires the implementation of a combination of strategies. However, by adopting their type of store design, displaying their products in the manner that they are displayed and taking other loss prevention measures, Harrods has drastically reduced the possibility of shoplifting.

Now contrast Harrods loss prevention strategy with a top ten UK retailer that I once worked for as a store detective.

A few years back, I was employed as a store detective for a leading retailer in the UK. On my very first day at work, whilst in the middle of briefing with the officer I was relieving, I noticed a couple walk into the store and head towards the coat section.

I stood there perplexed as I witnessed the lady remove one of the coats from the hanger, try it on, and then casually walk to the exit with her partner and scurry into the waiting getaway car. £900 walked out the door with such incredible ease, made me think "Holy cow! How can this sort of thing happen in broad daylight?"

The answer was actually quite apparent: The coats were prominently displayed right close to the exit.

Keeping this experience as a vivid reminder, any time I was assigned to a different store, I took great care to walk around and look for high ticket items that were not securely displayed. I would call the store manager over and advise that the items be relocated to more secure locations within the store. To my disbelief, most managers failed to take my advice – in their eyes, I am merely a store detective. What did I know about proper merchandising?

As a second example: I was working at a store in London Colney, immediately upon entering the store I noticed coats worth £250 prominently displayed near the store entrance. I located the store manager and expressed my concern to him.

I even joked with him how even the CIA Director at the time, George Tenant, could not possibly protect those coats where they were positioned. This manager ignored my warning. A few hours later, some of the coats were stolen, just as I had predicted.

When I approached the manager again, I figured he would pay more attention to me now that my gloomy prediction had come true. Once again, he failed to heed my warning only paying attention to me after 20 out of the 25 coats had been stolen.

At this same location, there are two big retailers who shared a single toilet facility located outside of both stores. Shoplifters knew this and would steal from one store, head to the direction of the toilet, pass through the other store and escape. When they were stopped and questioned by our store security, they would mention they were on their way to the toilet.

They were technically correct about the direction they were heading given the location of the toilet. The location of the toilet caused both stores to lose thousands pounds to shoplifting. Yet neither store's management could pin-point the location of the toilet as one of the primary causes of their shrinkage.

I share these stories with you to emphasize a very important point: Shoplifting occurs in most retail stores simply because it is allowed to take place.

> *Shoplifting is a crime of opportunity, eliminate the opportunity and you reduce its possibility.*

To increase sales yet fail to reduce profit draining activities is false economy. Many retailers feel loss prevention is something that they could do if they had the resources. The reality is: it is something that you cannot afford not to do because no retailer can become profitable without implementing effective loss prevention measures.

Inexperienced loss prevention managers

Ninety to 95% of retail loss prevention department managers are ex-service personnel. As a result of their law enforcement background, they take the law enforcement approach to their work. They focus mainly on arresting shoplifters and dishonest employees.

While it is true that shoplifting and employee theft accounts for almost 70% of retail shrinkage, they are not the sole cause of shrinkage. Furthermore, shoplifting and employee dishonesty cannot be tackled by solely arresting individuals. Preventative measures such as good store design and visual merchandise displays, as I mentioned in the case of Harrods, are the key to shrinkage reduction.

However, due to the fact that the majority of retail loss prevention managers know very little about store design and visual merchandising, they are unable to incorporate these aspects into their loss prevention strategies. As a result most loss prevention measures fail.

> *"The average retailer makes a 1% net profit out of each dollar and the average industry shrinkage percentage is 2.6%. This means that shrinkage is almost three times the average retailer's profit margin. By reducing retail shrinkage to 50% – from 2.6 cents to 1.3 cents, a retailer could more than double his profits: from 1 cent to 2.3 cents"*. (Crosset Company newsletter, June 2010)

Outsource Loss Prevention

Some retailers outsource their loss prevention department to outside contractors. As laudable as this may seem, it is a seriously flawed idea because retailers are sometimes incapable of clearly articulating their expected outcome.

When a job is outsourced, there is usually an expected outcome. However, if the retailer outsourcing the job cannot articulate their expected outcome, it is difficult to hold the contractor accountable.

Wal-Mart founder Sam Walton once described retail shrinkage as a "profit killer". He was right. High shrinkage is responsible for the death of many retail organisations.

The benefit of a good store design is to increase sales with the use of attractive merchandising display. However, attractive display does not necessarily mean designing your store without developing mechanism for crime prevention.

As you develop your store design blueprint, you need to ensure that the safety of the products is paramount. In the final analysis you are in business to make profit. You cannot make profit if you increase sales at the expense of the security of your products.

Without losing the original purpose of your store design, you can apply changes to the way fixtures are arranged in your store in order to decrease the chances of theft.

> *One way of doing this is to locate smaller items in places that are visible to employees. Furthermore, positioning employees in key areas of the store is a good shoplifting prevention strategy.*

Larger products need to be placed in small quantities to prevent the store from appearing cluttered. Poor display of large products can obscure the view of employees and increase the possibility for shoplifting.

Aisles and shelves need to be properly labelled to ensure customers can easily and quickly locate products.

In addition to labelling, installing proper lighting will attract buyers to products as well as allow your employees to observe the surroundings more effectively.

There is no fail proof way of preventing shoplifting. However, the installation of security systems such as CCTV and mirrors can reduce incidence of shoplifting in your store. Security mirrors optimize employee's view of the store and reduce blind spots.

How to increase your sales and simultaneously increase your profit?

The following are effective steps for increasing sales and profit with a good store design:

Step 1:

Locate smaller products close to areas that employees frequently visit to reduce the risk of shoplifting.

Step 2:

Reduce the number of large products on display to allow store employees unhindered views of the store.

Step 3:

Position employees in key locations of the store to increase overall security.

Step 4:

Security mirrors in the store to reduce blind spots and increase surveillance.

Step 5:

Use CCTV in areas that are not regularly frequented by employees and place high ticket products under cameras.

Step 6:

Ensure your loss prevention department is involved in the planning of your store design blueprint.

Years ago, shoplifting was conducted by homeless and drug addicts wanting to feed their habit. Today shoplifting is conducted by retail crime gangs using more sophisticated methods, never before seen in the industry. Within four minutes, an organised retail crime gang could steal seven thousand pounds worth of products from your store.

Think about this when developing your store design blueprint.

Chapter Ten

The Best Store Design Technologies

Technology can enhance the process of your store design and enable you to achieve your objectives of increasing sales and profit. However, in order to derive the maximum benefit from any technology; it is essential that you choose the most appropriate technology for your store and target market.

There is no one size fit all when it comes to the acquisition and implementation of technology. Consequently, prior to the acquisition of store design technology, it is imperative that you give consideration to the desired outcome of the technology.

Here are seven questions you should answer prior to investing in store design technology:

1) What are the types of store design technologies available?
2) What are their functionalities including features and benefits?
3) What constraints do they diminish?
4) Where can they be sourced?
5) What policies and procedures helped you to operate without those technologies?
6) What policies and procedures should you put in place now to adapt to the new technologies?
7) Are the technologies future-proof?

Answering the above questions would guide you in your decision of selecting the most appreciated store design technologies for your store.

The use of technology is essential for any retail operation. Whatever the size of the retail store, technology has both tangible and intangible benefits and helps to increase profit, increase productivity and improve customer satisfaction.

In order to provide convenience and a unique shopping experience for your customers, listed below are examples of the latest retail technologies in the market:

Information kiosk:

- Provides information on locating products in a store
- Is valuable for displaying promotional and advertising information
- It can be used in a shopping centre to show location of stores

Satellite navigation software:

- Helps shoppers find products by using an app that runs on Smart phones
- Speeds up shopping by showing customers a 3-D store map and the shortest route to pick up everything they need

Sensormatic Safer Electronic Article Surveillance (EAS) Solutions:

- With Sensormatic Safer Electronic Article Surveillance customers now have the freedom to openly select high value items without waiting for store associates. Specific area of the store could be fitted with the system.
- High ticket items have safe lock to prevent shoplifting

Radio Frequency Identification (RFID technology):

- Provides retailers with an advanced bar coding system as no line-of-sight is required to read a product with an RFID tag

- Automates the retail supply chain, reducing labour costs, human error and time spent checking in products
- Is less susceptible to damage as it is placed on a product or embedded in plastic to withstand harsh environmental conditions such as moisture, exposure to chemicals and outdoors

Point-Of-Sale system (POS Technology)

- Records sales as they occur and provides detailed inventory report
- Solves a variety of operational and record-keeping problems
- Can be customised to meet your specific requirements
- Can quickly locate sale prices and costs of all products
- Help determine the causes of shrinkage
- Records marked downs and discounts
- Tracks promotion successfully and easily
- Accurately reveals the effect of promotions
- Helps monitor store associate activity and productivity
- Ensures product prices are consistent in multiple retail operations
- Can be integrated into other software providers packages such as expenses, payroll or staff attendance software
- Helps in effective workflow distribution to accurately monitor activity of each store associate
- Provides accurate customer profile: buying behaviour, addresses or emails
- Facilitates an easy payment method

A lot of new retail technologies are constantly introduced into the market. I have chosen to focus on the main ones that can be integrated into other types of technologies. Most importantly, they can all be used for loss prevention purposes. It is a fact of life that new technologies are obsolete within three years of invention.

This means that you need to always be on the look-out for new technologies that would increase your productive capacity, staff productivity and ultimately your profit margin.

Part Two
Visual Merchandising Display

Chapter One

The Psychology Of Visual Merchandising Display

Visual merchandising is basically a truncation for marketing in retail. Selling takes place when customers and shoppers show interest in a product and the intention to buy a product on display.

However, before arriving at that conclusion; the individual needs to be sold which is why merchandising is very critical for a retail store. Most people do not buy because they are uninterested in a product or service been sold to them. And it is very difficult to sell to an unmotivated person.

So how do you motivate a person?

You do that by selling them what they want.

This brings us to the next question.

What does everyone want?

In marketing we are taught to believe that everyone wants a different thing.

This statement is true to an extent but it's not quite true. Human psychology has not changed since the dawn of time. The same desires we harboured when we lived in caves, we still hold dear today.

Every shopper, client or customer wants basically the following three things:

> ➢ Result

> Solution

> Relief from something

These three things manifest themselves in the form of the products and services we choose to buy. However, in the final analysis when someone takes out his credit card to buy a product or service no matter what that product or service is, they are doing so to satisfy all or at least one of the above.

Being aware of that, as you prepare to display your merchandise, the questions that need to be going through your mind are the following:

- Which one of the above three are you marketing to satisfy in a particular display?
- When someone passes your shop window, and they take a glimpse of your display, what emotion are you aiming to trigger?
- What result should they imagine the display is going to produce for them?
- What solution should they think your display would provide?
- Finally what pain is the display going to relieve?

This is classic marketing 101.

Your merchandise does not necessarily have to produce those results for the shopper; it just needs to produce the perception of the result in the shoppers' mind.

But there is a catch: the person creating the display needs to know the benefit behind the benefit (the solution the shopper is seeking).

It is only when your visual merchandiser know the benefit behind the benefit will they be able to create a beautiful attractive display that captivates their targeted audience.

I will use La Senza as an example. A woman passing by a La Senza store, spots a sexy lingerie on display in the window; her first thought is: I will look sexy in that underwear or that bra looks to be just right for me.

Figure 1: Think of the benefit behind the benefit in your display

But here is the interesting part, she would like the bra to prop up her cleavage not because she just wants them cleavage propped up. She wants her cleavage propped up to attract the attention of the opposite sex. (I must add a disclaimer that here that I am not trying to be sexist; I am just using this as an example).

Therefore as a visual merchandiser your aim in creating a display for that lady should not be about the cleavage, but the opposite sex. Your goal needs to be to match the thinking process that lady in your display.

Do not create a display to appeal to the beauty of her breast but the impression that the beautiful breast will have – on the opposite sex!

You see that with travel agencies. When you enter a travel agency, what do you see?

The images of a beautiful beach, with a couple or an individual sun bathing and a stunning hotel in the background.

No mention of the eight hours flight to get there, not to mention the two hours check in time at the airport, screaming kids on the airplane, the rude cabin crew and lest I forget…the sleeping air controller.

There is never any mention of those. All they paint for you is the picture of perfect get away that you cannot wait to buy.

As a visual merchandiser, this is the type of picture you want to paint with your display. A major part of visual merchandising is being able to analyse people's thought process.

The human thought process is complex and irrational. Even though he tries to rationalise his actions with artificial explanations of his environment, the reality this: we all do things for the same three reasons:

- Status
- Survival
- Sex

I am aware this might sound like a little over simplistic explanation of the complexity of the human thought process. However, the more you understand your target market, the more you will come to the conclusion that indeed all human actions can be reduced to the three.

As a visual merchandiser your ability to capture these three in your presentation is the key to your success.

The human has three brains:

- Reptile

- ➢ Mammal
- ➢ Thinker

The problem we face as humans, those three brains are not integrated. They all work separately and the thinking part of the brain is the least dominant of three, which why our thinking process is in most cases, irrational.

In his ground breaking book: "Blink", author Malcolm Glawell brilliantly illustrates this point when he introduces the concept of "the power of thin slicing" and "rapid cognition" which is the type of thinking process that occurs in a blink of an eye.

Thin-slicing is a psychological term for the ability to find patterns in events based upon minimal information. It means making rapid decisions with the least amount of information.

When someone walks through a shopping mall of three hundred stores or on a busy High Street on Saturday afternoon, his mind races and he thinks at a fast rate.

The decision as to which store he enters is made in the blink of an eye. It depends on the merchandise display that catches his attention. Except of course if he had pre-planned a visit to a particular store; he is thin slicing each store as he walks along.

Many of our actions, behaviour and thinking originate from the adaptive unconscious which the majority of us are unaware of. Almost all the time, our decisions are based upon triggers from the unconscious.

> *The good news is that other humans are capable of altering these unconscious biases just by tinkering with miniature details.*

Malcolm Glawell spoke about the tinkering or social engineering process in his first book "The Tipping Point". In "The Tipping Point" he outlines minute details of product packaging for example, that causes a product to tip (increase sales).

The retail landscape is changing rapidly. Endless choices, interruptions and information from all directions are either confusing customers or overwhelming them.

As the shopper walks through the shopping mall, there are a gazillion things going through his mind. Yours is not the only display in the shopping mall neither is it not the only display he has seen on that day.

There are clusters of information and displays all around them. Therefore your job as a visual merchandiser is to ensure that yours stand tall above the rest. That can only be done when you understand the psychology and design your display to suit customers' desire.

People don't like to be sold but they love to buy, therefore your visual presentation should sell to them without appearing to sell to them.

The most effective visual merchandise displays are those that speak directly to a customer's desire for:

- Result
- Solution
- Relief from something

Remember! It is all about:

Status

Survival

Sex

How to implement the psychology of a visual merchandise display

Starbucks has become the favourite hangout for many professionals. But if you went into a Starbucks you will notice that there is nothing special about it. It does not have special decoration or a seat that makes it stand out from all other cafés yet that's exactly what it does…standout above the rest of the cafés.

Apple retail stores are simple, there is nothing sophisticated and stylish about them yet they standout stores in any mall. Apple stores are fast becoming a favourite hangout for shoppers.

So what is it about Starbucks or Apple that makes them stand out?

Answer: Simplicity and elegance!

The fundamental principle that underpins an effective presentation is clarity of message and enhancement. Every presentation carries a message. It can be explicit or implicit; so long as it speaks to a targeted audience.

It is very important that your audience gets the message that your presentation is sending to them.

When the London 2012 logo was unveiled the head of the London 2012 organising committee went through pains of explaining what the logo depicted to the British public.

Figure 2: London 2012 Olympic logo confused everyone

Except for him and probably the designers of the logo, no one else in the UK seemed to have understood the logo. As far as most Brits were concerned, it might have been Greek or symbols from some Hindu alphabet.

When people were interviewed about what they made of the logo, some people described it as children drawing from a nursery…

For some it was an angry person expressing their feelings.

Not a single person associated it with the Olympics. That is a classic example of a presentation gone wrong.

Figure 3: what is the connection between bread and chewing gum?

This is the image of an ad I noticed at the bus stop on my way to the post office. It is an ad for a chewing gum. But as you can see it has the image of a big loaf of bread and the chewing gum on the side.

What exactly is the relation between a chewing gum and a loaf of bread?

As I walked around I constantly see ads on billboards and street corners that do not speak to any specific target audience.

Walking around the shopping mall and in retail store I cannot help but notice several visual merchandise displays even in large retailers that speak to no one in particular.

When creating a visual merchandise display you need to adhere to the following guidelines:

- The display has to be unambiguous so that it can be instantly understood by the targeted audience
- The display must invoke confidence in the brand
- The most important element of the display has to be the biggest and dominant feature of the display

Every single component of the display must be a part of the message you are trying to convey. There can be no component of the display that is there simply to make the display beautiful and more attractive; it must be a part of the overall message.

Colours have to be used sparingly. Colours have to complement one another and be in sync with the rest of the products in the store.

Visual Merchandise Psychology Process

Step One
Know thy customers – Identify your target market.

Step Two
Find out what result, solution and relief they are aiming to achieve with your product.

Step Three
Find the benefit behind the benefit they are trying to achieve (the guy with the muscular body for which they need that bra to prop up their cleavage).

Step Four
Create a visual display that speaks directly to their needs.

How to identify your target market

This is marketing 101 which every business should already know, therefore I am not going dig deep into it.

However, small retailers who might not have the luxury of hiring an expert visual merchandiser might find the following steps helpful:

Step One
After creating the display, speak to staff members and ask them to describe the display for you in their own words. If they explain it in words that you expect your customers to use then you know you have nailed it. This needs to be done every single time you tinker with the display.

Step Two
Speak to your customers – ask them what they think about the display. Ask them what message the display sends to them. If your customers describe your display using words that indicate that they got it, you know you have achieved your objectives.

Step Three
Ask your customers why they buy certain things from your store. When you know why they buy, you will know the result they are trying to achieve with your products.

Step Four
To be able to ascertain the benefit behind the benefit, find out what they intend to do with your products after they have bought it.

For example if a lady came to your store to buy lingerie. By asking her a few probing but un-intrusive questions as she tries them on, you will know if she is single and going out on a date or she is dressing for her spouse.

The more similar answers you receive the easier it would be to present your display to suite them.

Finally ensure your display does not look like the London 2012 logo. It should not confuse your audience; it needs to speak directly to their needs. When they look at it…blink they need to see the result, solution and relief they seek.

Chapter Two

How To Use Visual Merchandising To Increase Sales

Retail success depends on the image you create in your customer's mind about your merchandise as well as your provision of good customer services. Good visual merchandising also helps to create a positive customer image about your store and your products.

All of that results in increases sales.

But retailers tend to overlook the role visual merchandising plays in increasing sales.

Within the last few decades, the retail industry has recognised the role of visual merchandising display in increasing sales.

This is especially true for supermarkets that have mastered the art of visual merchandising display to the point of excellence.

Visual Merchandising display in a retail store:

- Enables consumers to easily locate products
- Keeps customers updated on the latest trends
- Influences customer buying decision
- Creates a pleasant shopping experience

Visual Merchandising display is basically what the shoppers sees either when passing by a retail store or when they are inside the store. It creates a positive image of the store which results in attention, interest, desire and action on the part of the customer.

Simply defined visual merchandising display is the art and science of displaying products to influence shoppers buying decision.

The most aggressive application of visual merchandise displays is used by larger retailers. For instance, sport brands such as Reebok spend 25% of their advertising on point of sale merchandising.

Furthermore, there has been a significant increase in impulse buying of certain products: that is directly attributed ingenuous visual merchandising display.

How to use visual merchandise to increase sales

Known in retail as the "silent salesperson", a good visual merchandising display:

- Presents the product to shoppers
- Invites the shoppers to get closer to the product
- Encourages shoppers to make a purchase
- Tells shoppers everything they need to know about products without the need to make inquiries

Visual Merchandising is a proven formula for increasing retail sales and customer satisfaction. It makes it easier for customers to see products on display as they walk around the store and aids in locating products easily.

The following are the three display structure used in retail stores. A retailer may choose to use the three structures in depending on his product range or he could use any of the three depending on his target market:

- Store-Front
- Window Display
- Found-Space Display

The most important element of visual merchandising display is the shop window display. The shop window display attracts shoppers as they walk pass and entice them to enter the store. There are lots of people who might have no intention of shopping on a particular day. However, the attractiveness of your window display could entice them into your store.

Display windows are usually facing the shopping mall or main shopping street and are geared towards attracting passers-by and enticing them to enter a retail store.

The storefront display is designed to build your brand image and tell the right story of your organisation. When developing the concept for your storefront, create the design from the customer's prospective.

Figure 4: The storefront display is designed to build your brand image and tell the right story of your organisation

You basically need to enter the customer's mind and ask yourself the question:

> What would my customers see when they look at my storefront display?
>
> What would they feel as they pass by my storefront?

The answers to those questions should inform your display design and structure.

When planning a window display take into consideration the following:

- The building façade
- The street
- Your target market and their perceptions
- Color harmony
- Lighting
- Viewing angles

Window displays are more successful when a central theme is carried throughout the display; whether the featured products are fashion-oriented, institutional or promotional in nature.

Window displays need to be constantly updated, preferably on a weekly basis or as often as possible. This sends a message to customers that there is always something new going on in the store.

Showcase Display

Figure 5: Showcase Displays feature expensive merchandises

Showcase Displays feature expensive merchandises retailers do not want to be seen in the front store window. They are usually exclusive items that require high security measures. These displays are usually located in high traffic areas in the store to ensure maximum customer attention. The lesser the items in the display, the more the perceived value, resulting in higher priced.

Found-Space Display

Figure 6: Found-Space Displays are displays of products at less prominent areas of the store

Found-Space Displays are displays of products at less prominent areas of the store, such as the top of shelves. When done right, they support your brand image and reiterate the story you want to tell with the display.

Below are points to consider when creating store displays for increased sales:

Install signage

Figure 7: Store signage needs to be appropriately installed

Store signage needs to be appropriately installed and placed in a position that allows shoppers to read the information written on them from across the aisle. A sign is a silent salesperson and a huge part of the shopper's first impression of your store.

Like Apple simplicity, clarity, elegance and legibility need to be the rule of thumb.

Use the appropriate colour

Figure 8: Your colour usage will significantly contribute to shopper's impression of your store

Your colour usage will significantly contribute to shopper's impression of your store as they pass by it. The store colour needs to be suitably chosen as it can influence your customer's mood.

The wall colours need to correspond with the carpet, floor tiles or the fixtures.

Lighting system

Figure 9: Lighting increases the visibility of the merchandise

The store should be appropriately lit and well ventilated. Lighting increases the visibility of the merchandise. A properly lit store contributes to the promotion of specific products and the store's image.

Store window lights should be strong enough to overcome the reflections from outside.

Contextual Product Display

Figure 10: Group together products in their respective racks

Group together products in their respective racks and place associated labels on the same shelves. This helps your customers locate products easily. The merchandise should be appropriately and neatly placed and should not fall off the shelves.

The latest trend items should be cleverly displayed on the shelves to attract customers and entice them to buy. Expensive and unique products should be placed on the right side of the store as most people are right handed and tend to gravitate towards the right side of the store.

Old merchandise should be removed as quickly as practically possible and placed on sale to create an atmosphere of constant freshness in the store.

Identify the right furniture and fixtures

Figure 11: All unnecessary furniture should be removed

All unnecessary furniture should be removed to create enough space for customers to move freely in the store. The more comfortable your store, the higher your chances of retaining customers, which will result in increased sales.

Maintaining an area for spouses or children to read or play and for physically challenged kids or elderly customers to rest also contributes to a good customer experience.

Providing resting space is a difficult concept to sell to store planners because of the cost of retail space. However, the payoff far outweighs the cost as the longer shoppers stay in your store, the higher the chances of them buying.

A changing room is an important component of a clothing store as it increases the possibility of the customer buying if they have had the chance of trying the cloth and it fits them well.

Separate changing rooms for male and female or a comfortable non-gender specific open space with individual cubicles will suffice.

Maintain good ambiance

Figure 12: The store ambience is essential for attracting new customers and retaining existing ones

Playing music that appeals to your target market can have a positive effect on your customers. Loud music is not advisable as it hinders effective communication between the customer and store associates.

Playing music that appeals to your target market is another strategy for keeping customers longer in your store.

The store ambience is also essential for attracting new customers and retaining existing ones. Customers shy away from untidy stores; therefore, ensure your store is tidy at all times.

The friendlier and more relaxing you can make your store, the longer your customers will stay and eventually make purchase.

Sometimes the store's appearance is more important than products in terms of a customer's decision to enter your store. Ensure your store entrance is welcoming; that your visual merchandise display tells the story of your store and merchandise display is resulting in higher sales.

How to implement a good visual merchandise display that increases sales

The following are the basic steps for creating visual merchandise display that increases sales:

Step One
Select a theme that tells the story
There needs to always be a theme or story that is being communicated to your potential customers in your display. Develop a theme around the reason why you decide to display some specific product in the window.

> Who are the characters in your display?
>
> Where are they going and why?
>
> How old are they?
>
> What jobs do they do?
>
> What merchandise would help you tell your product story better?
>
> If the story is about living a healthy lifestyle, what could you integrate into your theme to help you silently make this point in the display?
>
> If your story is about Christmas, Valentine or outdoor adventure, what are the details that will make your story come alive?

You can take your story to a whole new level with the use of props and mannequins. Just as if you were writing a story, your display needs to answer these questions:

> How old are your target market?

What do they do?

Where are they going?

What season is it?

You can also provide each mannequin a name to bring them to life. The key is to clearly understand who you are creating the display for and what message you want to convey to them through the display.

Step Two
Know thy customer

One of the major reasons for the failure of most retail ventures is that most retailers do not know their target market. This is marketing 101: It is critical for your success as a business. If you do not know who you serve, you might not be serving anyone.

- Who are your costumers?
- Are they teenagers, young professionals, college students or young couples?
- Are they housewives?
- Are they Single mums?
- Are they women in their 40's with lots of discretionary income?
- Do your customers want a bargain or are they looking for something unique?
- What interests them?

Answering the above questions will ensure that the message of your display is clearly understood by your target market. If your display does not target a particular segment of your market, it will not sell.

Step Three
Identify your Competitors

It is critical that you know who your competitors are; their product offering and service provision. By having an understanding of the strength and weaknesses of your competition, you can better prepare a display that either directly rivals or is better than theirs.

Competitive analysis is the key to the success of any business. Knowing the strength and weaknesses of your competition is a key element in your success as a retailer.

Step Four
Choose the right products for your store window

Your storefront is a window to your store. The products displayed their, provide potential customers an idea of the products inside the store. Consequently, it is imperative that you choose the products that are displayed in the shop window carefully.

You need to display products that are the most representative of products in your store.

Ensure that products that are displayed in the storefront are available in the store. It does not speak well of your store if shoppers are attracted to the store because of products they see in the storefront display but when they enter the store to buy that product, it is unavailable. Remember that the unavailability of product can result in a frustrated and unhappy customer.

Do not overcrowd the storefront with too much merchandise. The message you are trying to send to potential customers could be lost in an overcrowded window. Window displays should be in complete harmony with the entire atmosphere of the store.

Step Five
Observe the effect of display on your customers

An effective way to attract customers is to have good exterior and interior displays. As customers pass by your display, you need to have a procedure for measuring the effect of your display on them.

Does your display window inspire your customers?

Is it pleasing to the eye and does it have a welcoming effect?

Ensure you display your merchandise as it would be used in a real life scenario and that it is kept simple but striking to have a great impact.

Ensure that your window display can be seen from a distance to draw your potential customers inside your store. You might have the most creative idea, however, if you are incapable of displaying it in such a way that it grabs your shoppers attention as they pass by your store, you have defeated the purpose of the display.

The key to increasing retail sales; is an impressive and eye catching presentation of merchandise that attracts shoppers as they pass by your store. Encouraging sales through creative visual merchandise displays is the key to keeping a customer interested in your store.

Chapter Three

Challenges Facing Visual Merchandisers

Visual Merchandising display is the science of displaying merchandise in a retail store and storefront in a bid to increase footfall in a retail store. Besides your store design, visual merchandise display is the best and most effective form of promoting your store.

The most important element of visual merchandising display is that it is on the spot adverting. If a shopper sees a product on display that they like; they can make a purchase immediately and you can make a sale on the spot.

The most important aspect of your visual merchandising display process is in the message. It has to be clear and consistent. When the message is clear, it eliminates the possibility of appealing to the wrong target market and providing a bad customer experience.

Getting your display right is critical for the success of your business. Your display must reflect the quality and price of the products on sale. If you sell high a quality product, but your store design and merchandise display do not match the high end clientele you are intent on attracting, you will lose your target market.

By the same token, if your store appears high end but you sell low qualify products; you will scare off your target market. Consequently, it is essential that you ensure that your display speaks clearly and unambiguously to your target market.

Creativity and the love of design are the two essential requirements for becoming a good visual merchandiser. As a visual merchandiser you need to have the ability to come up with creative ideas about how you would like your display to look.

You need to be a good story teller with a kid like imagination. You need to stay current about developments in your sector and stay in touch with other visual merchandisers to stay abreast of the latest trends.

Challenges visual merchandisers face

Visual merchandisers face a number of challenges that limit their ability to create displays that woo shoppers in to a store. A good visual merchandising display strategy can result in increased sales, increased staff productivity and reduced shrinkage which eventually lead to increased profit.

However, getting visual merchandising right can be a mammoth task for most retail organisations.

The dynamic of the target market is one of the greatest challenges facing visual merchandisers. The volatility of consumer behaviour creates a nightmarish scenario for visual merchandisers who have to constantly invent creative ways to attract potential customers' attention.

The constant development of new products, scarcity of display space allocation and the constant change in consumer preferences all add to the challenging environment for visual merchandisers.

Below is an outline of a few of the challenges that visual merchandisers face:

Too much new merchandise

Figure 13: New products are produced every single day

New products are produced every day. This is a nightmare for visual merchandisers who are responsible for finding display space on the shop floor for new merchandise. The merchandising of fabric is not as difficult as groceries.

Because clothing is seasonal. At the end of each season, clothes belonging to the past season are either sold off or taken to the warehouse. However, the same cannot be said of groceries.

Tones of new products are produced every single day and the supermarket tests most products to see if they will resonate with consumers. It is the work of the visual merchandiser to ensure that each new product is given a space in the store and are visible enough for customers to notice.

This can be a nightmarish scenario especially if it is a low value or bulky product. Placing low value products in high traffic areas is a waste of space. In the same token placing new products in locations where they are not very visible reduces the chances of them being sold. Striking a balance between visibility and space allocation is a huge challenge for visual merchandisers.

Solution

One way of dealing with this challenge is to:

Reserve a specific section of the store for testing products. The only products that will be displayed in this section would be new products. This would make it easy for both visual merchandisers and customers.

If customers are aware that a particular section of the store is specifically reserved for new products, adventure seeking customers would go straight there to look for new products. It also makes it easy for the retailers to quickly gauge customer reaction to the product.

If a product placed there is sold out quickly, the retailer just as quickly recognise the need to order additional supplies fast; and can now move the display to a permanent location in the store. When a new product is placed amongst other products, it can sometimes be difficult to get an accurate picture of its popularity; due to its lack of exposure.

If it is a clothing store, again a specific section of the store can be exclusively set aside for new fashion. Imagine the response that you would receive from customers. They will visit the store specifically to look for the latest fashion.

The creation of such section for new fashion trends will now be multi-purpose: it would serve as a testing lab for new trends; it would provide convenience for customers because they will be able to find things easily and it would serve as a magnet for attracting customers who are bent on keeping up with latest trends.

Limited Display Space

Figure 14: Retail space is expensive; therefore, every inch of the store's display space needs to be maximised

Retail space is expensive; therefore, every inch of the store's display space has to be used to its maximum. However, with the constant introduction of new products, even hyper stores struggle for space to accommodate all the new products.

To cluster products in a bid to create more space is never a good idea as the store would appear untidy. Even in a store where clothes are replaced seasonally, there are still lots of new fashions that constantly come on the market. Therefore, it really is a struggle for visual merchandisers to decide which clothing or product to give priority in the display.

Solution

The best solution would be to place as much variety as possible but in small quantities. Staff need to keep a constant watch on shelves to ensure that they are not empty or well faced up. If it is a clothing store, the same rule applies. As staff walk around the store, they need to keep their eyes open for empty hangers and spaces between clothes. Every space needs to be immediately refilled.

If it is in a grocery, products also need to be displayed in small quantities. However, the aim has to be to display as much products as possible. Staff need to ensure that no shelf is left empty. The retailer needs to assign a specific supervisor whose job it would be to walk the store every hour checking all shelves and fill gaps as they notice them.

Supplier demand Premium Spacing

Figure 15: Suppliers compete for prominent and high traffic display space

Suppliers compete to have their products displayed in the most prominent and high traffic locations in the store. Here you must be on alert for signs of a conflict of interest between senior management; visual merchandisers and other staff.

The decision as to where products are displayed is often determined by senior management and the supplier; not by the visual merchandiser. Sometimes, what the senior management view as appropriate could prove difficult for visual merchandisers to implement. These conflicting interests result in lack of coordination and cooperation.

In retail, suppliers pay for their products to be displayed in store. There are locations in each store that are considered premium areas: they are mostly high traffic areas. Every supplier wants their products to be displayed in those areas because of a higher probability of increased sales.

And suppliers are will to pay handsomely for the privilege. The problem is sometimes their products contrast with the rest of the products in the department and fitting in their products might reduce the space availability for other products.

Solution

Suppliers and retail senior management need to be educated on the function of visual merchandising display in a retail store. This would help them to make an informed decision about the location of products in the store. Visual merchandising display is showbiz.

The objective is to:

- Attract shoppers as they pass by the store
- Entice them to enter the store
- Retain them for longer in the store
- Persuade them to buy

In order to achieve the above objectives, the placement of products on the shop floor has to be purposefully done, not done haphazardly to favour a few products.

Product security

Figure 16: Product security is very essential

Retail crime; including shoplifting, is responsible for the demise of most retail ventures. Years ago, shoplifting was done by the homeless and drug addicts who wanted to feed their habits.

Currently, shoplifting is conducted by organised retail crime gangs using sophisticated methods never before seen in the retail industry. Retail is a business and business is about making profit. In order to make a profit, a retailer has to increase sales and reduce shrinkage.

One of the best ways of reducing shrinkage is through creative merchandising that does not facilitate the easy pilfering of products from the store. It is therefore essential that visual merchandisers know their role in loss prevention and shrinkage management. The objective of visual merchandising is to attract customers. However, there has to be a balance between attracting customers and protecting products on the shop floor. It is therefore vital for visual merchandisers to be trained in and kept up-to-date with the basics for linking visual merchandising with loss prevention.

If products are displayed with loss prevention in mind, it becomes more difficult for them to be easily removed from the store. However, if the loss prevention aspect of the process is not taken into consideration, the products are at risk when they are placed on the shop floor.

The changing retail environment

Figure 17: The changing retail environment

The internet has removed the monopolization of the factors of distribution once held by a few. In the new retail environment, an individual can run a multi-million pound retail operation from the back of his car as long as he has an internet connection.

It also means that a small factory owner operating from his spare bedroom in China can now compete with a multi-national retail organisation in the West. As it stands, the retail environment demands a different approach to visual merchandising display.

You can no longer continue to view visual merchandising display as just another component of your operation. Visual merchandising along with store design needs to be considered a key component of a retail operation.

Visual merchandising is free advertising for your store. However, despite the fact that it is free; in order for it to be effective, all the fundamentals of advertising need to apply.

In his book "Breakthrough Advertising" Eugene Schwartz wrote "This is the core of advertising—its fundamental function: To take an unformulated desire, and translate it into one vivid scene of fulfilment after another; to add the appeal of concrete satisfaction after satisfaction to the basic drive of that desire. To make sure that your prospect realizes everything that he is getting—everything that he is now leaving behind him—everything that he may possibly be missing"

Below is a list of the fundamental principles of advertising:

- "The only purpose of advertising is to make sales. It is profitable or unprofitable according to its actual sales. It is not for general effect. It is not to keep your name before the people. It is not primarily to aid your other salesmen. Treat it as a salesman. Force it to justify itself. Compare it with other salesmen. Figure its cost and result. Accept no excuses which good salesmen do not make. Then you will not go far wrong".
- "Human nature is perpetual. In most respects it is the same today as in the time of Caesar. So the principles of psychology are fixed and enduring. You will never need to unlearn what you learn about them".
- "Use pictures only to attract those who may profit you. Use them only when they form a better selling argument than the same amount of space set in type".
- "Changing people's habits is very expensive. A project which involves that must be seriously considered. To sell shaving soap to the peasants of Russia one would first need to change their beard wearing habits. The cost would be excessive".

- "Prevention is not a popular subject, however much it should be. People will do much to cure trouble, but people in general will do little to prevent it".
- "We must learn what a user spends a year, else we shall not know if users are worth the cost of getting".
- "We must learn the percentage of readers to whom our product appeals. We must often gather this data on classes. The percentages may differ on farms and in cities".
- "Competition must be considered. What are the forces against you? What have they in price or quality as well as claims to weigh against your appeal? What must you do, to win trade against them? What must you do to hold trade against them when you get it? How strongly are your rivals entrenched"?
- "Almost any question can be answered, cheaply, quickly and finally, by a test campaign. And that's the way to answer them — not by arguments around a table. Go to the court of last resort — the buyers of your product".
- "Consumers all over the world still buy products which promise them value for money, beauty, nutrition, real relief from suffering and social status".

How to Resolve Visual Merchandisers Challenges

The following steps can help to bring relief to visual merchandisers:

1. Make effective use of a planogram to address the challenges of constant new product flow into the market.
2. Study your target market very well to determine product preference.
3. Group products according to make, model and size to enable easy display.

4. Ensure high ticket products are given priority in the display process.
5. Create an illusion of display with a few products that appear to be a lot.
6. Display smaller numbers of each product, especially slow moving products and ensure you make maximum use of the display space allocated.

Chapter Four

How To Burst The Price Myth With Creative Merchandise Display

I visited Harrods for research for this book and my book on store design. Harrods, for anyone reading this book who might not know, is the Mecca for retailing. Royalty, A-list celebrities and the 'who's who' from around the world fly into London just to shop at Harrods.

You can now imagine my anticipation when I visited Harrods. In my mind everything in Harrods was made of gold. I was disappointed; when I noticed a toy bus I had purchased for my son from Asda, was also being sold in Harrods. It was exactly the same toy bus, in exactly the same packaging as the toy in Asda.

A question popped into my mind: why is it that exactly the same bus, probably manufactured in exactly the same factory in China, is sold in Harrods for twice the price that it is sold for in Asda?

> *The answer is decisively simple – Asda sells a 'toy bus, but Harrods sells a 'classy toy bus'.*

There is a difference.

This is marketing 101: people buy emotionally but justify their decision logically.

Customers who shop at Harrods do not shop there to buy Harrods' products; they shop at Harrods to buy 'elegance and class.' Harrods sells them class.

Figure 18: Harrods customers buy 'elegance and class'

How do Harrods pull this off?

They achieve it with the combination of an elegant store design and attractive visual merchandising displays. When you move from one department to the next in Harrods, it is like moving from one store to another.

Their ability to use their store design to create the illusion of variation is one of the keys to Harrods' success. Harrods understand their customers; they know what their customers want so they design their store and display their products to satisfy the desires of their customers.

The common myth in the retail industry is that people buy more when merchandises are cheap. That is just a myth. In this new retail environment where the monopoly of the factors of distribution has been broken, no retail store can be cheaper than the internet. Even pound stores are not cheaper than the internet.

The main reason people still visit retail stores is either for convenience or to actually feel the products before purchasing them. Some people might visit a retail store just for the fun of shopping.

It is true that 30-40% of people will buy on the basis of price only. However, the large majority of people still buy on the basis of value and convenience.

I am a one click buyer in Amazon. I buy a lot of books because of my line of work. I was pleasantly surprised to learn that I could even buy white board and all my stationary from Amazon.

I cannot remember the last time that I entered a bookstore. I have a lot of friends like me who do the majority of their shopping on the internet. They shop for clothes and even groceries on the net.

Why would I and many of the people do our shopping over the internet?

We are sold on the convenience.

These days there are people who will check things up on the internet, but before placing an order on line; they visit a retail store to see how they look.

The 18th century was about speed of production in order to increase capacity. The 19th century focused on quality. With the increased in production leading to over capacity, the focus shifted from speed to quality.

In the 21st century the focus has shifted from quality to value and total customer experience. But many retailers have failed to grasp the concept.

> **Here is the secret, despite the fact that people conduct research on the internet, the large majority still don't trust information found on the internet.**

That is why books are still highly rated even though the information in most books can be found on the internet.

People still trust other people and prefer to interact with people. So despite the internet, bricks and mortar retailing will still survive. However, there is a new dynamic and retailers need to understand this.

The consumer of today is better informed than the consumer of ten or twenty years ago. Consequently, today's retail staff need to be better informed than retail staff of ten or twenty years ago.

One cannot navigate the 21st century with a 19th century skill set – it will not work.

Richer Sounds a UK based electronic and entertainment retailer has been featured in the Guinness Book of Records for the past 20 years as having the highest sales per square foot of any retailer in the world.

Coincidentally, their staff continue to top the 'Which" survey for excellent customer service and product knowledge. They are not necessarily the cheapest entertainment retailer in the world but they are the most profitable. Why? Because of the total customer experience that customers receive when they visit their stores.

Since the economic crisis, many middle or low tier retail stores have gone bust or struggling to survive. Yet the luxury sector of the retail market remains buoyant.

Even in recession hit Greece and Spain, the luxury retail market continues to flourish. The explanation that most people would have for this is that the rich are getting richer.

Even though this might be true, this is not the main reason for the continuous buoyancy of the luxury retail market.

The explanation lies in the fact that luxury retailers take the concept of total customer experience to the extreme.

When you visit Harrods, there is staff within an arm's length of each and every customer. On the other hand when you visit some retail stores, you can hardly find anyone to speak to when you need help.

I know of retailers in the UK who advertise on billboards in prime locations around the country. However, when shoppers visit their stores, they can hardly find a staff member to serve them and those in the store might have absolutely no knowledge about the products in the store.

To succeed in the 21st century retail environment, it is the little things that make the difference. As a retailer if you still believe that price is what is going to entice people to your store and make you successful, you are on the wrong end of the stick. 21st century retail is about value and total customer experience.

So as a retailer your focus needs to be on value drive strategies. An essential component of a value driven strategy is an attractive visual merchandising display. As Michael Porter puts it, "cutting prices is usually insane if the competition can go as low as you can".

Maintaining pricing integrity can be challenging in the face of fierce competition. But it can turn out to be a smart business decision in the long run. The concept of value is perceptive.

What might constitute value to one person might not be that valuable to another. However, there is a universal perception about value that exists in the mind of every customer: *cheap is poor quality and expensive is high quality.*

Despite the fact that this concept has proven time and time again to be untrue, like most things in life, it is the perception that matters.

Below is a list of the pricing strategies currently been used by retailers?

Price-matching guarantee

Price-matching guarantee is mostly used by consumer and industrial retailers. Retailers using price-matching guarantee frequently state that they are the 'lowest' priced store, and they will match the competitors.

A store with price matching guarantee will not lose customers to price cuts from other retailers even if it charges higher price to its loyal customers. Price-matching guarantee is an anti-competitive tactic that warns competitors not to attempt to steal market share by undercutting price.

Price slashing

Price cutting is a price strategy used by retailers such as Wal-Mart under their so-called "rolling back prices" price technique to eliminate competition. The core of the strategy is to reduce prices to a level low enough to eliminate competition.

Retailers use this strategy to under-cut the competition and offer the best price to the consumer. The objective is not to sell at a loss, but to reduce price to a point that competition is unable to compete.

Discounting

Discounting is a pricing strategy favoured by most retailers. It is done in the form of coupons, advanced purchases, loyalty cards or bulk buying. Coupons and promotions give buyers an incentive to buy from certain retail stores.

For some customers taking advantage of discount offers can be an attractive proposition. However, for the retailer concerned, discounting of products is never a smart business strategy as it eats into their profit margin.

The following are steps that prevent the need for product discounting:

Step One

Identify and understand your target market.

Like in the case of Harrods, customers visit a particular store for a reason. Your job is to find out who your customers are and what they want.

Step Two

Instead of discounting your current line, you could consider resizing.

As an alternative to discounting their menu, Quiznos took to a decision to resize its sandwiches.

Thus it offered a lower price for the smaller size. Probably there are ways that you could repackage your products in ways that it makes financial sense to discount without eating into your profit margin.

Step Three

Emphasize benefits of the products instead of the price. There is no getting away from the fact that it is very difficult to differentiate one commodity from the other. But it can be done if the retailer places emphasis on other intangible aspects of the buying decision.

Step Four

Emphasize the soft aspect of your offering such as great customer service, knowledgeable staff, easy access to merchandise, easy to locate merchandise or an easy to navigate store.

This might sound trivial, but in marketing, it is the things that are overlooked that count. The everyday thing that you think might not be important to the customer may well be what is really important to them.

The price discounting game is a losing one, do not play it, it is not a good business strategy.

When developing your pricing strategy you need to analyse the market place for sensory acuity. It can be done through the following means:

Competitive analysis

Conduct a competitive analysis of the pricing structure of your competition. When analysing your competitor's prices, your focus should not only be on the amount they charge but also their offering. You need to examine their entire service provision to be able to make an accurate assessment of the reason behind their pricing structure.

Maintain the ceiling price

If you decide to go for the highest price point, ensure it is the ceiling price. The ceiling price is the maximum price the market can bear. It is the price point that if you went above, you might scare away your customers.

Be aware that the price that might be the highest price currently in the market may not be the ceiling price.

Adhere to price elasticity

Price elasticity gives the percentage change in quantity demanded in response to a one percent change in price.

Price elasticity is almost always negative. Only goods which do not conform to the law of demand have a positive PED.

In most cases, the demand for goods is said to be inelastic when the PED is less than one. What this means is that changes in price have a relatively small effect on the quantity of the goods demanded.

The demand for goods is said to be elastic when the PED is greater than one. This means that changes in price have a relatively large effect on the quantity of goods demanded. As you develop your pricing structure, pay attention to these fundamental principles.

The following are steps for implementing an effective pricing strategy; when setting your prices to avoid selling at a loss:

Step One
Determine you cost
Calculate the cost of the product and add corresponding overheads such as: rent, utility bills, staff salary and benefits, marketing, credit cards or bank fees and professional fees.

Step Two
Know competitors prices
After calculating your cost, you then need to check out your competitor's prices for similar products. It comes down once again to ceiling price. If you notice that your price is lower than that of your competition, you will want to check out their offering before drawing conclusions.

On the other hand, if your price is higher, you cannot just reduce your price to match your competitors and operate at a loss. You also need to check out their offering and supply chain.

It is possible that despite the fact that their price is lower than yours, your offering might be more valuable than theirs. If that is the case, you need to ensure that your marketing stresses the fact that your offering is better.

You also need to pay close attention to their supply chain. The reason most grocery retailers struggle to compete with the likes of Wal-Mart and Tesco is because they have stronger bargaining powers when negotiating with suppliers.

This makes it possible for them to drive down their prices. So maybe instead of attempting to go head to head with to bigger players in your market who have strong bargaining powers, you can try changing your offering.

Step Three
Know thy customers
If you understand your customers better than your competitors, you will know the types of price they can bear. Again it is not about the cost of the product; it is about the total customer experience when they enter your store.

Harrods sell the same made in China products, however, it is able to sell it twice the prices of other retailers in the UK because its customers do not only buy at Harrods because of the products, but also because of Harrods total customer experience.

Step Four
Take the market into consideration
It is the market that sets the final price. Your final price would be determined by what the market can bear. The best strategy for testing the market is to start at the highest possible price point.

If you notice that sales are not being made as a result of your price point, you reduce the price and test again. Continue the process until you arrive at a pricing equilibrium.

As you test your prices, ensure that you have an accurate system in place for measuring the result of your pricing test.

How to handle price wars

Price wars are common place in retail. As stated previously, price is the most common strategy for differentiation in retail. Prior to deciding on your course of action during or even before engaging in price wars, you first need to consider this question:

Is the current price of the competition a short-term promotional strategy or a long-term pricing strategy?

If after analyzing your competitor's pricing strategy you reach the conclusion that it is just a short-term promotional strategy instead of log-term pricing strategy, you can either choose to ignore it or develop your own short-term strategy to counter theirs.

On many occasions, a price war is declared because retailers fail to analyse their competitors pricing strategy well.

Below is a list of possible responses to a price war:

Reduce price

You can choose to reduce your own prices in response to the competition's pricing strategy. This would seem on the surface the most logical action to take, but doing so would result in reduction of your profit margin.

Maintain price

You could ignore your competitor and maintain your current pricing strategy and hope that your competitor has made a mistake. This is a risky strategy because if in the process your competitor manages to lure your customers into their store, there is no telling that they would return to your store when the price war is over.

Use split market pricing strategy

This strategy is basically using different price point for similar products. This can be done by restructuring your product offer to promote a certain aspect of the product as basic and another part as premium.

Change your offering

The most effective way of winning a price war is to change your offer and service provision. Providing additional services such as home delivery or free shipment can increase the value of your offering tremendously.

How to implement a value driven strategy?

The best antidote in a price driven market such as retail is to focus on a value driven strategy instead of a price driven strategy. As I pointed out in the case of Harrods and the luxury retail market that is flourishing despite the economic downturn, price is never a good differentiator; therefore it is imprudent for it to be used as a long-term business strategy.

In this 21st century customer centrist environment where the definition of value has shifted from seller to the customer; where competition is fierce and the monopolisation of the factors of distribution has been broken, leaving the field wide open for anyone to enter; success as a retailer would no longer be dependent on 19th century marketing strategies.

> *Succeeding in the 21st century retail requires rethinking your approach to services provision.*

It is now about providing sustainable, durable, reliable and high quality products at reasonable price.

Thousands of retailers are going bust while a few are succeeding beyond their wildest imagination. The retailers that are succeeding understand that the 21st century customer is better informed than customers of the last few decades.

They understand that succeeding in the 21st century retail environment requires a different approach. As a retailer, if your desire is to succeed in the 21st century retail environment, your best course of action should be to update your current operational processes to reflect the realities of the new retail environment.

Below is a list of quality improvement processes used by the most successful companies in the world. Adapting these into your current modus operandi would bring your retail organisation in touch with the realities of the new retail environment.

Hoshin Kanri

Hoshin Kanri or policy deployment; is Japanese for strategically capturing and strengthening strategic goals and developing the means to bring the goals into reality.

Hoshin translated from Japanese to English means shining metal compass, or pointing the direction and Kanri means management or control. As the name suggests using Hoshin planning aligns an organisation toward focusing on the accomplishment of a single goal.

It is a strategic planning and strategic management methodology based on the concept that each person is an expert in his or her own job.

Japanese TQC (Total Quality Control) is designed to use the collective thinking power of all employees to make their organization the best in its field.

This concept was made popular in Japan by Professor Kaoru Ishikawa. In his book "What is Total Quality Control" he asserts that senior and middle managers need to be bold enough to delegate as much authority as possible.

Professor Ishikawa's also believes that a sure way to establish respect for humanity is to adopt management system in which all employees top to bottom participate in the decision making process.

Hoshin Kanri's real aim is to help companies:

- Create common goals
- Communicate those goals to every employee
- Involve all employees in the planning and execution of the plan for achieving the goals
- Create a mechanism for accountability for every participant

Kaizen

Kaizen is Japanese for continuous improvement or change for the better. It is a philosophy that focuses on continuously improving any process.

It can be applied to any work process whether it is manufacturing, engineering, sport, government, healthcare, banking and any ongoing activity.

The main objective of kaizen is to eliminate waste and create a benchmark for constantly moving up from one stage to the next.

Kaizen is originally a Buddhist term which comes from the words "renew the heart and make it good".

The adoption of the Kaizen concept in any business demands a change in the very 'heart' of a corporate culture and structure.

Kaizen requires businesses to intertwine their vision with every aspect their operational practices.

Kaizen gradual step-by-step process of improving every aspect of a business while at the same time developing employee skills through training and increased participation in the process.

The key areas Kaizen can be implemented in a retail environment are:

- Shop floor – GENBA,
- Product – GENBUTSU
- Training – GENJITSU

By pursuing improvements in the three 'GENs', a retailer is able to spot issues as they arise and can gradually make changes to the key operations – product, service and total customer experience.

Poka-Yoke

Poka-yoke is Japanese for mistake prevention or "mistake-proofing". A poka-yoke is any mechanism that helps a worker avoids mistakes.

The main objective of poka-yoke is to eliminate mistakes by taking preventative and corrective actions prior to an error occurring. Poka-yoke was adopted as a modus operandi by Shigeo Shingo of Toyota as a part of the Toyota Production System.

The fundamental of poka-yoke is to design behavior-shaping constraints into the working process, to prevent incorrect activities by employees.

Below is a list of ways of triggering the thinking process for improving your retail organization:

- The needs of the customer
- It is possible to improve anything
- Quality is the responsibility of all employees
- The employee assigned to a particular job knows more about the job than management
- People should be respected
- Teamwork is critical for success
- Differences should be respected
- Participation in results and commitment
- Support results in success
- Every employee makes the difference

This book is about visual merchandising so why have I taken the trouble of including information on price and quality improvement. As I have reiterated continuously, the 21st century retail environment is a new environment.

The old modus operandi of previous centuries will not work in the 21st century retail environment. To succeed in retail in this century demands a change from the old way of working.

Visual merchandising has always been perceived in terms of the design and presentation of products. The 21st century visual merchandiser needs to understand the reason behind the process and 21st century senior retail management needs to understand the bigger picture of visual merchandising.

It is no longer just about the presentation of products. It is the thinking process behind the presentation of products that matters the most.

Chapter Five

The Best Merchandise Display Strategy

Shelves and display spaces are the most valuable spaces in a retail store. Consequently, retailers tend to work hard to ensure they maximise return on investment on each square foot of store space.

They display as many products as possible to ensure the maximum utilisation of their display space. Displaying too many products can result in wastage, while displaying too few could result in loss of sales.

The trick is to strike the balance between the two: ensuring customers are able to easily find the products they went into the store to buy and in the process reducing shrinkage.

Visual merchandising display is basically the physical presentation of products for the purpose of increasing sales. Visual merchandising is essential for maintaining the balance between shelf and warehouse stock.

Visual merchandising display is commonly referred to as the silent salesman because a good display effectively sells the products.

The core objectives of visual merchandising are to:

- Enable shoppers to closely examine products
- Maintain the customer's interest in the product
- Encourage them to lower their psychological defences
- Make the purchasing decision easy

However, the most successful retailers do not view visual merchandising as just the display of products on the shop floor. They see it as a marketing tool.

Because they view visual merchandising as a marketing tool, when creating a display, they do not only focus on the physical aspect of placing the products on the shop floor or storefront, they focus on all aspect of the process.

In fact their main focus is on the thinking behind the process rather than the actual process of displaying the products. I will diverge here a little to make this point clearer.

I do a lot of internet marketing, for that I attend lots of internet marketing events taught by the most successful internet marketers in the world. In event after event that I have attended or bought, I continued to observe an interesting trend; the most successful internet marketers do not teach people how to succeed on the internet. Instead they teach marketing fundamentals.

The way they see it, like visual merchandising, the internet is only a vehicle through which they can apply timeless marketing fundamentals. The likes of Google, Facebook, YouTube, Amazon, eBay and many of the successful internet success stories are not successful because their ability to use the internet better than their competitors. They are successful because they applied timeless marketing principles using the internet as an instrument.

There is similar situation with social media. The myth goes that social media can generate loads of customers. As the most successful internet marketers know, social media does not bring anyone business or customers.

It only effective use is to draw traffic to a business's website, the business has to apply timeless marketing principles if it intend on converting those visitors into customers.

The principles of marketing like any principle have never changed. The application might change but the principle itself endures for ever. The fundamentals of marketing have never changed since the beginning of time because human behaviour has never changed since the beginning of time.

This is what one of the world's legendary marketing gurus Eugene Schwartz had to say about this point.

> *"Human nature is perpetual. In most respects it is the same today as in the time of Caesar. So the principles of psychology are fixed and enduring. You will never need to unlearn what you learn about them…Consumers all over the world still buy products which promise them value for money, beauty, nutrition, real relief from suffering and social status".*

Marketing is what determines the success and failure of any business. Your ability to acquire and retain customers at the most cost-effective rate would determine your level of success in your retail business.

In Value Migration, Adrian Slywotzky stated that:

> *"A business (model) design is the totality of how a company selects its customers, defines and differentiates its offerings (or responses), defines the tasks it will perform itself and those it will outsource, configures its resources, goes to market, creates utility for customers and captures profits. It is the entire system for delivering utility to customers and earning a profit from that activity".*

In their paper "while the term 'business model' is often used these days, it is seldom defined explicitly." Chesbrough and Rosenbloom point out that there are six specific functions of a business model:

- *Articulate the value proposition – the value created to users by using the product.*
- *Identify the market segment – to whom and for what purpose is the product useful; specify how revenue is generated by the firm.*
- *Define the value chain – the sequence of activities and information required to allow a company to design, produce, market, deliver and support its product or service.*
- *Estimate the cost structure and profit potential – using the value chain and value proposition identified.*
- *Describe the position of the firm with the value network – link suppliers, customers, counterparts and competitors.*
- *Formulate the competitive strategy – how will you gain and hold your competitive advantage over competitors or potential new entrants.*

Joan Magretta wrote in the Harvard Business Review in May 2002:

"A good business model answers Peter Drucker's age-old questions. Who is the customer? And what does the customer value? It also answers the fundamental questions every manager must ask. How do we make money in this business? What is the underlying economic logic that explains how we can deliver value to customers at an appropriate cost"?

As you make plans for your visual merchandise display I want you to give some thought to the above messages. The main objective of a visual merchandise display is to motivate customer interest in your products. Displays should also be able to provide information about the products; show customers how to use the product.

A good visual merchandise display strategy answers the following questions:

- Does the display fit your brand image?
- Is it attractive enough to capture the customers' attention?
- Does it have a story to tell to the customer?
- Does it have a clear and specific message for the customer?
- Is it focused on the product?
- Is the information of the display easy to read?
- Does the lighting system bring out the best in the display?
- Is the display well organised?

The answers to the above questions will result in:

- Increase footfall
- Increased impulse buying
- Good brand positioning
- Effective use of display space allocation

In the fiercely competitive retail market you need to ensure you provide your customers the total shopping experience they crave. Taking the time to think through your merchandise display process – applying fundamental marketing principles will provide you huge competitive advantage over your competitors.

What is a good merchandise display strategy?

So how can you influence your customer or potential customers' buying decision through the creative use of a visual merchandise display? You can do that by simply asking yourself:

What catches your attention and persuades you to enter a particular store amongst three hundred stores in a shopping centre?

An answer to this question would bring you closer to answering the question of how to influence your customer's buying decision.

A creative visual merchandise display must have the following:

Balance
Balance refers to the manner in which the products are arranged around an imaginary centerline. When the phrase formal balance is discussed in relation to a visual merchandise display, this means that a product is on one side of the line, and a similar product is displayed at the same distance from the line between both products in the display. Balance encompasses the symmetry and weight of products on two sides of a display.

Emphasis
Emphasis is using one product in the display as the centre of attraction. The product would be core of the display around which the rest of the display is arranged.

The emphasis in a display is where the potential customer is expected to look first and it is deliberately arranged by the visual merchandiser to be the most prominent component of the display. All good visual merchandise displays have an emphasis.

Proportion
Proportion is the dimension and spacing of products in a display. Proportion can refer to the relationship between the product used as emphasis and the rest of the products in the display.

When the word proportion is used in relation to a merchandise display, it refers to the relative association of every piece of the display in relation to the: distance, size, amount and degree of differentiation.

Rhythm

Rhythm is the measurement of systematised movement from one product to the next in a merchandise display. Rhythm is an inexplicit guide tactically placed in the display to guide the customer's eyes from product to product in the display back to front and/or side to side.

The rhythm is also necessary for leading the eyes of the customer from the product of emphasis to the rest of the products on display as they look at them.

Harmony

Harmony conveys the mood and emotions of the display. It is obviously the most important aspect of the display. However, because it is not a tangible object, its essence could be lost in the display. Harmony is the story and message within the products on display. It is what brings the display to life and gives it character.

There are self-service and full-service displays

Self-Service

The Self-service display is a display in which the products on display are the ones on sale. If customers see a product in the display that they like, they can select the product and take it to the checkout counter.

Full-Service

A full-service display on the other hand is a mock display of the products. The main products are kept in the warehouse or behind the customer services counter. If customers see a product in the display that they like, they need to call one of the store associates who will go and collect the product for them.

This sort of display is usually used for expensive or large products and it is frequently used in luxury and upscale retail environments.

Big retailers often use a combination of both self-service and full-service.

How to conduct a good merchandise display strategy

The two types of displays are window and interior displays.

Window Display

Window displays are merchandises displayed in the shop window to attract shoppers as they pass by the store. The main objectives of a window display is to attract shoppers attention and entice them to enter the store.

Consequently, window displays are often brightly and impressively colored and lit. Window displays are usually season and occasion related; for example a window display for Valentines would be done in red and white colours and hearts reflecting love.

Interior Display

An interior display as the name suggests is the display of merchandise inside the store. Interior displays are also strategically located in various locations of the store to attract customers' attention as they move from one part of the store to the next.

The main objectives of interior display are to increase customer desire for the merchandise, show what merchandises are available, and stimulate both impulse and planned buying.

There are three types of interior displays: Open; closed, and Point-of-Purchase.

Open Display

An open display is one in which customers have access to the merchandise. They can touch, feel and try on merchandises in an open display.

Closed Display

Closed displays are displays that restrict customer access. Merchandises are usually kept enclosed in display cabinets and behind the cashier checkout counters.

Point of Purchase Display

Point of Purchase Display refers to products that are displayed close to the checkout counter. The main objective of this display is to encourage impulse buying. The Point of Purchase Display can be used to introduce new products, announce special offers or stimulate "no brainer" purchases such as lip balms, pens and small items.

When planning your visual merchandise display, take the following into consideration:

Your Brand Image

Is the display consistent with your brand image?

As a retailer, you represent a certain image to the public.

That image needs to be reflected in all of your marketing materials, messages and visual merchandise displays.

As you plan your display, the question that needs to be core to the process is, does the design represent the brand image you are known for?

Your target market

The next point that needs to be considered is: does the design appeal to your target market? I am making the assumption that you already know your target market. So as you prepare your design story board, the question that your need to be asking is, does this message speak to our target market?

If the answer is yes, then your display is effective. If no, you will need to tweak it until it speaks directly to your target market.

What's the concept?

What is the concept of the display?

What would it be communicating to your target market?

The most effective displays are the ones in which the products are displayed exactly how they are to be used. It could be a clothing display in which the item is dressed on a mannequin the way someone is expected to wear it or in a furniture store where furniture are arranged in a way that they are expected to be arranged in a room.

The display structure

Considerations have to be given to the area in which the display is to be located. The location of the display has a significant impact on how it is to be designed? In retail store displays are usually located in: windows, walls, cases, gondolas or islands. The specific area in which the display is to be located within the store would determine its size and shape.

Promotional displays

Displays created for promotional purposes need to be different from the rest of the displays in the store. Promotional displays need to be located in the front of the store for a short period after which they should be moved to the back of the store if you intend on carrying on the display for a long time.

Customers who are interested in bargains will find it no matter the area of the store it is located.

Your customers need to be treated to new and exciting displays every week to create a sense of freshness in their heads. Always ensure that you have enough products in stock during promotional periods to cater to customer demand.

The following steps for creating displays that would increase your sales:

Step One
Determine the goal of the display
Every display needs to have a specific goal. The questions with which to determine this are: Is the goal of the display to promote new products; to carry on promotion; to attract a new target market to your store?

There needs to be a goal for each and every display.

Step Two
Choose the right merchandise
The merchandise on display needs to reflect the types of merchandise you sell. To ensure this takes place, the questions you need to answer are:

Does the merchandise on display match the quality of your product?

Does it reflect your brand image?

Your merchandise displays need to contain the right product for the right time. If the display is for Valentine, every product on the display needs to be related to valentine.

Step Three
Choose a theme

Every display needs to have a theme. The theme of the display is the story behind the display. You need to be able to identify the message you want the display to send to your target market. The theme of your merchandising can be a way to communicate a seasonal message to your target market.

Step Four
Select props

Props are the items used in a merchandise display to physically support merchandises that form part of the display theme. Props are essential for strengthening the message of a display.

Prop characters are essential for determining the overall appearance and feel of a display hence the reason why it is essential to get the appropriate props for your display.

Step Five
Create a contextual display

Create contextual displays by merging similar products together. This makes buying decisions easier for customers. For example: putting together shirt and ties or shoes and socks.

When products are grouped together, they make it easier for customers to make their choice. It also results in increased sales as it encourages a lot impulse buying.

Step Six
Develop signs

Ensure your signage is visible enough to complement the merchandise on display. There needs to a balance on the amount of signage placed on a display to avoid confusion.

The objective of signage in a display is to provide information such as the price of the products on display. It needs to be brief and easy to read. Signage should also prompt customers to move around the store. The sign should basically covertly inform that there are more great products to be seen in the store.

Step Seven
Design the lighting

Your lighting system is the most important element of your display. You need to ensure that the lighting system used for your display is the most appropriate one. The lighting system is also very crucial for your display because the right lighting system enhances the appearance of the products.

A good lighting system can also create an illusion and make products in the display appear more valuable than they actually are.

The light should be enough to enable the customer to examine the display and read the signs related to it. You can use a spotlight to highlight specific items in the display.

Ensure the lighting system does not cause glare and shadows around the display area. This is done effectively when you have different lighting sources.

Finally, displays must be neat and simple.

A cluttered display sends a bad impression of your store.

A confusing display would result in poor sales.

Therefore, it is very important that displays are:

    Neat

    Uncluttered

    The display area clean

There are no unrelated things lying about

The objective of the display should be to:

- Attract customers as they pass by the store
- Entice them to enter the store
- Retain them for longer in the store
- Persuade them to buy

Remember visual merchandising display is first and foremost a marketing tool, therefore the design has to be infused with timeless fundamental marketing principles.

Chapter Six

How To Maximise Display Space Allocation With Creative Display

Maximising display space to achieve the maximum return on investment per square foot ought to be a main objective of your visual merchandising display strategy. The cost of retail space by square foot is on the increase. So too is the variation of products. Creative use of display space is particularly relevant for retailers who sell low value products.

There are only so many products that can be crammed on a shelf in a small retail space. This means that space needs to be used creatively, to result in maximum profit for the retailer.

What Is Creative Space Use?

Creative visual merchandise space is the efficient use of retail space to maximise its potential capacity while retaining the sense of present-ability. This allows the products for presentation to appear neat and eye catching to the passing customer.

The efficient use of retail display space has several benefits:

- The ability to stock more products

The more space you have to display merchandise the more products you can display in your store.

- More supplier support

With fierce competition in the retail marketplace, all suppliers want their products to be allocated a space in a store, preferably in the high traffic areas. Consequently, suppliers are willing to bargain for marketing support and higher space rental just to get the space that they want.

- More organised and controlled displays

An organised and well-controlled display area results in the maximisation of space. When your store is well-organised it is easier to monitor your products. There is also less incidents of pilferage and theft.

- Increased consumer satisfaction

Aside from good quality products and services that the store offers, availability is also very important to the consumer. Product prices prove irrelevant in comparison to convenience and quality.

- Increased sales and profit

Increased customer satisfaction results in increased sales and profit. Word of mouth advertisement based on personal experience is the oldest but still the most effective marketing tool.

For example, grocery items displayed on end caps and promotional merchandise situated near the store entrance are more likely to attract customers' attention than if they are positioned in a side aisle or in the back of the store.

- It helps prevent out-of stock and inadvertently lose sales

When you display your merchandise properly on the shop floor, they can be easily monitored by staff to ensure that the spaces are constantly refilled. In most cases when customers notice that a product is not on a display only a few customers who desperately need the item would bother to ask store associates. The majority would just assume that it is unavailable in the store and go somewhere else and buy.

The effectiveness of a visual merchandise display space would depend on a few key factors:

- The type of merchandise you sell
- The location of the building
- Your store design
- The amount you are willing to allocate to the process

Display space allocation is the most complicated challenge facing most retailers. New products are constantly been introduced into the market. As those new products are brought into the store, the visual merchandiser is charged with the responsibility of finding display space for all of the new products.

One-third of the products each year in an average retail, are new products. Each new product brings with it the accompanying challenge of finding a suitable spot on the shop floor.

To ensure an effective use of your display space, take the following into consideration:

Set a realistic budget

The first thing that needs to be taken into consideration is your budget. How much will you realistically spend on visual merchandising; knowing fully well the benefits of the process?

Answering this question would help you set budgetary priorities to ensure you focus your spending on essential elements such as lighting, display area, fixtures, shelving, storage units and furniture as well as floor and wall coverings.

Create a blueprint

A blueprint of your display space taking into consideration you product line is another point to consider when developing your visual merchandising display plan.

You need to monitor your sales volume, price point and profit margin to ensure that you are effectively using your display space. By monitoring your results, you can keep tweaking your blueprint to ensure you are making maximum use of your display space.

Plan the traffic flow

Customers need to be able to properly examine the products from all angles to make an informed buying decision. Ensure you allow sufficient space for aisles and give consideration to the projected traffic flow.

Remember, you would want your customers to move through your display areas and to the checkout counter with ease. Designing customer flow and accessibility into the visual merchandising display blueprint would help make the process smoother.

There are three basic visual merchandising display space structural frameworks:

Open Structure

An open structure enables customer flow from one product to the next without any barriers or obstacles. The open structure enables the separation of space; however it is done in such a way that it does not hinder the movement of customers around the display.

Grid Structure

In the grid structure, products are displayed in enclosed spaces according to product categories. Adequate segregation is provided on every product category. If the store carries a lot of different product categories extensive efforts are made to ensure each product category is well separated from the next.

Boutique Structure

With the boutique structure, products are placed next to each other. This allows the customer the freedom to choose at will. The drawback of this structure is it can be difficult for the customer to navigate through the products.

In retail; space means money. The store has to be designed in such a way that it optimises the selling area and minimises the non-selling areas.

The selling area is used to present the merchandise and the non-selling section is taken up by passage space, aisles, staircases, lifts, facilities, and the back area. The area mix in a usual department store is: selling area about 65%, circulation area 15% and back area 20%.

In a ready-made garment retail store; setting up the size of the selling space starts with a wardrobe audit where a sample size of the customer section is intercepted and their wardrobe mix of garments and accessories planned out.

This will determine the number of styles and the range width of the same category. Then a store design is made based on the space integration. The selling space is then planned in terms of size and place of merchandise and based on the mix of staple, convenience and impulse merchandise.

How to use space well

The display of a good retail store with attractive windows and an inviting entrance attracts the customer to enter. The customer enters the store and often keeps walking inside following the walkway wherever it leads or sometimes takes a while to look for directions within the store. Sometimes the customer's attention is drawn to certain displays and merchandise presentations before he moves on.

Merchandise can be efficiently displayed on a variety of fixtures such as gondolas, tables, cubes, mannequins, waterfalls and other racks. Display cases and manufacturer point-of-purchase displays are also handy.

A fixture should not only match the merchandise, but also the environment created in the store. Each fixture is presenting the merchandise to the public and as such acts as a silent salesperson.

The space must be specially designed for the type of product being sold in that section. For example, a bookstore requires many shelving units to hold some products that can be arranged by category. On the other hand, a clothing store will need more open spaces to fully display all its merchandise. Once within the store, the customer needs to be guided silently to where he/she wants to go and also expose him/her to the entire store offering. This can be achieved by setting up the flow and the location of the merchandise.

The aisles forming a pattern flow can be of different types based on the store arrangement. The section occupied by the aisles is normally 12-15% of the store carpet area.

Below are some types flow layouts you can choose from:

Free Flow

This layout is used in stores where the merchandise and fixtures are grouped in clusters.

Grid Flow

This type is usually used in supermarkets where the aisles and fixtures are at right angles to each other.

Race Track

This is generally utilized in larger and wider stores where the customer is made to circle around the floor and get back to the beginning, usually the lift or the staircase lobby, to move to the next level of the store.

Herringbone Flow

This is used most of the times for a narrow store of at most 40 ft. wide wherein the freeway is a single two-way one, bisecting the store along its length with "side roads' leading to the walls from it.

The proper utilisation of store space will require the retailer to focus on these three important steps simultaneously:

Step One
Get the appropriate space and product assortment

Retailers optimise and rationalise their assortments based on enhanced analysis of profitability and the apprehension that variety may be overwhelming for customers.

They know they need to do a better job of understanding the assortment. So they assume the role of selector and chief buyer on behalf of the consumers. The positions of various goods are chosen carefully to ensure that the customer is exposed to the entire store; thus increasing the possibility of a purchase.

Step Two
Systematize strategies to manage space

Retailers should re-evaluate their business operations; standardise new and revise older formats. They should competently segment and align their retail space to consumer needs and purchasing behavior.

At the same time they should explore other opportunities for growth.

Step Three
Integrate online and offline channels

The increasing importance of online shopping is changing notions of space management. It introduces the concept of the "endless aisle" and encourages retailers to treat the Internet as an integral part of their operations.

The retail business is very competitive, with thousands of contending retail establishments vying for attention, space management does not end with optimisation.

It creates greater opportunity for merchandise promotion and presentation, which will not only result in higher profit margin but also customers retention.

Below are additional important tips for optimising your store space relative to effective utilization of your fixtures:

Use modern fixtures

An article titled "The Psychology of Shopping," looks at retailing nearly four decades ago. It revealed that the retail giants of the 1970s relied heavily on the philosophy of "pile it high; sell it cheap" and they found success with that philosophy.

Although retailers are currently using more sophisticated ways of capturing the attention of shoppers, this philosophy remains pervasive. To successfully compete in the contemporary retail environment requires you change your philosophy along with your fixtures to more modern eye-catching fixtures.

Choose fixture to match your target market

Pick displays and fixtures that are distinctively suited to your target market.

>Who is your target market?
>
>What type of customer do you have?

Take a detailed look at your own store. In what ways are the store fixtures and displays matching the types of customers you wish to attract?

Plan your display strategies

Plan your space using display systems that make it trouble-free for your customers.

The width of the aisles needs to be selected according to the density and traffic pattern.

The main aisle or 'highway' in a department store is six feet wide, which is the width of a double doorway. It facilitates easy passage in both directions. The side aisles or 'side roads' that branch out are three or four feet wide.

In supermarkets, the aisles are three feet wide and form a denser grid around the fixtures.

When planning you display space, you need to take into account the following:

- The average person's field of vision tends to be around 170 degrees
- The number of product categories in the store
- The percentage of space to be allotted to each category
- The volume of merchandise in each category
- The relative placement of each category

How to implement good space allocation

The primary purpose of retail space is to stock and sell product to consumers. The spaces must be designed in a way that promotes an enjoyable and hassle-free shopping experience for the consumer.

The shelf space problem is quite different depending on whether we take the perspective of the manufacturer or the retailer.

Manufacturers want to maximise the sales and profits of their products, and as such always want more and better space to be allocated to their brands.

Retailers want to maximize category sales and profits, regardless of brand identity; they must allocate a fixed amount of shelf space in the best possible way.

Here are a few things to consider when allocating display space:

Fixture arrangement

One of the most common fixtures in stores are gondolas – movable shelving that are accessible from all sides.

They should be lined up in rows as in grocery, hardware and drug stores or used singly to form an island.

When placing racks, progress from small fixtures to large fixtures near the back walls. When working with hard goods, place cubes in the front with gondolas to the rear of the department or store.

Higher end stores require fewer fixtures because there are less merchandise. Use primarily T-stands and four ways to create an illusion of space for selective goods.

This is necessary to sell higher ticket products.

Contextual Merchandising

Similar merchandise should be grouped together on the end-cap and gondola sides. The end-cap should indicate the type of related merchandise on the gondola sides. For example, golf balls displayed on an end-cap should indicate that related golf accessories are located on gondola sides.

End-caps are units at the end of aisles. End-caps are important selling fixtures that should be used for high ticket impulse or seasonal merchandise.

Centralise high ticket products

Customers usually look to the center of gondola sides first before looking either to the left or right. Additional high ticket impulse items should be placed in the center of gondola sides and other related merchandise to either the left or right.

Larger more expensive merchandise should be placed to the right.

Furthermore, high ticket items should be placed at eye level.

Allow contact

If possible, remove a sample from packaging to allow customers to touch and feel the items. Old merchandise should be cleaned and pulled forward as new merchandises are added to the display.

Use a starter gap in which at least one item is missing, so the customer will not feel like they are messing up a neat display.

Create rainbow presentation

Make stimulating displays with mass merchandise by using quantity and color. A good way of arranging merchandise on a gondola is by color. People think of colors in a rainbow pattern and are comfortable with that sort of presentation.

Display merchandise in quantity on quads, round and T-stands; use cubes for folded goods.

Restock the display before it gets down to the last item so customers will not get the impression that something is wrong with the item.

If merchandise are broken the remaining items should be moved to the bottom shelves of the gondola.

Use geometric pattern

A well-planned geometric aisle pattern works best to maximize sales. Place aisle displays in an island rather than wing fixtures.

Fixtures that work well for sale items include tub tables, round racks and rectangular rackslay product. Allow need to be three feet between racks.

Leave fire exit free

The aisle leading directly to the fire exit is considered a major aisle. Do not block the fire exit with fixtures or extraneous materials. Legal requirements for aisle width vary from four to eight feet.

The most common aisle width is six feet. Check your local codes for the your local requirements.

Your goal should be to have enough products of display, not overcrowded fixtures and walls. In addition, clearly delineated product categories. Maximising fixture practice requires fresh eyes and a creative spirit alongside a desire to drive sales.

The new representation for retail success includes not only space utilisation but an integrated approach to space management that will drive traffic, increase sales and profitability.

Retailers should understand the changes in consumer behavior and preferences and align their space management strategies accordingly.

Chapter Seven

The Benefits Planogram Software

More and more retailers as well as manufacturers are now using planogram to create images shelf strips, shelf tags and back tags to help store associates produce prompt and accurate visual merchandising display.

A planogram is a marketing instrument used in retail stores. It is an illustration or drawing that provides details of where a product should be placed on a shelf and how many facing that product should be. It is used by a retail store to increase sales and by suppliers to justify the space allocated of brands and new products.

Retailers employ planograms so they come up with product displays that draw customers' interest and help them to sell more products as a result. The complexity of a planogram may differ by the size of store, the software used to create the planogram and the need of the retailer.

Why is planogram good for visual merchandising?

Figure 19: Planogram makes merchandising display easy

As competition heats up; an increasing number of retailers as well as distributors are becoming more aware of the importance of marketing their products. They are beginning to realise that better marketing leads to improved sales.

Planograms are an accurate way of presenting new ideas for product placement, testing merchandising principles and understanding best possible inventory requirements. It is a schematic of shelve and fixture positioning of products on those shelves or fixtures.

Successful retail space planning and management is an important part of the merchandise planning and execution. A well-designed shopping environment catches the attention of customers, prevents stock outs, enhances inventory productivity, reduces operating costs and most of all boosts the financial performance of the store.

Here are the advantages of utilising planogram for visual merchandising:

Guaranteed product placement

Figure 20: Planogram ensures optimum supply chain efficiency

Accurate store-specific planograms ensure optimum supply chain efficiency that results in higher availability to shoppers, maximum stock turn over and the most efficient use of space.

Improved sales

Targeted store-specific planograms direct maximum in-store compliance, resulting in an accurate understanding of product distribution and eventually increase sales.

Tighter inventory control and reduction of stock outs items

Focused store-specific planograms leads to increased sales and profitability, easier product replenishment, reduction in stock and operational costs and an overall enhancement in bottom line contribution.

Satisfying customers with a better visual appeal

Improves customer satisfaction by making it easier to shop in shelves that are well-organised and reduces the time it takes to arrange stock in the store. Influence customer behaviour for trade-up and impulse buying, which result increased sales.

Effective communication tool for staff

Tailors assortments including product launches and group-specific go-to-market strategies so that you can improve cluster results and meet true local demand and effectively communicate with your staff.

Assigned selling potential to every inch of retail space

Enables better management of inventory by allocating shelf space and facings based on movement, which in turn reduces out-of-stocks; streamlines space and floor planning, so that you can increase your space productivity and optimise your capital investment.

Merchandising Tactics

Figure 21: Planogram Enables better inventory management

Improved merchandising best practices by testing and comparison of cause and effect in like stores; translates merchandising strategy into tactics; so that you can drive consistent store execution of your corporate strategic and assortment decisions.

Planograms will give you a good idea of how a display will look before you physically dress that merchandise on to the shelves in your store. This saves you time and ensures you are not frequently distracting and irritating your customers, by always dressing and re-dressing shelves until you find a product layout that works.

Planograms can be as easy as a photo of a preset section or more thorough with numbered peg holes and shelf notches showing exact position of each item.

Planogram diagrams received by a store may be imprecise or worse nearly impractical to implement because the category size, orientation, or shelving in a particular store may not match the planogram.

In some cases, resetting can be hampered by shelf tags and layouts that rely on shortened names.

Product positioning and enhanced sales are just two important reasons why a retailer should be implementing planograms in their stores. Using a planogram helps a retailer design different product layouts and compare them side by side.

Below are some things to consider when implement planogram in your store:

Quality

Includes shelf heights, merchandise placements and the quantity of facings. Shelf heights depend on the volume of the products and ease of reach for the customers.

Merchandise placement illustrates which shelf and where on that shelf a product should be placed. A facing is a row of products.

Thus, if a product has two facings, there are two rows of that product on the shelf.

Importance

The arrangement and number of facings merchandise has will considerably change its sales at the store. It will also change the store's overall performance. It is recommended that the product be placed at eye level and have the maximum amounts of facings.

It is significant for the store to let its most profitable products have the most facings and be located at eye level. And avoid wasting space by placing low ticket slow-moving products with low profit margin in premium locations.

Purpose

The objective of the planogram is to increase sales and offer the most popular product the best spot to attract customers. A store should regularly modify the layout of all of its fixtures.

For example, the design of the children formula section in a supermarket will be different every few months depending on what is hot in that period.

The stores use a planogram to make a decision on how the section will look and what merchandise will be most available to the customer. Besides, with each layout of a planogram, the store will make the fixtures appear more aesthetic to the customer.

Time Schedule

Planograms are typically planned a few weeks in advance of its implementation. A company that specializes in planograms and merchandising will design them using specialized software. Then they will be tested on pilot shelves to ensure they are suitable for the store before deploying it.

How Planogram is used

For a chain of retail stores, planogram guarantees the uniformity of product placement at all locations and wholesalers use the sketches to implement the display of their product. In effect, it gives them the highest sales volume.

Independent retailers use planogram to make the best use of shelf space and improve the look of products. Operating with an efficient planogram is one way to ensure products are replenished and maintained in a way that develops the quality of the display.

A good retailer should understand that the key to increased sales is proper merchandising. A planogram is one of the best merchandising tools for presenting products to the customer.

Listed below are the types of commonly used planogram:

Box with text

The most basic form of planograms utilises box shapes to represent to different goods, with the name of the item typed inside the box.

For example, a planogram intended for a noodle aisle might have rows of larger rectangular boxes to packs of instant noodles.

The brand of instant noodles will be written inside of the box. There may be two rows of each brand depending on the store's requirement.

If the store is usually selling more of one brand, there will be more facings of the high seller. These planograms are typically black and white, two-dimensional diagrams intended for use in grocery stores or areas of retail department stores where merchandise are moving fast.

Pictorial

Pictorial planogram is normally used in clothing and department stores wherein displays are more important and arrangement is essential.

Pictorial planograms are more difficult and thorough compared with the basic planograms.

Pictorial planograms include images of the product and how it should be displayed.

It may show how shirts should be arranged on the shelf or it may demonstrate how dishes or small appliances should be displayed. These planograms are generally flat, two-dimensional, computerised illustrations.

They are typically drawn more precisely to scale and are in color to give an exact representation of how the items are to be displayed.

3-D

Planogram application differs by retail sector. Three-dimensional planograms are usually drawn to scale and include aerial views of the area. As technology advances, so to do the applications and software used to create planograms.

The 3-D type includes whole department layout. Computer generated photographic illustrations of how the department, including promotions and displays should appear. These technologies have led to the growing popularity of three-dimensional planograms.

Fast-moving consumer product industry and supermarkets most of the time use text and box based planograms that optimizes shelf space, inventory turns, and profit margins.

Department Stores are more focused on presentation therefore use pictorial planograms that project "the image" and also identify each product.

Factors to consider when implementing planogram that makes the buying process easier for the customer, which simultaneously result in increased sales for the store are:

Planned Category

Customers might need a product but prior to going to the store have not determined which brand, size, quantity and flavour they require. Having planned category help make customer decision easier.

Impulse buying

A customer might not have plans of buying an item, but seeing the item on display might trigger their desire to buy it.

Substitution

An appropriately merchandised planogram can influence trade-up or trade-down purchases. For example, a customer originally plans to purchase Brand 'A' but proper planogramming directs the customer to Brand 'B' which is offered as a better value.

Triggered

The busy customers frequently appear at the store knowing what they want to purchase; they just don't have a specific list. A "triggered" purchase takes place when they see the product on the shelf which serves as a reminder and that encourages them to buy.

Contextual

Making sure that product category is accurately placed through the aid of correct planogramming will lead to larger transactions and happier consumers.

An incremental purchase is completed as a result of purchasing another product. For example, a customer purchases paint and the appropriately arranged planogram reminds them of the need for a brush, tape, and other items needed to perform the task.

One very essential rule of good quality planogramming is "always anticipating the customer's need." Picture strips and tags are well-liked by shoppers because it helps them understand "product-to-price" identification and let customers know that an item is sold even if it is currently out of stock.

How does planogram work?

The goal is to take full advantage of the quantity of merchandise on display and the amount of sales by arranging merchandise in a way that they will look enticing to customers.

Planogram was designed aim of:

- Increasing sales
- Increasing profits
- Creating a proper way of introducing a new product
- Supporting a new merchandising approach

Deviating from the planogram defeats the rationale of any of the above stated goals.

The full benefits of planogram can be best achieved if the following steps are being followed:

Step One
Identify the purpose
Decide product positioning and sales betterment are few reasons why you should implement planogram. Outline the kind of display you plan on implementing.

Step Two
Map out the display
The display cases and shelves are the most important elements of a planogram. Start by illustrating the backdrop and draw as accurately as possible so it can be used literally as instructions for organising your shelves.

Step Three
Organize your merchandise
Try out different ways of arranging your merchandise so that they fit as best as possible and will be easily seen.

Decide where you want the products to be positioned using shapes that have the same dimensions and forms of the actual products.

Step Four
Add Labels
Using labels and product images will give you the absolute feel of what you have arranged. It will also let anyone involved in the planning envisage the display.

Step Five
Implement It
Use the illustration to create the life size display. If all of your dimensions are accurate, you should be confident that everything will fit as you planned.

To fully appreciate the value of planogram, any retailer deciding to implement planogram should first be able to read and understand diagrams.

Here are a few pointers to help you read and understand planogram:

Determine whether you have the appropriate planogram for your store. Some retail chains will have different planograms to accommodate the various sizes of stores.

To ensure you are merchandising the right product, match the bar code on the product with your SKU list. This is a listing of all the products and the number of facings, or the number of times each product is to be merchandised on the shelf.

Most planogram software takes some time to master fully, so start with a small display area in your store which contains only a few lines. Locate the lead-in arrow, in the bottom left corner of the schematic. This shows the direction in which the planogram is to be set.

When implementing planogram it is recommended you allocate space based upon product sales performance. A basic rule of planograming is to ensure there are enough products on the shelf to meet the customer's requirement.

Knowing how to read a planogram is a key component of a successful visual merchandising display strategy. It aids in speeding up product placement on the shop floor and increase performance efficiency.

What can you do in your store right now to implement planogram?

Here are some things to consider when implementing planogram:

Location

>Where in the store located?
>
>Are there secondary placements?

Category Space Allocation

How much space will be allocated to each category?

Product Space

What will spaces allocation be based upon: sales, movement, mandates or inventory thresholds?

Layout

How will the planogram be structured based upon: price, brand or manufacturers?

Labels/ Signage

How would the category or section benefit from signage or point of purchase materials?

Planogram makes the work of your employees easy at store level as they do not need to do the thinking about where products are to be placed, increasing staff productivity and decreasing shrinkage.

Chapter Eight

How To Profitably Display Merchandise

London based Harrods is one of the most successful retailer in the world. Royalties, A-list stars and the "Who-is-Who" from around the world fly to London just to shop at Harrods.

What is responsible for Harrods spectacular success?

There are three factors responsible for Harrods phenomenon success...

- Good store design
- Attractive visual merchandise display
- Effective loss prevention strategy

The subject of loss prevention is something that has never been taken seriously by the retail industry even though the industry spends billions every year on loss prevention. In the last ten years loss prevention spending has increased tremendously. In 2011 the total cost of retail crime plus loss prevention was $128 billion; but retail shrinkage rose to $119 billion.

So why is it that despite the huge amount spent on loss prevention, retail shrinkage continues to rise?

To answer this question, I will give you a quick tour of Harrods.

Harrods store design and visual merchandising displays are definitely factors in its success. The key factor to Harrods' success though is its ability to remain profitable. Profit is king in retail. In retail the formula for making profit is to increase sales and reduce shrinkage.

Increasing sales requires a good store design and attractive visual merchandising; whereas reducing shrinkage calls for an effective loss prevention strategy.

This is what Harrods and most successful retailers have over the rest of the retail industry: their ability to simultaneously increase sales and reduce shrinkage. Most retailers know how to increase sales, however, when it comes to reducing their shrinkage, they are challenged.

Getting the two right is the fundamental principle of retail success. No retailer can succeed without simultaneously increasing sales and reducing shrinkage.

Why do shrinkage reduction or loss prevention measures fail in most retail organisations?

Loss prevention measures fail in retail is a result of the following reasons:

- Lack of understanding of the subject
- Senior management's failure to prioritise
- Outsourcing loss prevention without a mechanism for accountability
- Inexperienced loss prevention managers
- Ineffective use of loss prevention technology.

Harrods is the first retail store that I have ever entered that has no visible blind spots. I am not saying that there are absolutely no blind spots as I managed to spot a few.

However, the difference with other stores is that they are not visible to the unprofessional eyes.

Anyone deciding to shoplift in Harrods would have to be:

- A professional shoplifter or part of an organised retail crime syndicate
- Really brave
- Really stupid

Products are displayed in such a manner that each department seems wide open. Store staff can stand at one end of a department and have a clear view of the entire department.

Figure 22: Harrods drastically reduced the possibility of shoplifting

There is CCTV in every corner of the store; in addition store assistants buzzing around like bees make it difficult for anyone who might intend to shoplift.

I will not go as far as to say that it is impossible to shoplift at Harrods; because I know shoplifting prevention requires the implementation of a raft of strategies.

However, by designing their store as they have done; by displaying their products in the manner that they do and by taking loss prevention measures seriously; Harrods have drastically reduced the possibility of shoplifting.

Now contrast Harrods loss prevention strategy with a store in the top ten UK retailers that I once worked for as a store detective.

This was a few years back. On my very first day of work, as I was in the middle of a briefing with the officer I was to relieve, I noticed a couple walk into the store and head for the coat section. I stood there perplexed as I witnessed the lady remove one of the coats from the hanger; put it on and then casually walk to the exit with her partner and scurry into the waiting getaway car.

£900 walked out the door with such incredible ease, making me think "Holy cow! How can this sort of thing happen in broad daylight?"

> **The answer was actually quite apparent: The coats were prominently displayed right close to the exit.**

Keeping this experience as a vivid memory, any time I was assigned to a different store, I took great care to walk around and look for high value items that were not securely displayed. I would call the store manager over and advise that the items be relocated to a more secure location within the store. To my disbelief, most managers failed to take my advice – in their eyes, I was merely a store detective. What the heck did I know about visual merchandising?

As a second example: I was working at a store in London Colney; immediately upon entering the store I noticed coats worth £250 prominently displayed near the store entrance.

Without hesitation, I located the store manager and expressed my concern to him. I even joked with him how even the CIA Director at the time, George Tenant, could not possibly protect those coats where they were positioned.

This manager chose to ignore my warning and a few hours later, some of the coats were stolen; just as I had predicted. When I approached the manager again, I figured he would pay more attention to me now that my gloomy prediction came true. Once again, he failed to heed my warning. I finally got his attention but only after 20 of the 25 coats were stolen.

At this same location, there are two big retailers who shared a single toilet facility located outside of both stores. Shoplifters knew this and would steal from one store, head to the direction of the toilet, pass through the other store and escape.

When they were stopped and questioned by our store security, they would always mention they were on their way to the toilet. They were correct about heading in that direction; given the location of the toilet.

The mere location of the toilet caused the stores to lose thousands of pounds to shoplifting. Yet neither store's management could pinpoint the location of the toilet as one of the primary causes for their shrinkage.

I share these stories with you to emphasize a very important point: Shoplifting occurs in most retail stores simply because it is allowed to take place.

> *Shoplifting is a crime of opportunity; eliminate the opportunity and you reduce its possibility.*

Figure 23: To increase sales yet fail to reduce profit draining activities is false economy

To increase sales yet fail to reduce profit draining activities is false economy. Many retailers feel loss prevention is something that they could do if they had the resources.

The reality is: it is something that you cannot afford not to do because no retailer can become profitable without implementing effective loss prevention measures.

Senior management's failure to prioritise

Ninety to 95% of retail loss prevention department managers are ex-service personnel. As a result of their law enforcement background, they take the law enforcement approach to their work. They focus mainly on arresting shoplifters and dishonest employees.

While it is true that shoplifting and employee theft accounts for almost 70% of retail shrinkage, they are not the sole cause of shrinkage. Furthermore, shoplifting and employee dishonesty cannot be tackled by solely arresting individuals.

Preventative measures such as good store design and visual merchandise displays; as I mentioned in the case of Harrods, are required to make any preventative measure effective.

Figure 24: Many retail loss prevention managers know very little about store design and visual merchandising

However, due to the fact that there are still retail loss prevention managers who know very little about store design and visual merchandising; many of them are unable to incorporate these aspects into their loss prevention strategies. As a result most loss prevention measures fail.

Outsourcing loss prevention without a mechanism for accountability

> "The average retailer makes a 1% net profit out of each dollar and the average industry shrinkage percentage is 2.6%. This means that shrinkage is almost three times the average retailer's profit margin. By reducing retail shrinkage by 50% – from 2.6 cents to 1.3 cents, a retailer could more than double his profits: from 1 cent to 2.3 cents. (Crosset Company newsletter." June 2010).

Some retailers outsource their loss prevention department to outside contractors. As laudable as this may seem, it is a seriously flawed idea because retailers are sometimes incapable of clearly articulating their expected outcome.

When a job is subcontracted, there is usually an expected outcome. However, if the retailer outsourcing the job cannot articulate their expected outcome, it is difficult to hold the contractor accountable.

Wal-Mart founder Sam Walton once described retail shrinkage as a "profit killer". He was right. High shrinkage is responsible for the death of many retail organisations.

The benefit of a good store design and visual merchandising display is increased sales. So as you develop the plan your store design or visual merchandising display plans, you need to ensure that the safety of the merchandises remain paramount.

In the final analysis you are in business to make profit. And you cannot make profit if you increase sales at the expense of the security of your merchandises.

Without losing the original purpose of your store design and visual merchandising display, you can apply changes to the way in which fixtures are arranged in your store in order to decrease the chances of shoplifting.

One way of doing this is to locate smaller items in places that are visible to employees. Furthermore, positioning employees in key areas of the store is a good strategy to raise the apprehension of shoplifters.

Larger products need to be placed in smaller quantities to prevent the store from appearing cluttered. Poor display of large products can obscure the view of employees and increase the possibility for shoplifting.

Aisles and shelves need to be properly labelled to ensure customers can easily and quickly locate merchandises.

In addition to labelling; installing proper lighting will attract buyers to merchandise as well as allow your employees to observe the surroundings easily.

There is no fool-proof way of preventing shoplifting. However, the installation of security systems such as CCTV and mirrors can reduce incidence of shoplifting in your store. Security mirrors optimize employee's view of the store and reduce blind spots.

How to increase your sales and simultaneously increase your profit?

The following are effective steps for increasing sales and profit with a good store design and merchandising display:

Step 1:

Locate smaller products close to areas that employees frequent to reduce the risk of shoplifting.

Step 2:

Reduce the number of large products on display to allow store employees unhindered views of the store.

Step 3:

Position employees in key areas of the store to increase overall security.

Step 4:

Install security mirrors in the store to reduce blind spots and increase surveillance.

Step 5:

Use CCTV in areas that are not regularly frequented by employees and locate high ticket items under cameras.

Step 6:

Ensure your Loss Prevention Department is involved in the planning of your store design and visual merchandising display.

Years ago, shoplifting was confined to the homeless out for food and drink or drug addicts wishing to feed their habit. Today shoplifting is conducted by retail crime gangs using more sophisticated methods, never before seen in the industry.

Within four minutes, an organised retail crime gang can steal seven thousand pounds worth of products from your store. Think about this the next time you develop your store design and visual merchandising display strategy.

Part Three
The Most Effective Retail Loss Prevention Strategies

Chapter One

The Culture of Loss Prevention

Introduction

Time after time we hear of once healthy retail businesses getting into trouble or being swallowed up by their competitors to save them from collapse. During the recent recession, thousands of retailers bellied up, blaming their shortfalls on the recession. Meanwhile, in that same period, UK supermarket giants such as Morrison's and Sainsbury's almost doubled their profit margin and Tesco went on to become the second most profitable retailer in the world.

Why did a few retailers shine during the recession while others struggled?

Answer: Successful retailers have a built-in mechanism for profit protection within their organizations.

The most successful retailers are those with the lowest shrinkage level because they understand that low shrinkage equals high profits. They have robust loss prevention cultures which permeate throughout the DNA of their organizations. They create a culture in which every single employee is willing to help in the fight against shrinkage.

This book provides strategies retailers can use to create the sort of infrastructure that will allow them to achieve phenomenal results, results achieved only by a few in the midst of a recession.

The Conventional Approach to Loss Prevention

The fundamental principles which reinforce any successful business are the increase in profits and decrease in expenditures. The strict application of the above principles has been responsible for the success of most businesses. On the other hand, failing to apply these principles has been responsible for the demise of the majority of failed businesses. Similar principles apply to the retail industry. Over 50% of retail ventures go bust before their 3rd birthday.

The reason for this being, in the retail industry, the main performance indicator (KPI) is increasing sales without the application of decreasing expenditures. The key question that most retailers need to ask themselves is this:

Does an increased sale really lead to increased profit?

In order to increase sales, a retailer has to carry out additional promotions, advertising and improve customer service or offer a huge discount. Even though these measures are not guaranteed to increase sales, with their implementation there is a chance that sales could be increased. On the other hand, decreasing expenditures means one thing to most businesses: dismissing employees!

However, these techniques are antiquated and have no place in the modern retail environment. The key element that guarantees a healthy return on investment (or increased profit) is increasing sales and decreasing shrinkage. The average retailer makes a 1% net profit out of each dollar, and the industry shrinkage percentage is 2.6%. This means that shrinkage is almost three times the average retailer's profit margin. If you take the above calculation, you will see that if retailers reduced shrinkage by 50% – from 2.6 cents to 1.3 cents, they could more than double their profits: from 1 cent to 2.3 cents. (Crosset company newsletter. June 2010.)

Instead of following the conventional practices of cutting staff in order to create decreased expenditures, the above calculation shows that retailers have the opportunity to increase their profit margin without necessarily giving away their goods or reducing their workforce.

How can Retailers Decrease Shrinkage?

This question has formed the core of "loss prevention" discussions in many quarters. Expert after expert has come up with their own suggestions of how shrinkage can be reduced. Although many of these suggestions make for great sound bites, they have not been able to produce the desired results.

The shrinkage rate for 2005-2010 in North America remained stable: 1.48% to 1.49%. In Europe it stayed at 1.23% from 2006 to 1.33% in 2009. (Global Retail Theft Barometer Report 2010. Bamfield, J. 2010). However, within the same period, loss prevention spending continued to increase to the highest rank of 0.46% in the US. Despite the increase in loss prevention spending, each year over the last 10 years, retail shrinkage either plateaued or decreased by just a few percentage points, which does not correlate with the amount spent.

Why? To answer this question, I will relay two stories:

On Monday 06/12/2010, I visited the Trafford Centre in Manchester, UK. On my way out, I noticed that the Electronic Article Surveillance (EAS) gates at John Lewis were located outside of the store and there were no staff members around monitoring the gates. The first problem is obvious, even if the gate sounded; there were no staff members around to confront the person involved. The second problem with this situation is the simple fact that the gate was outside of the store, instead of inside, rendered it useless.

This is a classic example of the misuse of technology and the wrong application of loss prevention strategy. To place an EAS outside the store is to defeat the objective for which it was installed.

During my research for this book, I stumbled upon some perplexing suggestions made by a group of loss prevention experts. These experts gathered at the 2009 RILA Loss Prevention, Auditing, Safety, and Security Conference held on the 5th of May at the Gaylord Palms Resort in Orlando. Below is the list of the suggestions that were made:

- Institute cross-training of LP (Loss Prevention) staff with sales associates and managers, to include combining LP with operations at the district manager level.
- Utilize Loss Prevention Foundation LP Qualified training for both sales associates and store management.
- Increase the visibility of CCTV and increase signage regarding use of new LP technologies.
- Train and authorize store managers and district managers to conduct employee theft interviews.
- Implement and encourage a "culture of honesty" program in all stores.
- Implement an automated returns management system that is rules based.
- Enlist shoppers to report acts of shoplifting or employee theft in real time by using their cell phones.
- Enlist the help of apprehended shoplifters to consult on effective deterrence ideas.

- Rehire employees who have been caught in small scale dishonest employee incidents. This idea is based upon the old adage, "the devil you know is better than the devil you don't know." (Loss Prevention Magazine. July – August 2009, p.16)

While I have a lot of respect for these guys as the finest and brightest in our trade, I found some of their suggestions bewildering to say the least and quite frankly impractical.

To start with, the suggestion of enlisting shoplifters to serve as consultants is ridiculous. While it might seem the most expedient thing to do, you will not get very far with this. The most successful shoplifters that you might gain valuable information from, don't get caught and if they were caught, it's highly unlikely they'd 'play ball' with you. They are either part of an organized retail crime gang or professionals who make a living from shoplifting.

How much should retailers pay shoplifters to stop shoplifting?

What valuable information can retailers glean from a possible drug addict or alcoholic that loss prevention personnel don't already know?

The suggestion to "re-hire" employees who were caught in the act of theft goes against the grain of common sense. The most important cardinal rule for preventing employee theft is to hire honest people to begin with.

The above examples clearly illustrate why, despite the increased spending on loss prevention, shrinkage levels have remained the same. Thinking outside the box and common sense are imperative!

Why Loss Prevention Is Critical to Retail

In the retail industry, the approach to loss prevention is retroactive. The good guys (loss prevention personnel/experts) pitted against the bad guys (shoplifters and dishonest employees). The problem with this approach is many retailers are hiring ex-service personnel in the roles of loss prevention management. Their experience and training are based on "law enforcement" techniques, lacking basic business knowledge.

What is loss prevention?

Loss prevention is the series of activities that are geared towards the reduction of loss in a retail environment.

What is loss or shrinkage?

Shrinkage is the loss in value of the goods from the time they are received by the store, to the point of sale.

What is profit protection?

Profit protection is a series of activities geared towards inventory and asset protection which ultimately result in sustainable profit.

What causes this loss in value?

It is caused by the following factors:

[Figure 1]

The above chart [Figure 1] demonstrates that shrinkage goes far beyond just theft. Shrinkage is a combination of factors that largely result from little to inadequate or non-existent policies and procedures.

Senior retail executives perceives shrinkage as associated with theft, and therefore overlook or pay little to no attention to the other factors.

Loss prevention must be at the heart of any retail operation because loss prevention is profit protection! If retailers continue to increase sales and ignore the effects of profit "draining" activities, it will be impossible to grow as a successful business.

Below illustrates the current thinking within the retail industry:

1. The Perception that shrinkage is just theft
2. Loss prevention activities managed by-service men with no business background

3. Senior management do not understand the correlation between loss prevention and profit therefore do not give the issue the deserved attention
4. Shrinkage remains a challenge

As a result of this quartet of views there is no culture of discipline in the industry, consequently making it difficult to gain proper traction with shrinkage reduction.

Loss Prevention Spending VS Return On Investment

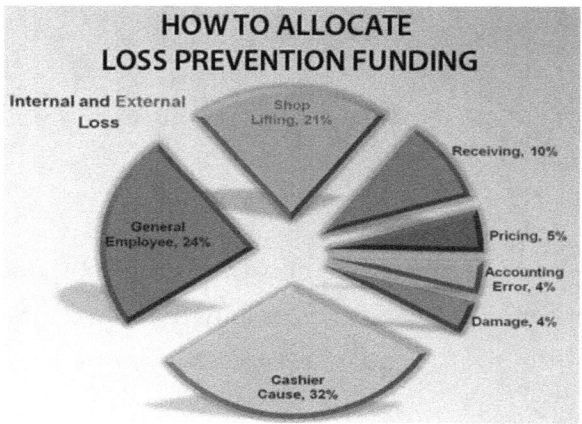

[Figure 2]

The above pie chart [Figure 2] breaks down retail shrinkage by department. According to the chart, cashier cause 32% (theft, fraud and error) accounts for the highest amount of retail shrinkage followed by general employee causes 24% (theft and error). Shoplifting accounts for 21%. This is followed by other contributors including receiving, pricing, damage and accounting errors.

Backing the Wrong Horse:

When it comes to spending on loss prevention, retailers spend more of their resources on methods that produce little or no return on investments (ROI).

Example:

In 2009 the total retail shrinkage for the UK was £4 billion. £1.8 billion resulted from shoplifting, £1.5 billion employee theft, £642 million for administrative error and £175 million for supply chain theft. (Global Retail Theft Barometer Report 2009). (See Figure 3 below).

2009 UK RETAIL SHRINKAGE FIGURES

Total Shrinkage	£4 billion
Shoplifting	£1.8 billion
Employee Theft	£1.5 billion
Administrative Error	£642 million
Supply Chain Theft	£175 million

[Figure 3]

In the same period, UK retailers spent £772 million on Total Loss Prevention, spending: £271 million on Contract Security, £163 million on In-house Security, £224 million on Security Equipment, £62 million on Cash Collection and £52 million on other LP spending. (Global Retail Theft Barometer Report 2009). (See Figure 4 below).

2009 TOTAL LOSS PREVENTION SPENDING

Total LP Spending	£772 million
Contract Security	£271 million
In-House Security	£163 million
Security Equipment	£224 million
Cash Collection	£62 million
Other LP Spending	£52 million

[Figure 4]

However when it came to Return on Investments, retailers gained 50% ROI for training employees which they spent only 6.8% of their revenue on, 2% for security personnel after spending 56.2% of their resources, 45% on security equipment on which they spent 29% on. They gained 3% ROI on signs and other measures through a spending of 8% of their loss prevention revenue. (Global Retail Theft Barometer Report 2009, RIG 2009) (See Figure 5 below).

RETURN ON INVESTMENT FOR LOSS PREVENTION SPENDING

Measures	Spending	ROI Achieved
Trained Employees	6.8%	50%
Security Personnel	56.2%	2%
Security Equipment	29%	45%
Signs and Others	8%	3%

[Figure 5]

It is not hard to see why the current loss prevention strategy of the industry is ineffective. When you spend 56.2% of your resources on measures that give you only 2% ROI, someone must reason there has got to be something seriously wrong with this picture. It is a matter of misallocation of resources to the wrong measures. Consequently, if retailers want to gain better ROI from their current loss prevention spending, the first step they need to take is to conduct a comprehensive analysis of their current spending, their current ROI, and then look for alternative ways of utilising their resources to achieve maximum ROI.

What You Are Losing

If your total annual turnover is £10 million the calculation below gives you an idea of what you are losing on a daily basis.

WHAT YOU ARE LOSING

Percentage Of Shrinkage = 1.37%
Total Sales = £10,000,000
Total Annual Shrinkage = £137,000
Total Monthly Shrinkage = £11,417
Total Weekly Shrinkage = £2,635
Total Daily Shrinkage = £375

[Figure 6]

Just imagine what **£375** per day added to your profit will do for your business.

Profit vs. Sales Calculation

The belief in the retail industry is:

- "We must increase sales, we must increase sales!"
- "As long as sales are up the rest does not matter!"
- *However, does an increase in sales really lead to an increase in profit?*
- *Does it occur to retailers that an increase in sales simultaneously results in an increase in shrinkage?*

The calculation below illustrates this point better:

PROFIT VS SALES CALCULATION

	Store 1 (Sales)	Store 2 (Sales)
Amount Of DVD's Sold Weekly	450	300
Average Sales Price	£7.00	£9.00
Profit Margin (%)	14%	33%
Average Profit Margin (£)	£1.00	£3.00
Operating Profit	£450.14	£899.91
Weekly Shrink (Units)	20	13
Weekly Shrink (£)	£140.00	£117.00
Weekly Profit Contribution	£310.14	£782.91

[Figure 7]

As demonstrated in the above calculation:

- Store 1 had a promotion on that week and sold 450 DVD's.
- Store 2 operated without promotion and sold 300 DVD's.
- Store 1 sold DVD's for £7.00 per unit, while store 2 sold for £9.00.
- Store 1 had a profit margin of 14% while store 2 had a profit margin of 33%.
- The average profit margin was £1.00 for store 1 and £3.00 for store 2.
- This resulted in an operating profit of £450.14 for store 1 and £899.91 for store 2.
- The weekly shrinkage for store 1 was 20 and 13 for that of store 2
- The weekly shrinkage in monetary value was £140.00 for store 1 and £117.00 for store 2.

- At the end of the week, the profit for store 1 was £310.10 while that of store 2 was £782.91

What this calculation illustrates is even though store 1 increased sales by 150 units more than store 2, when it came to profit, store 2 achieved almost twice the amount of profit as store 1 because store 1's shrinkage increased simultaneously with its sales.

Increased sales will eventually lead to increased shrinkage. Consequently, it is incumbent upon retailers to ensure that while they are focused on increasing sales, they simultaneously focus on reducing their shrinkage.

During holiday seasons, store sales increase to record highs. Retailers use this opportunity to boost sales, offering tremendous discounts to lure customers into their shops. Many stores make their biggest sales within a single week or month. While the sales process is planned meticulously in advanced, the issue of loss prevention is never taken into account.

Only on very rare occasions are loss prevention personnel invited into sales planning meetings. Loss prevention is never called upon to provide advice, on the level of security required, for the weeks or days within a holiday. This is the reason why, despite the fact that retailers increase their sales tremendously, their profits remain the same or even lower.

Key Points

Question: How can retailers get their employees' willingly participating in drives for shrinkage reduction?

Answer: By creating a culture of loss prevention.

KEY POINT 1
Retailers cannot reduce shrinkage only by:

- Being tough on shoplifters
- Prosecuting dishonest employees
- Or even closing their store in which case they will not have a business

KEY POINT 2

Creating an environment that is pleasant for employees. Make employees feel valued and respected. These are actions that create loyalty from employees and create a culture in which employees are willing to help with loss prevention. Policies, procedures and guidelines are fine but cannot reduce shrinkage on their own. It is people who create shrinkage and it is those same people who can prevent it.

How to Create a Culture of Loss Prevention

I attended one of our sites due to an officer running late. Upon arrival, I conducted the daily patrol of the premises. After my patrol I sat next to the reception as my officers always did while on duty. The deputy manager of the hotel informed me that she did not want me sat down apparently doing nothing. I asked her what she'd prefer me to do. She responded that she didn't know, all she knew was she didn't want me to just be sitting down.

We had provided security for this hotel for about 18 months. About two months prior to the above incident, I received an email informing me of a change of management in the hotel. I emailed the new manager requesting a meeting to formally introduce ourselves and most importantly to discuss any changes she felt necessary to our assignment instructions.

During my discussion with the deputy manager I informed her that I had attempted to contact her manager to establish a new brief of what they expected from our officers and our company. She was unsure why the manager had not met with me and didn't know what was expected of us.

They were not willing to brief us on their expectations, however they complained about our work. Perhaps if I wasn't there on that day and had received a call or email to say that my officer was failing to perform his duties, I would have held him to task when it wasn't entirely his fault.

Clarity of expectation, clarity of delivery, and clarity of results is almost non-existent in the security industry. This is because businesses contract security without knowing exactly what they need the security for or why they need it. According to Gallop approximately 50% of employees do not know what is expected of them at work. When employees know what is expected of them their productivity increases anywhere between 5% – 10% and there is a 10% – 20% reduction in work related accidents. (Twelve Elements of Great Managing. Wagner, R. and Harter, T.)

The deputy manager wasn't aware of the role our security officers were to perform and her manager didn't make things easy for her by failing to brief us on her expectations. However, the most important lesson to be learnt from this story is that the hotel management did not have a coherent security policy that was communicated to the various branch managers. The company's policies and procedures needed to be communicated from above. When this is not present it hinders the functionality of the system.

Like any professional service, people purchase security to fulfil a particular need. This concept has still not filtered down to the security buying public yet. Security is perceived as a grudge purchase by many security service users. For the average person on the street, a security officer is the guy who is stood at the entrance of a business doing nothing, only acting when he is asked to do something.

Due to this perception, many organisations do not give the issue of purchasing security any serious thought therefore is left to junior management to handle.

The majority of times when people call for security, it is the secretary of the senior manager who places the call. When asked to speak to her boss to get more information before providing a quote, the usual response is "We just need an idea of rates. The boss will call you when you are chosen". That is the nature of the beast when it comes to the role of security in business.

Many businesses don't understand that a safe and secure environment is essential for business to flourish, when properly utilised security can add directly to the bottom line.

A similar approach exists within the retail industry with regards to loss prevention. Firstly, in the retail industry, many retailers still cannot distinguish between security and loss prevention. Secondly, even those who can make the distinction, still see loss prevention as something unrelated to retail operations.

Security is retro-active, responding to events after they have occurred. Loss prevention on the other hand is supposed to be pro-active, preventing the incident from occurring even before it occurred. Security is concerned with theft and fraud while loss prevention encompasses every area of loss within a retail operation.

The main function of security in a retail environment is to either prevent fraud or deal with employees or customers suspected of fraud. The primary function of loss prevention is to prevent any area of loss within a retail operation whether it is to do with theft, fraud, error or procedural failure.

Loss prevention is at the core of any retail operation as shrinkage is almost three times the profit margin of a retailers business.

Let us repeat our previous calculation to illustrate this point. The average retailer makes a 1% net profit out of each dollar and the industry shrinkage percentage is 2.6%. This means that shrinkage is almost three times the average retailer profit margin. Therefore if we reduce shrinkage by 50% – from 2.6 cents to 1.3 cents – we could basically more than double our profits: from 1 cent to 2.3 cents. (Crosset company newsletter, June 2010)

This is an indication that loss prevention departments should not be considered an isolated element in retail operations; it is the core of the operation. Loss prevention or profit protection should be on a par with increased sales in the retail industry.

What is the benefit of increasing sales without making profit?

The correlation between sales and profit is like that of an hour glass [Figure 8]. Retailers do ring the till when they increase sales; however, they also increase the possibility for shrinkage which eats into their profit.

RELATIONSHIP BETWEEN PROFIT AND LOSS PREVENTION

[Figure 8]

Let's use another calculation to further drill down this point:

RELATIONSHIP BETWEEN PROFIT AND LOSS PREVENTION

Sales Breakeven = Fixed Costs / (Selling Costs - Variable Expenses)
We Are Selling 1500 Books
The Books Have Fixed Costs Of £ 10,500
1 Book Sells For £11
Each Book Has A Variable Expense Of £1.50
Sales Breakeven = 1105 Books

[Figure 9]

In the above calculation figure 9, the book retailer spent £10,500 to buy 1500 books and now he sells each book for £11.00.

Each book has a variable expense (overheads, etc.) of £1.50.

In order to break even, the retailer needs to sell 1105 books.

RELATIONSHIP BETWEEN PROFIT AND LOSS PREVENTION

The Books Have Fixed Costs of £10,500
Each Book Sells For £11
Increase Shrinkage Of £0.50
Each Book Now Has A Variable Expense Of £2.00
Sales Breakeven Is Now = 1167 Books
Sales Breakeven Increased By 61 Books
In Order To Breakeven We Must Now Sell 5.6% More Books Or Increase Selling Price To £11.50

[Figure 10]

In the above illustration Figure 10, the retailer sells the same amount of books – 1500.

Each book sells for £11.00.

The retail now has shrinkage (theft, fraud or error) of £0.50.

Each book now has a variable expense of £2.00.

In order for the retailer to break even, he will need to sell 1167 books.

Sales breakeven has now increased by 61 books or 5.6%.

In order to breakeven, the retailers will either need to sell more books or will have to increase the price of the books to £11.50.

With competition right around the corner, raising the price does not seem a sensible option. Neither can he guarantee that he will be able to sell more books as that is dependent upon other factors beyond his control. What is the most viable option? Reduce shrinkage.

RELATIONSHIP BETWEEN PROFIT AND LOSS PREVENTION

Variable Expenses Reduced Due To Loss Prevention
With A Shrink Reduction Of 68% or £1.02
The Books Have Fixed Costs Of £10,500
Each Book Sells For £11
Each Book Now Has A Variable Expense Of £0.48
Sales Breakeven Is Now = 998 Books
Sales Breakeven Reduced By 107 Books
£1,179 Additional Profit

[Figure 11]

Let's see what happens when shrinkage is reduced (see Figure 11):

The retailer sells the same amount of books: 1500.

He sells each book for £11.00.

Each book now has a variable expense of £0.48 as there has been a reduction of £1.02 resulting from effective loss prevention measures.

Sales breakeven point is now 998 books a reduction of 107 books.

Now his profit increase by **£1,179** compares to figure 10.

We used the above calculation to illustrate the point that loss prevention is indeed profit protection. It is the most effective profit generator in retail. No retailer has control over their sales cycle. They can make the most educated guesses yet in most instances they end up being wrong as they are dependent on factors beyond the control of the individual retailer. However, loss prevention is totally within the control of a retailer, he and only he can decide on the level of effective shrinkage control measures he would like to implement.

Effective Shrinkage Management Strategies

The most effective method for shrinkage management and achieving the above result is the creation of a culture of loss prevention.

How can a retailer create a culture of loss prevention?
By taking the following steps:

1. Gain Senior management commitment
2. Train employees
3. Measure the scale of the problem
4. Accurate management of accounts

5. Create awareness

6. Continuous education and discipline

7. Create mechanism for monitoring compliance

8. Set measurable targets

9. Take advantage of technology

10. Make adjustments to current policies and procedures

11. Shift focus from increase sales to profit protection

12. Solicit employee buy-in

Senior Management Commitment

Senior management must first and foremost realise the concept of loss prevention is basically profit protection. Therefore loss prevention should never be an isolated department it ought to be an integral part of their operations. The annual goal for increasing sales and profit must align with the goal to decrease shrinkage. Senior management need to communicate the importance of shrinkage reduction to their regional managers who will in turn converse this to their supervisors and store associates.

Senior management need to communicate the fact that low shrinkage equals high profit and high profit means job security for everyone.

The starting point needs to be the establishment of a goal for the organisation. This might sound simplistic but it may come as a shock to many that a lot of organisations do not have a goal or vision. Nine out of ten entrepreneurs start their business without an outright vision of where they would like their organisation to be in the future. This is not an easy exercise whether for an individual or an organisation. But failure to set specific goals for the future has been responsible for the failure of the majority of retail businesses. This is not limited to small retailers alone it goes to the grain of most retail operations. When you set a goal, you create a plan to help you achieve that goal. When a retailer sets a goal, he will discover there are certain critical pieces that are required to succeed. The most critical component to succeeding is having the right people.

Jim Collins in his book "Good to Great" explained that the most important component required to transform an organisation from good to great is getting the right people on board and placing the right people on the right seat. It is after you have the right people on the bus and place them on the right seat that you can contemplate moving the bus in any direction. (Collins, J. Good to Great. 2007). A true life example of this is the case of Sir Terry Leahy of Tesco. When he took over in 1997, Tesco was lagging behind many of the big retail giants in the UK, but upon his departure, Tesco has become a major player in world retail. This is a classic example of having the right person in the right place which produces fantastic results. See figure 12 below for a summary of his achievements.

Sir Terry Leahy's Wall of Accomplishment

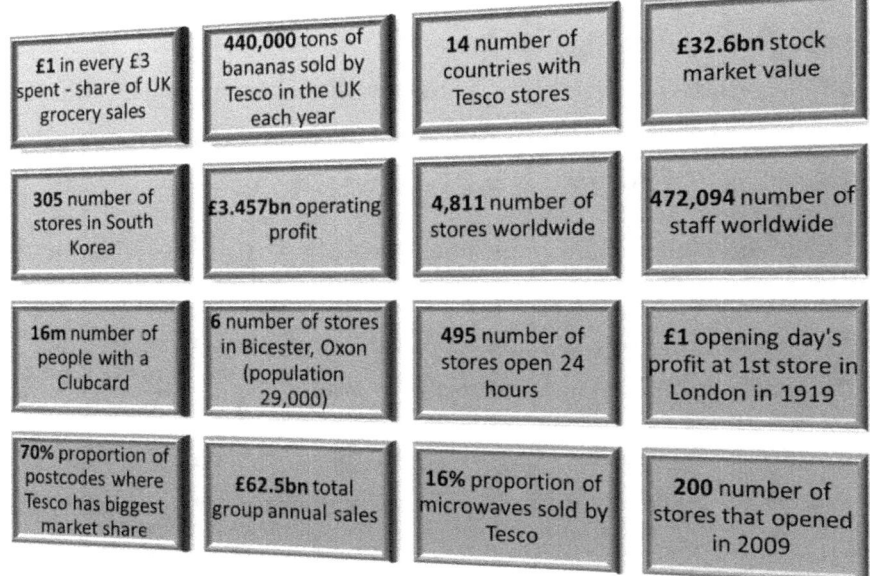

[Figure 12]

Two brilliant steps he took upon taking over was firstly identifying Tesco's core customer base; focusing exclusively on serving them and secondly focusing on shrinkage reduction by introducing the traffic light system.

Every Tesco manager knows he must keep shrinkage to a certain level. When a store goes to "code red" the manager of that store immediately gets a call from head office. Today Tesco has one of the lowest shrinkage levels in the retail industry; it is therefore no coincidence that Tesco is the second most profitable retailer in the world.

I must put a footnote to this comment that: *Tesco still has a lot to be desired in terms of its supply chain practices. Getting that right would reduce its shrinkage even further and skyrocket its profit.*

Wal-Mart is the most profitable retailer in the world despite its size because Wal-Mart has managed to maintain one of the lowest shrinkage levels in the industry year after year. The late Sam Walton, founder of Wal-Mart, arguably the most successful retailer who ever graced the planet earth, once described shrinkage as "top profit killers". (Associated Press. 14th June 2007)

Consequently he instilled the need to fight shrinkage ferociously into the genetics of the company. Wal-Mart invests in the latest loss prevention technology because senior management understand that shrinkage reduction equals profit improvement.

When senior management understand the role shrinkage and loss prevention play in determining the success of the organisation, the right policies and procedures are developed and implemented.

Employee Training

Despite the fact that there are cost implications associated with training employees, an educated workforce will pay more dividends in the long run compared to an uneducated one. Everyone who has been to university knows that the one thing you are taught in a university is how to think. This is because when you know how to think you can execute better. Training retail staff to think and execute better can make a tremendous difference to the success of any retail organisation.

For example the table below demonstrates that providing employees with shoplifting awareness training is a more effective tool against shoplifting than any other measure employed. See figure 13 for the statistics.

WHY RETAILERS NEED LOSS PREVENTION TRAINING

Method	Effectiveness
Employees	33%
Cameras	31%
Management	17%
EAS	14%
Signs	3%
Guards	2%

[Figure 13]

The above table, Figure 13, indicates that employees trained in shoplifting awareness reduced shoplifting by 33%, CCTV cameras by 31%, store management by 17%, Electronic Article Surveillance (EAS) systems by 14%, signs by 3% and security personnel by only 2%.

The least utilised weapon in retailers' fight against shrinkage is the most effective.

Measure the Scale of the Problem

How many store managers or senior retail managers know the scale of their shrinkage problem?

How many really know which department of their store is responsible for the highest amount of shrinkage?

Step one for loss prevention requires an accurate assessment of the causes, effects and costs of shrinkage.

At the beginning of a financial year, retail financial planners estimate a figure they consider an acceptable level of loss. As long as store managers stay within this figure it is acceptable by senior management.

This approach does not encourage store managers to investigate the causes of shrinkage or take personal responsibility for shrinkage within the bounds of the budgeted figure set by senior management; in their minds senior management have already given their approval to those numbers. Shrinkage prevention and reduction requires a systematic approach which begins with:

Thorough internal inventory of all merchandise within the store, both in the warehouse and shop floor.

Implementation of robust policies and procedures for receiving, merchandising, theft and fraud control and error prevention.

A comprehensive analysis of these areas will present a clearer picture of the stores' current problem, allowing store managers the opportunity to implement the most appropriate mechanisms for dealing with their shrinkage challenges.

Mechanism for Accountability

Detailed and accurate transactional reports are vital as they show top management and store managers the monetary values of shrinkage. Management accounts detailing profit and loss enable management to assess their performance and pin point areas for improvement.

Awareness Campaign

The organisation's policies and procedures regarding loss prevention and shrinkage management must be constantly communicated to every single employee within the organisation. Top management has the ability to shape the behaviour and actions of their employees by effective communication which clearly outlines the managements' goal for shrinkage reduction. This is the 'carrot and stick' approach in which employees are made aware of the benefits that will accrue to them for cooperating while at the same time making it absolutely clear that management adopts a zero tolerance stance on shrinkage.

An improvement in any area of life is not an event, it requires daily practice. The same theory applies to loss prevention. In order for it to be effective, it needs to be reinforced by top management on a daily basis. Store managers and team members need to acquire the requisite training whilst managers need to lead by example by ensuring their daily actions do not contradict their policies.

Top management need to show their commitment by providing the resources that store management require, whilst allowing operational staff the opportunity to assist in the creation of the appropriate policies and procedures.

Create Mechanism for Compliance

People do not voluntarily submit to authority or comply with rules and regulations. It is important that senior management understand that it is human nature to do what is fun and easy. Unfortunately most of the activities that produce results are not fun and easy to accomplish. People therefore may shy away from those activities and focus on tasks that are easy to complete. Senior management must keep a constant vigil on the activities of their employees.

The best way of accomplishing this is to communicate regularly with store management and supervisors to identify employees that are in need of additional support. Regular employee appraisals and daily evaluations will identify those employees that would benefit from additional support and training. This operational practice is one of the most important as it ensures preventative measures are implemented before an issue becomes a problem.

Make Effective Use of Technology

It can be difficult to quantify the benefit of technology. Many technology providers struggle to explain the return on investment (ROI) for their products. It is the exact opposite when it comes to loss prevention technologies. The latest loss prevention technologies have transformed the retail industry. From the time the technology device is installed to the point where retailers begin to accrue benefit is shorter than in any industry. Loss prevention technologies provide an amazing 50% ROI within a very short space of time. The retail industry is a fiercely competitive sector that is changing rapidly. Practices and procedures can change dramatically with the introduction of a single technological device. Technology has made the receiving and auditing processes more accurate and ordering and forecasting easier.

However, technology must be tailored to support the issues of each individual store. Technology on its own is not a cure. We need to ensure that relevant training and support is offered to all levels of employees who are expected to use the devices.

Set Measurable Targets

Goals that get measured get achieved. The human mind is a goal seeking organism that operates best when it has a target to aim towards. Senior management need to establish a form of measurement through which staff can measure their progress. When staff can focus on daily, weekly, monthly and annual targets for shrinkage reduction, they will have a goal to aim towards.

The statistics need to be published at the back of the store on a regular basis for all employees to see as this will provide motivation for them. When staff are motivated and aiming towards a common goal they are willing to give their best.

Targets set must be SMARTER:

S • Specific

M • Measurable

A • Achievable

R • Realistic

T • Time-Based

E • Evaluated

R • Reviewed

The New Retail Environment

Author Chris Anderson in his book 'The Long Tail' describes the rapidly declining brick and mortar retail store. He pointed out it is fast becoming the era of the niche or aggregate market. The coming of age of the internet is breaking down the monopoly of the factors of distribution held by a few. *(Anderson, C. The Long Tail, 2006)*

The advent of Google, YouTube and Facebook means pretty much anyone can run a multi-million pounds retail operation from the back of his car as long as he has an internet connection. Gone are the days when people have to go to book stores to buy books, now all one needs to do is log onto Amazon and the book will be delivered the follow day.

Shopping as we know it will never be the same again, however, traditional shopping will never go away. The act of going to the shops for some people is an event that they look forward to. But those people are fast becoming the minority. Christmas shopping was the time when retailers were looking to make a kill. Today with the internet and the availability of literally hundreds of thousands of alternatives, retailers are struggling to keep up with the trend.

Many retailers have now gone online to get a piece of the online spoils and this has made a lot of difference to their bottom line. The only problem being it also comes with a price tag – they have to incur additional costs of either shipping or delivering the goods.

The home delivery part of most supermarkets reads well on paper but do they deliver enough profit?

Loss prevention or profit protection remains the only safe bet for retailers.

At the beginning of this book, I made the statement that to make profit in any business, you need to increase sales and decrease expenditure. To make profit in retail, there needs to be an increase in sales and a decrease in shrinkage. Shrinkage reduction is the only, and I stress this word, the only avenue still open to most retailers to make profit.

Just in case any retailers haven't heard this news yet: the internet is not going to disappear. Y2K did not materialise. What this means is that retailers are going to be fighting for less and less foot count as shoppers increasingly turn to the internet. This is one problem that no amount of advertising is going to solve. Aggressive reduction of price simply translates into lesser margins. Excellent customer service – well is it not what everyone is claiming?

"Here is Edward Bear, coming downstairs now, bump, bump, bump, on the back of his head, behind Christopher Robin. It is, as far as he knows, the only way of coming downstairs, but sometimes he feels there really is another way, if only he could stop bumping for a moment and think of it". (A. A. Milne, Winnie the Pooh).

Increasing sales is not the only way to make profit; it might not even lead to increased profit. There really is another way of making profit in retail. It is our hope with this book that retailers stop bumping their heads and think of it. Effective loss prevention (profit protection) and shrinkage management is that way.

The Ultimate Retail Profit Protection Formula

CORE PROBLEM:
- Shrinkage accounts for 1.36% of retail turnover

OBSTACLES PREVENTING OVERCOMING THE PROBLEM:
+ Lack of top management commitment
+ Lack of top management understanding of the issue
+ Lack of mission and value statement
+ Lack of core values
+ Lack of security measures
+ Inadequate policies & procedures
+ Lack of & ineffective use of technology
+ Poor auditing
+ Lack of mechanism for monitoring & compliance
+ Lack of shrinkage awareness programme

SOLUTIONS TO THE PROBLEM:
+ Policies & Procedures:
  + Clear job description
+ Top management understanding of the issue
+ Periodic & random auditing
+ Top management commitment
+ Company core values
+ Shrinkage Awareness programme
+ Select appropriate people
+ Proper mechanism for monitoring & compliance
+ Proper training

+ Security Measures:
   + Access control
   + Key control

= Reduce Shrinkage by X%

The Ultimate Retail Profit Protection Formula Explanation

Step one for solving any problem is to first identify the root cause of the problem. The retail profit protection formula diagram was developed to help retailers identify the core constraints that are serving as a hindrance towards the achievement of their goal of making profit.

Identify the Goal

The first step in the diagram (from the top) is to identify the goal this is the ultimate target that they are aiming for. In the above diagram the goal is to reduce shrinkage by X% in 90 days.

Identify the Core Problem

The second step is to identify the core constraint… what are the obstacles that are preventing a retailer from reaching their goal of reducing shrinkage by the target date. To aim to reduce 'shrinkage' is too broad; therefore address shoplifting as our example. The goal is now to reduce shoplifting by 10% in 90 days.

What are the critical success factors we need to install to be able to achieve our goal?

Shoplifting might be symptomatic of a deeper structural problem within the organisation – maybe the core problem is poor merchandising, lapse in policies and procedures or untrained staff etc. Any of the above could be the core constraint.

List all of what you consider obstacles and ask yourselves why they exist by answering the following questions:

Question: Why do merchandising problems exist?
Answer: Because those responsible for merchandising problems have inadequate knowledge of loss prevention.

Question: Why do they have inadequate knowledge of loss prevention?
Answer: Because they haven't received any loss prevention training.

Question: Why haven't they received any loss prevention training?
Answer: Because the organisation has reduced its training budget.

Question: Why has the organisation reduced its training budget?
Answer: Because they didn't receive an adequate return on investment for previous training.

Question: Why didn't they receive an adequate return on investment for previous training?
Answer: Because the training provider couldn't deliver value.

By following this method and repeatedly asking "why", you will be able to identify your core issues. It is always a single constraint or a few constraints that when removed from the organisation will enable it to function smoothly.

Identify the Critical Success Factors

In this section, we need to identify the critical success factors that are required to be in place to allow us to move to the solution stage. For example, one of the critical success factors required to reduce shoplifting would be to make the right merchandising decisions.

In order to make the right merchandising decisions those responsible for merchandising must receive loss prevention training.

In order for them to receive loss prevention training, senior management needs to buy-in to the idea and accept that when merchandising staff receiving loss prevention training they will be able to make well informed merchandising decisions which will result in a reduction in shoplifting incidents.

In order for senior management to buy-in, they must be convinced that shoplifting prevents them from reaching their overall objective of making profit.

For senior management to see shoplifting as a hindrance store managers must be able to demonstrate the cost implications of shoplifting to senior management.

Identify the Solution

The final step in the process is the solution stage. It is at this stage that we arrive at the solution to the problem based upon the findings from the first two stages. At this stage we identify the best solutions to address the core problem. In most cases identifying the solution is very easy if we were honest with ourselves during the first two processes. If we have identified the core problem and critical success factors, once those conditions are in place we can easily solve the problem.

We have identified merchandising as one of the core problems that makes shoplifting possible in stores. In order to solve this problem; retailers need to implement simple changes to their merchandising strategy, for example:

- Place goods in more secured parts of the store
- Attach security tags to high value goods
- Provide loss prevention training to merchandising managers
- Ensure coherent communication, with regards to merchandising, between store managers and head office

Please Note:

We have created a template that will assist retailers identify the core constraint that is preventing them from reaching their objectives in relation to shrinkage management.

We are aware that the dynamic in every organisation can be different. Therefore, the formula should only be used as a template to guide them in finding solutions to their own core constraints.

Chapter Two

Employee Theft

Introduction

In 2008, we secured a store opening event in Liverpool for one of the world's biggest sportswear companies. To mark the event there was a football goal scoring competition. Besides chaperoning the attending football stars, we were responsible for ensuring the return of all football boots, issued to the competitors in the competition. When providing service to a large organization, I always ensure that I am present at all times. This is not because I do not trust my team but to provide that added 'air cover'.

Prior to the start of the competition I asked one of the staff, supervising the event, if boots are usually lost during these types of promotional events. He stated they lose, on average, 10 pairs of boots per event. Armed with this information I briefed my officers appropriately. One officer was to stand at the entrance and the other at the exit to ensure no one walked away with any of the boots. We also carried out spot checks and counted the boots every 15 minutes.

By the end of the event we were pretty confident that we had supervised the event to the satisfaction of the organizers and managed to prevent anyone from walking away with any of the boots.

However, when the final count was made, we were quite surprised to discover three pairs of boots were mysteriously missing. We were certain no one had walked away with any boots.

The mystery was solved within a few minutes when we noticed one of the staff selling a pair of boots to a member of the public. We had clearly focused only on the public and overlooked employees, who were having a field day.

This was an important lesson for us as loss prevention professionals and a timely reminder that sometimes the thieves are actually within the organizations.

Employee theft is the number two source of retail shrinkage in many parts of the world. In the US, Canada and Australia, this is the leading cause of retail shrinkage (Global Retail Theft Barometer Report 2010). The 2010 Global Retail Theft Barometer Report stated that employee theft accounted for 35.3% of retail shrinkage ($37.8 billion), while in the US it accounted for 43.7% ($17.2 billion). The average cost of employee theft in a supermarket is $93,000 and approximately $243,000 to a hypermarket annually.

Taking advantage of their positions (access to security information, keys and security codes etc.), dishonest retail employees are capable of inflicting more damage on their employers than shoplifters. The average customer related theft costs a retailer £66, while the average employee theft is estimated to cost retailers £1,318. Due to their proximity to the system, employee theft is difficult to detect. It takes an average of 18 months to detect a retail employee theft. Most instances of employee theft go undetected for years, especially if the individual involved is a store manager or in a senior management position.

Is employee theft an inevitability that retailers have to learn to live with? The answer to this question is an emphatic 'no!'

Employee theft can never be totally eliminated, however, with the correct policies and procedures, it can be minimized. This e-book will give you details regarding employee theft and show you step-by-step ways of minimizing it.

Why Do Employees Steal?

The Dr. Donald R. Cressey "Fraud Triangle" theory revealed three factors that explain employee theft: the individual's financial situation, the opportunity and their ability to justify their actions.

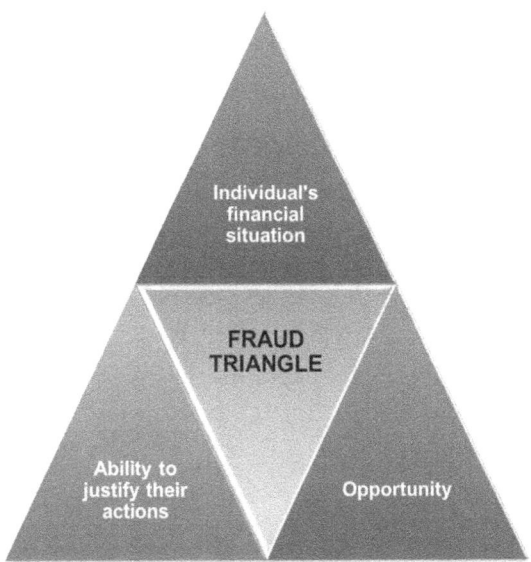

The Process of Employee Theft

OPPORTUNITY
- If merchandise is placed in inadequately secured locations, for example, high value items placed in warehouses without locks, merchandise not strategically placed on the shop floor, placed close to an exit or positioned in a place which easily facilitates their removal from the store.

PERCEPTION
- If the employee perceives the consequences to be less severe to dissuade them from carrying out the act.

BENEFIT
- If the benefit from stealing the merchandise outweighs the perceived cost of being caught they will be willing to take the risk.

RATIONALE
- If they rationalise their decision by saying something like "I am not paid enough for the work I am doing", "the organisation is rich therefore will not be affected by this or everyone else is doing it anyway".

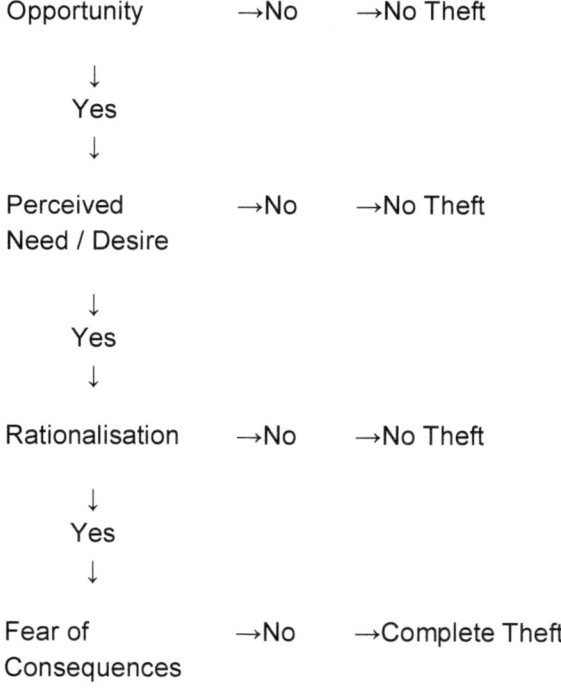

The above diagram demonstrates that *"opportunity"* is the main reason for employee theft. The organization involved might not have the appropriate policies and procedures in place to limit the occurrences of theft. For example, in many retail warehouses, high-value items are left lying around without any form of security. Furthermore, newly hired employees are not given clear and concise policies and procedures regarding employee theft. The lack of policies and procedures and inadequate security of goods (especially high value items), sends a signal to employees that no one cares.

However, there is one very important aspect of opportunity that has repeatedly been ignored by many writers on the subject of employee theft. They have mostly placed the onus on the employees or have presented the employees as antagonists who are disloyal to their employers. Furthermore, when the issue of opportunity is discussed it is done in terms of location of goods not in terms of organizational structure.

Most retail organizational challenges (whether it is to do with employee theft, error or shoplifting) are systemic.

Many retail organizations are run like "sweat shops", with no proper organizational structure/policies/procedures. This "sweat shop" concept is not limited to small retailers alone, big multibillion pound retail organizations conduct similar "sweat shop" practices albeit on a larger scale. Indeed larger retail organizations might have fancy documents detailing their organizational missions, values, policies and procedures, written by some management consultant, yet the practices in those organizations leave a lot to be desired. Therefore, when I talk of opportunity in this sense, I mean the systems within the organizations that allow the theft to occur in the first instant. When an employee notices that there are no coherent policies and procedures and top management have not demonstrated core values that others within the organization are expected to aspire to, then they have no reason to be loyal to the organization. I will get into this in more depth when I address the issue of prevention.

To briefly summarize this point, what creates the most opportunity in many retail organizations for employee theft is the lack of top management adherence to any form of core value.

Signs of Employee Theft

PRODUCT THEFT

SITUATION

- *An employee hides or takes products without paying*

WARNING SIGNS:

- A preference to park his/her car behind the store or next to the outside bins
- Seldom takes breaks with colleagues.
- Bagged merchandise stacked next to the till
- Stashing away goods in the store
- Shows a preference for inappropriately large work bags.
- Always first in and last to leave
- Taking goods to and from toilets or changing room
- Product or packaging found in the vicinity of bins or compactors
- Discarded empty product packages found in warehouse or areas of assignment
- An eagerness to take out rubbish especially just before a break or home time

NON SCANNING

SITUATION

- *Cashier regularly marks down selling prices without authorisation*

WARNING SIGNS:

- A price discrepancy as multiple items not scanned at the same price
- Cashier who manually enters instead of scans items
- Cashier who has access to spare barcodes at the till
- Cashier with a below average customer spend for all periods
- Items on till records do not tally with the items covered in the transaction

Employee Stealing Cash

SITUATION

- *An employee steals cash*

WARNING SIGNS:

- Above normal use of the 'no-sales' key
- Use of calculator or other counting aids to track cash removed.
- Frequent refunds
- Employee who regularly borrows money from colleagues
- Habitually closes tills or cashes up early.
- Till open for long periods after transactions
- Cash drawer remains open from one sale to the next
- Cashier holds on to cash and puts it aside instead of in the till
- Regularly adding vouchers to the till.

FRADULENT REFUNDS

SITUATION

- *A customer service employee creates a false refund and takes the equivalent in cash from the till.*

WARNING SIGNS:

- Receipt not given to customer resulting in customer complaint
- Customer receipts found on customer service counter or in the bin
- Processes a refund with a colleague's log on code
- Processes a fictitious refund with no customer present
- Processes a refund for an accomplice without returning merchandise
- Failing to issue customer receipts
- Falsified customer details on refund records

COLLUDING WITH SHOPLIFTERS

SITUATION

- *An employee colludes with shoplifters and alerts them of loss prevention activities*

WARNING SIGNS:

- Employee supplying customers with extra carrier bags
- Employee receiving lots of visitors during working hours
- Employee who unusually avoids management
- Employee monitoring the movements of loss prevention personnel or other store employees
- Employee who strikes up friendships with loss prevention or security officers.

FALSIFIED VOIDS

SITUATION

- *a) Cashier annuls a valid transaction and takes the equivalent in cash*

- b) *Cashier conspires to void items after they are scanned to reduce the actual amount to be paid*

WARNING SIGNS:

- Annulled sales is followed by no-sale
- Multiple negative transactions.
- Supervisors manually register a transaction sale or sanction personal voids
- Customer receipts from that day discovered at the till or in bin next to cashier
- Cashier registers sizable overcharges repeatedly
- Cashiers with exceptionally low scanning average
- Cashiers failing to issue customer receipts
- Signs of calculating aids (i.e. paper/pencil, calculator, paper clips)

CASH OFFICE FRAUD

SITUATION

- a) *A cash office employee fakes accounting figures thus enabling the removal of cash*
- b) *A cash office employee falsifies payroll or time sheets*

WARNING SIGNS:

- Abnormal cash discrepancy
- Cash shortages discovered following audits of safe/petty cash
- Statements from bank do not correspond with store deposits records
- Totals from cash office are out of sync with figures from bank deposit
- Your bank says deposit is short

CREDIT/DEBIT CARD FRAUD

SITUATION

- a) Cashier deliberately processes a stolen credit card as payment
- b) An employee refunds to their own or an accomplice's account

WARNING SIGNS:

- Employee records a customer's credit/debit card number
- Employee retains the customer's copy of a credit card receipt
- Differences in cash and credit totals
- Employee takes card away from the presence of the customer

MOST COMMON SIGNS TO LOOK OUT FOR

GENERAL SITUATION

- *Retailers need to be mindful of the below signs which may signal theft in their store.*

WARNING SIGNS:

- Employee who is extremely friendly with loss prevention personnel – he/she maybe monitoring their activities
- Employee constantly at odds with company's policies and procedures – discontented with superior
- Employee who doesn't take part in activities with other staff members.
- Increase in variant prior to an employee holiday
- Employee who is always absent during audit and impedes audit of financial records

How to Calculate the Cost of Employee Theft

(A) Total Sales = £10,000,000
(B) Percentage of Shrinkage = 2%
(C) Total Shrinkage = £200,000
(D) Percentage of Employee Theft = 47%
(E) Total Value Of Employee Theft = £94,000

[Figure 14]

The above calculation shows a turnover of £10,000,000 **(Box A)**. A shrinkage level of 2% **(Box B)**; will amount to total shrinkage of £200,000 **(Box C)**. Employee theft accounts for 47% **(Box D)** of total retail shrinkage. Therefore, a retailer with a turnover of £10,000,000 would be losing £94,000 **(Box E)** per annum to employee theft. Multiply that by the numbers of stores you have and you will be able to determine how much your business is losing to employee theft.

How to Prevent Employee Theft

There are two effective measures for preventing employee theft these are: *intangible* and *tangible* preventative measures.

INTANGIBLE PREVENTION

We read many books and conducted hours of internet research prior to writing this e-book. The single theme that ran concurrently throughout all the materials was that employees who stole from their employers were branded as disloyal criminals. While it is true that stealing for whatever reason cannot be justified it is important that we put the issue into context.

In their book *'Built to Last'*, authors Jim Collins and Jerry I Porras made an important point with regards to the key ingredient required to build a great company. One of those ingredients was "purpose beyond making money and core values". They stated that all of the companies that are built to last are those companies with operational practices which were in congruence with their core values. Those values are communicated throughout the blood stream of the organisation from the CEO to the cleaner. They live and breathe those values in their daily activities.

Another vital ingredient for creating greatness is creating a culture of discipline…where disciplined people take disciplined actions without the need for hierarchy. When an organisation has a culture of discipline, people are willing to perform their duties independent of top management directives.

During a training session for some retail executives from the Middle East, I mentioned to my trainees that one of the most effective tools for preventing employee theft was to incentivise them. One of the delegates responded to this suggestion by saying employees were being paid for a job therefore he saw no reason for incentivising them. To an extent he was right, yet the fact of the matter is every employee is a volunteer. Whether they are paid or not, they volunteer their time and a piece of their lives working for an organisation. They could choose to work for another organisation but they chose your organisation, therefore they deserve to be treated with respect.

How do you show them respect? You do so by demonstrating genuine appreciation for their work. You treat them like people not numbers and you genuinely care for them. My trainee works for an organisation that has introduced the concept of "Saudinisation", however, almost all of their store managers are foreign.

What would motivate a Saudi to work and see a future in this company when most of the senior management is foreign? If the company introduced a program in which foreigners are brought in to train Saudis to take over from them in a few years, it is only at that point there will be an alignment between what is being pronounced and what is actually practiced.

Like my Saudi friends, in many retail organisations, there is no alignment between what is written in a staff handbook and what is actually being practiced in the stores. Employees do not see senior management as people who have their interest at heart therefore they see no reason to be loyal to them. The mentality in many retail organisations is that of a mini tyrant leading a group of worker bees, who are supposed to be at their beckon call.

Employee theft prevention 101 is this: people do not respond to tyranny.

A friend of mine visited her doctor, during the consultation, the doctor preached to her about the benefits of eating healthy food. However, on his desk, were sugar filled soft drink and chips. When she came out she told me how surprised she was that her doctor was advising her to eat healthily while he was munching on such sinful foods. *Do you think she gave his advice any thought?* Similar scenarios play out daily in most retail organisations. While senior management are preaching honesty and integrity, their actions shout out something entirely different.

If there is one thing any retailer must get from reading this book (and if they get it, it would be worth their while) is this: you cannot function in the 21st century with antiquated 18th century business practices. In the 18th century, people were factors of production. In the 21st century, employees are partners in the business. Today there are cries around the UK that big supermarket chains such as Tesco, ASDA and Sainsbury's are killing independent retailers and town centres.

Are those statements really a well-founded fact or sentiment?

I believe it is the latter. Change is the only thing that is constant and if people fail to master change, they will be victimised by it. Things are rapidly changing in the 21st century and anyone in business who wants to survive in this century must adapt. Most of those independent retailers in town centres must adapt to the changing world.

One of those essential changes is this; they need to treat their employees like partners in order to get the best out of them.

Employee theft prevention 102 – treat employees with the utmost respect.

Employee theft prevention 103 – top management must demonstrate genuine care for them.

Employee theft 104 – top management must operate with organisational core values in mind.

It should not only be in their pronouncements, but also in their actions. Only after top management has demonstrated that they are guided by a set of core values and principles that they can succeed in implementing the other measures that follow.

What do you stand for as a senior manager or owner?

What is your implicit or explicit promise to your employees?

Your answer to the above questions will determine your employee's loyalty to you.

TANGIBLE PREVENTION

- Have a robust recruitment process

We cannot emphasize this point enough. Hiring the right people in the first instance can make a huge difference to preventing employee theft. Marks & Spencer (M&S) learnt this lesson the hard way when one of their managers, Mr. Mistry used his staff ID number to make cash refunds to his debit card totalling £6,700 in July and August 2009, from the M&S Trafford Centre store. (Thompson. D. 2009) He had a previous police caution for stealing a lottery scratch card from Morrison's supermarket, where he formerly worked. If M & S implemented a robust recruitment process which included conducting thorough background checks, they would have discovered his previous misdemeanour and not employ and allow him to rise to a managerial position.

Peter Drucker, the management guru, once said:

> *"The ability to make good decisions regarding people represents one of the last reliable sources of competitive advantage, since very few organisations are very good at it"*

By having a robust recruitment process that involves; pre-employment screening, proper background/credit checks and a thorough examination of past employment history/ references, it is quite possible the retailer can avoid recruiting the thief in the first place.

Employee Theft Policies and Procedures

The following policies and procedures are essential for reducing employee theft:

Proper Key And Access Code Management

- Entry and exit access to the store must be controlled, employees must only use designated entrances to the store
- A search policy must be in place for employees entering or leaving the store (Including subcontractors, salesmen and company reps).

- Maintenance personnel and sub-contractors who have to work within business hours should always be accompanied by security.
- Entry and emergency exits must be monitored
- Keys and lock codes must be changed periodically. Restrict this information to only authorised staff
- Keys must be counted on a regular basis.

Scanning, Void, No-Sale Policies

- Clearly spell out and include essential points in procedures for the manual inputting of barcodes and scanning of items
- There must be crystal clear guidelines for using the multiple quantity key function
- Policies regarding the authorisation of negative transactions such as refund, void and no-sale must be clearly written and communicated to employees
- To ensure the integrity of the process, only designated supervisors and managers must be authorised to perform those transactions

Employee Shopping Policy

- There must be a policy that indicates times employees are allowed to shop. The times must be limited to periods when they are either on break or off duty.
- In this policy there must be clear stipulations that no special treatment including discounts should be given to staff members, friends and family members outside of the company's courtesy offers.
- Receipts must be kept with their purchases at all times and employees must not be permitted to scan their own shopping.

Markdowns Policy

- After every markdown all records must be amended to reflect the current inventory situation.
- All markdowns must be carried out by assigned employees only
- All markdowns must be authorised

Receiving Policy

- All incoming deliveries must be physically counted and confirmed against delivery notes.
- At the end of the process, receipts must be given to the vendor or receiver confirming the consignment as complete or incomplete.

PERIODIC AND RANDOM AUDIT

Periodically auditing vulnerable areas is another effective preventative measure that retailers can use to strengthen their defence against employee theft. By conducting periodic and random audits, retailers will be able to detect thefts before they get out of control. The mere fact that employees are aware that they could be audited at any time will serve as a deterrent. Areas that need to be audited are:

Sales
Shrinkage Report
Inventory
Purchase

SHIFT ROTATION AND MANDATORY HOLIDAYS

Many instances of employee theft go undetected for months, even years, because the employee's knowledge of the organization's system gives them the ability to cover their tracks. Therefore, staff shift partner rotation makes it possible for other staff members to quickly detect fraudulent activities.

Employees who fail to take their statutory holiday need to be of concern to retailers, this could be an indication that they are trying to conceal something. Consequently, it is incumbent upon retailers to ensure their employees use their holiday entitlements. Not only is it good for their productivity but the absence of a staff member could result in some very interesting revelations about their activities on the job.

How Technology Can Help Prevent Employee Theft

Except in situations where employees are blatantly dishonest, their actions can go undetected for months or sometimes years. Consequently, the effective use of loss prevention technologies can result in tremendous decrease in instances of employee theft.

However, prior to investing in any of the below listed technologies, retailers need to answer the following questions:

- What are the functionalities of the technologies including features and benefits?
- What constraint does the technology diminish?
- What is the ROI of the technology?
- Where can the technology be sourced?
- What policies and procedures helped them to operate without the technology?
- What policies and procedures should they put in place to adapt to the new technology?
- Is the technology future-proof?

Technology is beneficial only if it removes a constraint. Therefore to identify the constraint that a technology is expected to remove; retailers need to ask themselves the following questions:

- *What is the core constraint they are aiming to remove?*
- *Is employee theft the core constraint or is it a symptom of another deep rooted structural problem?*
- *Are they attempting to cover up a lapse in policies and procedures with technology?*

It is only after they have conducted a comprehensive synopsis of their current situation and come to terms with the findings that they need to consider investing in technology as a solution to their problem.

Below are some of the most effective retail technologies, currently available, which can assist in reducing retail employee theft.

Exception-Based Reporting (EBR)

Exception based reporting (EBR) helps to identify instances of fraudulent activities that are likely to occur. EBR has increased retailers ability to identify suspicious activities without having to examine mountains of sales records.

EBR also analyses and encompasses all areas of the operation from the point of sale, to purchasing, receiving to merchandising.

How Does It Work?

STEP 1
- An employee commits fraud at the point of sale.

STEP 2
- The data is transmitted to loss prevention.

STEP 3

- Loss prevention checks the data to detect evidence of inconsistency or fraud.

STEP 4

- An investigation ensues with evidence from CCTV and reports. The evidence is precise to the time the incident occurred.

STEP 5

- The suspected employee is apprehended and disciplined.

Point of sale systems (POS) use complicated algorithms to track people and merchandise. These systems pick up items on the counter and determine whether someone is actually stood by or standing next to the counter. It allows loss prevention personnel to witness a transaction in real time as the system is shown on a computer screen or monitor that is connected to the CCTV system.

The data collected is stored and used to identify correlations between POS transaction reports and exception reports.

The data and video analytics give loss prevention personnel the ability to detect fraudulent cashier behaviours. It has proven to be very effective in cases involving void manipulation, merchandise passing and discount fraud.

How Does It Work?

STEP 1

- A cashier commits theft or fraudulent activity.

STEP 2

- Point of sale video analysis detects and records the fraudulent behaviour.

STEP 3

- Loss prevention personnel are alerted, they view the video analytics data, POS transaction reports and exception reports and make comparison for correlations.

STEP 4

- If there is evidence of wrong doing, an investigation is launched and employee responsible is disciplined.

Electronic Journals record information of all transactions in a retail store. They collect information regarding credit card, gift card, refunds and void transactions at the point-of-sale.

Electronic Journals

How Does It Work?

STEP 1

- Customer enters the store and makes a purchase with their credit card.

STEP 2

- The electronic journal records the customer's credit card number.

STEP 3

- The store can then retrieve the information when they print receipts for the customer.

STEP 4

- The customer will then be able to link the purchase with their credit card information when they receive the receipt of the purchase.

Ultimate Employee Theft Prevention Formula

CORE PROBLEM:
- Employee theft accounts for x% of retail shrinkage

OBSTACLES PREVENTING OVERCOMING THE PROBLEM:
+ Opportunity:
  + Poor Merchandising
  + Lack of core values
  + Accounting fraud
+ Lack of proper p&p
+ Personal financial pressure
+ Part of ORC network
+ Lack of mechanism for monitoring & compliance

SOLUTIONS TO THE PROBLEM:
+ Policies & Procedures:
  + Robust recruitment / screening / background checks
  + Staff handbook / disciplinary procedures
  + Staff purchase
  + Refund
  + Cash office & cash handling
  + Cashier:
  + Void & no sales
  + Multiple item entry
  + Receiving / warehouse
  + Merchandising
  + Bank office
  + Search
+ Proper Security Measures:
  + Secure all high value items in warehouse

+ Key control

+ Access control

+ Random search of staff

+ Locker room

+ Location of locker room

+ Backroom design

+ Store design

+ Create open relationship between management and staff (periodic appraisals)

+ Company must have mission and value statement from top down and communicated to all staff

+ Effective use of technology

+ Proper mechanism for monitoring & compliance

= Reduce Employee Theft by 2% in 90 Days

Ultimate Employee Theft Prevention Formula Explanation

Step one for solving any problem is to first identify the root cause of the problem. The retail profit protection formula diagram was developed to help retailers identify the core constraint that are serving as a hindrance towards the achievement of their goal of making profit.

Identify the Goal

The first step in the diagram (from the top) is to identify the goal. This is the ultimate target that a retailer is aiming to achieve. In the above diagram the goal is to reduce employee theft by 2% in 90 days.

Identify the Core Problem

The second step is to identify the core constraint... what are the obstacles that are preventing us from reaching our goal of reducing employee theft by the target date.

What are the critical success factors we need to install to be able to achieve our goal?

Employee theft might be symptomatic of a deeper structural problem within our organization – the core constraint might be limited or non-existent policies and procedures, the existence of the opportunity, inadequate recruitment and screening practices, etc. Any of the above could be the core constraint.

We list all of what is considered obstacles and ask yourself why they exist by answering the following questions:

Question: Why do inadequate recruitment and screening policies exist in our organization?
Answer: Because the HR department has not made the correlation between employee theft and recruiting dishonest staff.

Question: Why has the HR department not made the correlation between employee theft and recruiting dishonest staff?
Answer: Because HR personnel haven't received any loss prevention training.

Question: Why hasn't HR personnel received any loss prevention training?
Answer: Because senior management perceives the loss prevention department as a separate entity from the rest of the operations.

Question: Why does senior management perceive loss prevention as a separate entity?

Answer: Because shrinkage is perceived as just another word for shoplifting.

Question: Why is shrinkage perceived as just another word for shoplifting?
Answer: Because that is the norm in the retail industry.

By following this method and repeatedly asking "why", you will be able to identify your core issues. It is always a single constraint or a few constraints that when removed from the organization will enable it to function smoothly.

Identify the Critical Success Factors

In this section, we need to identify the critical success factors that are required to be in place to allow us to move to the solution stage. For example, one of the critical success factors required to reduce employee theft would be for HR personnel to receive loss prevention training.

In order for HR personnel to receive loss prevention training senior management need to accept that there is a direct correlation between inadequate recruitment and screening policies and dishonest employees.

In order for senior management to accept the correlation between inadequate recruiting and screening policies and employee dishonesty, they need to be presented with evidence of this fact.

In order for senior management to be provided with evidence, store managers must conduct a comprehensive analysis of the situation of employee theft in their stores.

By completing this exercise, we are able to determine the sequences of events or steps required before reaching the solution stage.

Identify the Solution

The final step in the process is the solution stage. It is at this stage that we arrive at the solution to the problem based upon the findings from the first two stages. At this stage we identify the best solutions to address the core problem. In most cases identifying the solution is very easy if we were honest with ourselves during the first two processes. If we have identified the core problem and critical success factors, all that is required is to put those conditions in place and we can easily solve the problem.

We have identified inadequate recruitment and screening policies as the core problem in relation to employee theft and we also identified training deficiencies as the critical success factors required for us to overcome the problem of inadequate recruitment and screening policies. It is vital that HR personnel are provided with the requisite training in order to conduct their duties efficiently.

We need to provide senior management with evidence to convince them of the correlation between inadequate recruitment and screening policies and dishonest employees in order to get their buy-in.

Please Note:

We have created a template that will assist retailers identify the core constraint that is preventing them from reaching their objectives in relation to employee theft.

We are aware that the dynamic in every organization can be different. Therefore, the formula should only be used as a template to guide them in finding solutions to their own core constraints.

How to Apply the Lessons from This Part to Your Business

Tangible

- Scanning Policies & Procedures
- Void & No-Sale Policies & Procedures
- Pre-employment Screening & Recruitment Policies & Procedures
- Refund Policies & Procedures
- Employee Shopping Policies & Procedures
- Receiving & Deliveries Policies & Procedures
- Mark-Down Policies & Procedures
- Access & Key Control
- Periodic & Random Audit
- Security Measures
- Shift Rotation & Mandatory Holidays

Intangible

- Value & Mission Statement: Embed Core Values into Company DNA
- Incentive Scheme
- Bonus & Shares Scheme
- Education & Training
- Effective Communication of Policies & Procedures
- Create a Positive Working Environment
- Team Building
- Staff Discount

Chapter Three

Retail Employee Error

Introduction

The issue of employee error has never been on the radar of loss prevention experts when devising policies and procedures for retail profit protection. Most of the concentration has been focused on employee or customer-related theft and fraud. This approach to loss prevention in many retail organizations has allowed employee errors to go on unnoticed and unabated.

Furthermore, even when the issue is discussed, the focus is primarily on simple errors such as pricing, administrating or accounting; very little, if any, attention is paid to merchandising, procurement or procedural errors that are actually responsible for a larger percentage of losses within retail organizations.

I stumbled upon an interesting insight during one of our training sessions. Addressing the subject of employee error, one of the delegates said he believed there was an important aspect of employee error that I had omitted, which was procurement error. He went on to explain that in his organization, supplies are usually distributed amongst stores. However because most of the purchasing decisions are based purely on price, the procurement department will end up purchasing surplus merchandise for stores that do not require the amount of stock that was shipped to them.

For example: they could purchase a large quantity of rice, because vendors offer them a special discount when purchasing a certain quantity. While this may seem sensible on the surface, in practice much of the rice ended up staying in the warehouse until it decays and must be thrown away. Sometimes large quantities of rice were shipped to stores with the wrong demographics in mind – population that consume less rice than they think. This is because procurement works independent of the store management.

Purchasing decisions are not based upon previous transactional records of the stores; their focus is solely to get the best deal from the supplier. This approach ends up creating avoidable losses to the company. This is particularly common in clothing stores where buyers purchase large amounts of a particular line hoping that it would be rushed off the shelves; yet by the end of the season, the clothes are still stacked somewhere in the warehouse. The first step retailers must take to address employee error is to acknowledge the cost of it to their organizations and pinpoint the particular areas where it occurs to enable them to be reduced. This does not have to be a costly task; by implementing the appropriate policies and procedures employee errors can be prevented and indeed minimized considerably.

It is not the cost of an error that retailers need to focus on, but rather how much it would cost to rectify that error. An 18% turnover (which is £36,000 for a store with a £10 million turnover) might appear insignificant on the surface. However, when you consider that it would require sales of £3.6 million to recover the £36,000 losses resulting from employee error, you will easily realize it is much more cost-effective to prevent the error in the first place. To put this in perspective, simply consider the amount of time and money necessary to accumulate sales of £3.6 million (if shrinkage level is 2% and profit margin is 1%).

What Is Retail Employee Error?

Retail employee error occurs as a result of pricing, accounting, unintentional damage, and over- or under-ordering. Examples of employee error could be a cashier ringing up the wrong item into the wrong department, inventory counting inaccuracies, or distribution error that results in shortage or surplus in some stores as well as receiving mistakes.

These can all be caused by individual mistakes or could be systemic; they could result from a poor, disorganized warehouse, poor administrative practices, and a lack of training or simple procedural error. Eliminating errors is virtually impossible in any working environment. Fast paced activities, constant employee turnover, low wages and lapse in adhering to procedures all help to increase the possibility of multiple employee errors. However, with the creation of the appropriate policies and procedures, well-trained staff and introduction of adequate mechanisms for monitoring compliance, these errors can be drastically reduced.

How to Calculate the Cost of Employee Error?

To calculate the cost of employee error, you need to multiply your total turnover by your shrinkage level; then multiply the result by the industry percentage of employee error (in this calculation we used 18%). This will give you the cost of employee errors to your store. The table below illustrates this calculation:

How to Calculate the Cost of Employee Error

(A) Total Sales = £10,000,000
(B) Percentage of Shrinkage = 2%
(C) Total Shrinkage = £200,000
(D) Percentage of Employee Errors (pricing, accounting & receiving) = 18%
(E) Value Of Employee Errors = £36,000

[Figure 15]

How to Calculate Additional Sales Required to Recover Losses Caused By Employee Error

To find the additional amount of sales required to recover the loss made from the error above, you will need to multiply your total turnover by the industry percentage of employee error and then divide it by the value of your net profit. The table below illustrates this calculation:

How to Calculate Additional Sales Required to Recover Losses Caused By Employee Error

(A) Value of Sales = £10,000,000
(B) Percentage of Net Profit = 1%
(C) Total Value of Profit = £100,000
(D) Value Of Employee Errors (pricing, accounting & receiving) = £36,000
(E) Additional Annual Sales Required To Recover Profit Lost To Error-Related Shrinkage = £3,600,000

[Figure 16]

Prevention Is Better Than Cure

From the above calculations, retailers can see that it is far cheaper to prevent employee error than to make up for it after it occurs. With the implementation of good policies and procedures, retailers can minimise error.

Policies and procedures you have control over; whether you can increase foot count to your store is something entirely beyond your control.

Types of Employee Error

Procurement Error

- **A buyer orders more stock than needed for A particular store**

Effect:

- Over ordering causes unnecessary expiration of perishable goods, damage to products or tying down valuable capital that could be used to order more products or expand the business

Solutions:

- Ordering must be made in conjunction with sales data and demographics
- Buyers must coordinate with store managers when choosing the types of products required for a particular store.
- Buyers must not solely focus on discount or percentage of saving they will make when ordering; they must consider the speed of sales and the logistics of warehousing the products.
- Senior management must hold buyers accountable for large errors in buying that causes the company to lose huge amounts of money.

Merchandising Error

- **Products not securely merchandised on the shop floor**

Effect:

- When goods are not merchandised securely on the shop floor, it can easily facilitate their removal from the store by either shoplifters or dishonest employees.
- Failing to secure goods on the shop floor sends a signal to shoplifters and dishonest employees alike that the company does not take the issue of loss prevention seriously.

Solutions:

- Involve store manager in the selection of location for merchandising of goods on the shop floor.
- Involve the loss prevention department when making decisions on merchandising of goods in the store
- Store design must take into account stock vulnerability and blind spots.
- Take the appropriate precautions to ensure store design does not impede security.

Receiving Error

- **Failure to maximise supplier credit opportunity**

Effect:

- In the contractual agreements between suppliers and retail organisations, there is always stipulation for credit for products that expire or are damaged. However, it is the receiver's responsibility to request those credits as vendors would not voluntarily take back damaged or expired stock or offer stores credit.
- Furthermore, like the refund procedures of the stores themselves, suppliers have their own returns procedures. It is

incumbent upon store managers to ensure that they train their staff to follow the vendor return procedures.

Solutions:

- Designated receiving employees need to be properly trained on the appropriate ways of requesting credit from suppliers.
- Create a mechanism for monitoring compliance with suppliers credit procedures
- Ensure the procedure is organised and is carried on at a particular time each and every week
- Ensure all internal documentations reflects the inventory variations

Sales Floor Error

- **Pricing error**

Effect:

- Inaccurate pricing is another major employee error. Inaccurate low price errors can cause losses for the retailer; however, inaccurate high pricing error can cause customer dissatisfaction.
- Pricing errors usually occur during promotional or sales periods. If changes are made during one shift and the information is not transmitted to the next shift, it can result in avoidable error.

Solutions:

- Train a designated scan file maintenance coordinator.
- Designated scanning coordinator and department managers must be held accountable for pricing errors.
- Regularly check, compare and verify as necessary all prices on the sales floor to ensure accuracy.

Sales Floor Error

- **Failure to record damaged or distressed stock**

Effect:

- When damaged or distressed goods are discarded without a proper mechanism for accountability and adjustment of inventory records, it results in artificial inventory inaccuracy.

Solutions:

- Train employees to be honest and open about damaged products to ensure that they report it to their supervisors or line manager without fear of sanction
- Ensure damaged or distressed goods are returned to supplier for credit
- Create a log book in which all damaged and distressed goods are logged and investigated to prevent future occurrence
- Discounting and bulk selling damaged and distressed goods can minimise loss

Sales Floor Error

- **Lack of proper mechanism for product rotation**

Effect:

- The lack of adequate mechanisms for ensuring proper product rotation results in unnecessary wastage and product expiration

Solutions:

- Install mechanisms for accountability for product rotation
- Maintain constant vigil and ensure short shelf-life products are managed to prevent expiration

- Product rotation has to be included as a daily task and specific individuals have to be assigned to it each day.
- Ensure products are discounted before their expiration date.
- Managers and supervisors, when conducting their store walk must pay particular attention to perishable products to ensure that the appropriate discounts are applied.

Sales Floor Error

- **Damage caused by customer or shelf fillers**

Effect:

- When products are damaged or distressed by customers or employees filling shelves they either have to be discounted or discarded.

Solutions:

- Products on shelf should never exceed a certain height
- Shelf fillers must be properly trained in the correct handling of sharp tools used to open packages and crates.
- Regularly face up products to avoid situations in which customers have to struggle to reach them resulting in breakage
- Stock cages must be attended at all times especially when customers are in the store.
- Products have to be properly arranged by order pickers, placing fragile objects in their own cages and ensuring heavier items are placed at the bottom
- Order pickers must properly label fragile products to make it easy for shelf fillers to recognise them
- Products must be prearranged in the warehouse before being moved to the shop floor

Sales Floor Error

- **Causing risk of injury to customers during shelf filling**

Effect:

- Customers injured as a result of a cage or trolley used for shelf filling can result in costly injury claims.

Solutions:

- Shelves should be stacked to a specified limit
- All sharp tools must be carefully handled during replenishment
- Never leave stock unattended on the shop floor
- Regularly face-up stock during the day

Sales Floor Error

- **Failing to notice large gap in display shelf**

Effect:

- A large gap in display shelf is an indication of shoplifting or inventory shortage. This could result in inventory inaccuracy or customer dissatisfaction

Solutions:

- When a large gap is noticed in the shelf display, an immediate investigation needs to be launched to ascertain the reason why
- Check inventory and sales records and make comparisons
- Keep a constant vigil on all high value items and high risk areas
- Train store associates to recognise large gaps in shelf display and immediately report their findings to management

Sales Floor Error

- **Employees use stock for store operations**

Effect:

- The use of inventory for store operation results in shrinkage. While this may seem harmless if stock taken from store inventory are not properly recorded, it can lead to inventory shortage.

Solutions:

- Whenever store inventory is used for operational purposes, a proper record must be kept and all inventory records must be adjusted to reflect the new inventory position.
- Only permit supervisors and managers to remove inventory for store operations

Administrative Error

- **Inefficient procedures for managing the movement of money around the store**

Effect:

- Inadequate money movement management creates exposure to robbery and temptation for dishonest employees

Solutions:

- Never leave the till draw open after a transaction
- Ensure the till is neatly arranged separating cash from other forms of payment
- Keep accurate records of all cash pick-ups
- Set up an alert system that spots large cash build-ups and automatically calls for pick-up

- Cashiers should be held accountable for all variances in cash.
- Cashiers needs to be trained in the correct procedure for requesting cash pick-ups

Cashier Error

- **Accepting counterfeit money**

Effect:

- **Valueless notes in the till**

Solutions:

- Implement a procedure for cashiers to alert management whenever they receive counterfeit notes. Display procedure close to the till facing the cashier with a diagram.
- Train cashiers in the use of counterfeit identification pens and other security devices that detect counterfeit notes.

Cashier Error

- **Blind scanning of items, cashier passing products through the till without checking the price**

Effect:

- Due to the fact that most tills in retail stores scan automatically, many cashiers fail to check the products they are scanning.
- Cashiers need to be aware of current prices of products in the store so that in the event a customer swaps the sticker, they will be alerted to it.

Solutions:

- Cashiers must be constantly made aware of the changing prices of products in the store especially promotional items

- Train cashiers to look at product prices as they walk through the different aisles
- Ensure cashiers are made aware of high theft or high value items to enable them to be vigilant when ringing such items.

Administrative Error

- **Promotional items not properly communicated to cashier**

Effect:

- Misunderstanding of promotional items can result in customer services nightmare.

Solutions:

- Program tills to identify multiple promotional sales
- Brief cashiers on promotions and new ringing sequences at the start of their shift
- Retrain cashiers to ring promotional items correctly.

Cashier Error

- **Cashier incorrectly packs customer shopping**

Effect:

- Damages resulting from improper packing by the casheir causes shrinkage as the store will be forced to replace the items

Solutions:

- Train cashiers to properly handle fragile products
- Train cashiers in the best procedures to pack products safely

Cashier Error

- **Cashier inadvertently processes sales one department into another**

Effect:

- When the wrong product is scanned into the wrong department, it causes artificial shortage in one department and credit for another department

Solutions:

- Train cashiers to scan products into the right departments
- Confirm that information in the master register matches department information

Cashier Error

- **Irregular use of multiple items key**

Effect:

- This could result in expensive products being processed as low value items
- Errors could be compounded.
- This could affect inventory accuracy

Solutions:

- Require cashiers to scan items individually
- Train cashiers at regular intervals
- Regularly check cashiers scanning percentage to highlight training requirements, any issues or faulty equipment

Cashier Error

- **Cashier unaware of an item's price decides to make a guess**

Effect:

- This may result in shrinkage as cashier may charge lower to prevent conflict with a customer.

Solutions:

- Train cashiers to identify products
- Constantly check cashiers to ensure they are up to speed with scanning policies and procedures
- Never permit cashiers to guess prices
- Ensure quick price check system is in place
- Set up a clear and visible support system to help cashiers identify items

Cashier Error

- **Failing to correct scanning errors**

Effect:

- Cashiers display an unwillingness to delay customers or hold up their till queue.
- Untrained supervisors are unable to attend to cashier errors
- Cashiers may leave such errors uncorrected or try to hide them

Solutions:

- Develop an error alert system in which cashiers are instructed to call in supervisors as soon as an error is detected so that errors are addressed and corrected with minimal delay
- Provide cashiers with adequate training
- Train supervisors in the most basic correction procedures to prevent long queues and shrinkage

Cashier Error

- **Incorrect use of scales**

Effect:

- Inaccurate scales may register higher or lower weight

Solutions:

- Train cashiers to correctly use scales
- Calibrate scales daily to ensure accuracy

Backroom Error

- **Stock damage**

Effect:

- Damaged products lose part or all of their value

Solutions:

- Keep stock level in the warehouse as low as possible
- Keep busy areas of the stockroom clear of any obstruction
- Keep the stockroom tidy and organised
- Provide warehouse staff with adequate training
- Secure all high value items in secure locations in the storeroom

Backroom Error

- **Products disappear in warehouse**

Effect:

- Lost product results in inadequate inventory, over ordering and a waste of time trying to locate it

Solutions:

- Manage stock levels to ensure sufficient stock to satisfy customer demand
- Keep stockroom tidy and organised
- Keep stock level in the warehouse as low as possible

Backroom Error

- **Product is mistakenly thrown into the compactor**

Effect:

- When a warehouse is untidy, there is a possibility of good products being mistakenly thrown into the compactor resulting in preventable shrinkage

Solutions:

- Ensure compactor is used by only designated employees
- Ensure the compactor is locked at all times when not in use
- Maintain tidiness in the warehouse
- Keep the compacter far from the warehouse
- Recycle all recyclable items

Auditing Error

- **Inventory miscount**

Effect:

- Miscounted inventory creates a complete disorganisation in the organisation's inventory system potentially resulting in shortage or surplus.

Solutions:

- Conduct inventory count at specific intervals

- Every effort must be made to ensure that all items are counted and that the count is accurate
- Do not add stock arriving during an inventory stock take to the count.

Ordering Error

- **Order picking error**

Effect:

- Order picking error causes acute inventory inaccuracies as there might be adequate supply within the supply chain as a whole however, there might be shortages and surplus in some stores

Solutions:

- Train pickers to select products as accurately as possible
- Train pickers in product knowledge to ensure they are familiar with the products they are picking
- Use the latest technology to ensure accuracy of the process
- Assign accountability for error to supervisor and managers

How to Reduce Employee Error

Employee error can never be eliminated; however it can be minimized through the implementation of the following measures.

Ensure employees:

1. Receive thorough training for the job / tasks they are assigned to
2. Understand the company's policies and procedures
3. Are confident using the equipment
4. Are issued with clearly defined job descriptions

5. Regular oversight is essential for monitoring employee's progress.

Ultimate Employee Error Prevention Formula

CORE PROBLEM:

- Employee error accounts for x% of retail shrinkage

OBSTACLES PREVENTING OVERCOMING THE PROBLEM:

+ Lack of and ineffective use of technology

+ Lack of proper training

+ Lack of proper policies and procedures

+ Poor procurement process

+ Poor supply chain process

+ Lack of mechanism for monitoring & compliance

SOLUTIONS TO THE PROBLEM:

+ Policies & Procedures:

  + Clear job description

+ Proper Training:

  + Receiving

  + Cashier

  + Merchandising

  + Loss prevention

  + Supervisor training

+ Investing in the appropriate technology

+ Proper mechanism for monitoring & compliance

+ Supply Chain Process:

  + Proper Delivery Scheduling

  + Proper forecasting

+ Procurement:

+ Consumer data analytics correct ordering

+ Proper forecasting

+ Coordination between store management & buyers

+ Coordination between store procurement & supply chain

= Reduce Employee Error by 2% in 90 Days

Ultimate Employee Error Prevention Formula Explanation

Identify the Core Problem

To solve any problem, it is necessary to first identify the root cause of the problem. The retail profit protection formula diagram was developed to help retailers identify the core constraint that might be preventing them from reaching their goals of making profit.

Identify the Goal:

The first step in the diagram (from the top) is to identify the goal; this is the ultimate target that they are aiming for. In this example, the goal is to reduce employee error by 2% in 90 days. We place that at the top of the diagram.

Identify the Core Problem:

The second step is to identify the core constraint... what are the obstacles that are preventing you from reaching your goal of reducing employee error by the target date?

What are the critical success factors you need to install to be able to achieve your goal? Employee error might be symptomatic of a deeper structural issue within your organization – the core constraint might be limited or non-existent policies and procedures, untrained staff, lack of mechanism for monitoring compliance, etc. Any of the above could be the core constraint.

In this section, the aim will be to ask the necessary "whys". Only after a retailer has been able to answer the "whys" can they begin to contemplate asking the "how" question.

List all of what you consider obstacles and ask yourselves why they exist by answering the following questions:

Question: Why does employee error occur in your organization?
Answer: Because employee error is not perceived as a major cause of retail shrinkage.

Question: Why is employee error not perceived as a major cause of store shrinkage?
Answer: Because the idea of shrinkage has always been attributed to customer and employee-related theft.

Question: Why has shrinkage always been attributed to theft?
Answer: Because the entire concept of retail loss prevention has traditionally been focused in that direction.

By following this method and repeatedly asking "why", you will be able to identify your core issues. It is typically a single constraint or a few constraints identified enable the organization to function smoothly once eradicated.

Identify The Critical Success Factors:

In this section, you will need to identify the critical success factors required to be in place, allowing you to move to the solution stage. These things are vital if you are going to reach the solution stage. If the first two steps are not completed, the possibility of achieving your desired result is virtually nil.

For example, one of the critical success factors required to reduce employee error would be to change the perception that shrinkage is mainly attributed to theft.

In order to change the perception that shrinkage is attributed mainly to theft, store managers need to conduct a comprehensive shrinkage analysis of their store and break down each department's shrinkage according to root causes.

In order for store managers to be able to conduct a comprehensive shrinkage analysis of their store, they need the prerequisite skills to do that.

In order for store managers to acquire the prerequisite skills to conduct a comprehensive shrinkage analysis of their store, they need training.

By completing the above exercise in this manner, you are able to determine the sequences of events or steps required before reaching the solution stage.

Identify the Solution

The final step in the process is the solution stage, wherein you arrive at the solution to the problem based upon the findings from the first two stages. At this stage, you identify the appropriate solutions to address the core problem. In most cases identifying the solution is very easy if you have been honest with yourselves during the first two stages. If you know the core problem and know the critical success factors that must be in place, all that is required is to put those conditions in place, allowing you to easily solve the problem.

Lack of requisite skills hinders the store manager's ability to conduct a comprehensive shrinkage analysis of their store. You have identified training for store managers as the main critical success factor in order for managers to gain the prerequisite skills.

All that is required is to put the necessary mechanism(s) in place to ensure store managers are provided with the appropriate training they require to gain the skills they need.

You need senior management buy-in; this is accomplished by providing them with the evidence required to convince them of the correlation between store manager's inability to conduct a shrinkage analysis of their store and store profit margin without proper training.

Please Note:
We have created a template that will assist retailers identify the core constraint that is preventing them from reaching their objectives in relation to employee error.

We are aware that the dynamic in every organization can be different. Therefore, the formula should only be used as a template to guide them in finding solutions to their own core constraints.

How to Apply the Lessons from This Part to Your Business

STEP 1
- Use the Ultimate Employee Error Prevention Formula to identify the core problems with regards to employee error in your business

STEP 2
- Provide employees with the requisite training in order for them to fulfil their role within the organisation.

STEP 3
- Ensure employees understand the company's policies and procedures

STEP 4

- Ensure employees receive adequate training to be able to use any equipment they are expected to operate.

STEP 5

- Provide employees with clearly defined job descriptions.

STEP 6

- Develop proper mechanisms for monitoring employee compliance.

Chapter Four

An Efficient Receiving Process

Introduction

The receiving process is unstructured in many retail organizations, with no written policies and procedures. This results in receiving shrinkage, accounting for an estimated 10% of total retail shrinkage. In an average supermarket, this amounts to £37,750. (NNRG 2006) Supply theft and vendor fraud are responsible for the majority of receiving shrinkage.

The receiver plays a crucial role in every retail store. They are the first line of defence through which every item must pass before entering the store's inventory system. If the process and individual lack moral integrity, this will have a negative ripple effect throughout the entire store's inventory system.

When suppliers notice that receivers are ignorant of the merchandise they are receiving, they are certain to exploit the situation by either short supplying or charging for undelivered goods.

For this reason, it is imperative that every retail organization has designated and well-trained receivers, possessing adequate knowledge of the products they are expected to receive and the technology they operate.

How to Properly Receive Merchandise

Retailers, large and small, receive a mass of products on a weekly basis. Depending on the size of the operation and the amount of stores in the chain, the process can range from complex (with the use of automated systems) to a small store where goods are counted manually.

Regardless of the operation's size, the main purpose of the process remains consistent – to ensure that goods are received in good, sellable condition and that the amount received is correct.

Below is a checklist for an effective receiving process:

1. When preparing to receive goods, keep the warehouse clean and organised.
2. Rotate stock in the warehouse and move some to the shop floor as required.
3. Ensure extra staff are on hand to receive the goods.
4. Count the number of cages or pallets ensuring that where possible boxes are counted.
5. Inspect the consignment for damage, distress or leakage.
6. Record any shortage or surplus and ensure credit is requested from the supplier.
7. Rotate receivers to prevent collusion with suppliers.

Calculating the Cost of Receiving Shrinkage

Receiving shrinkage accounts for ten percent of retail shrinkage. In monetary terms that can have a significant impact on the bottom line for an average retailer.

However, the manner of calculating shrinkage can be complicated for many retailers. The formula below can be used as a template to aid retailers in calculating the cost of retail receiving shrinkage:

Receiving Shrinkage Calculation

Cost Of Merchandise = £400,000
Percent of Shrinkage = 10%
Annual Loss= £40,000
Amount Of Stores = 15
Total Receiving Shrinkage For All Stores= £600,000

[Figure 17]

The above formula illustrates that a retailer receives merchandise worth four hundred thousand pounds. The industry average for receiving shrinkage is ten percent. Ten percent of four hundred thousand pounds is forty thousand pounds. If you multiply that by the amount of store you have (in this example we used 15 stores) you will arrive at your receiving shrinkage level. Forty thousand multiply fifteen stores gave us six hundred thousand.

Vendor Theft & Fraud

Vendor dishonesty can occur in many ways including:

    Supplying less products than charged for.
    Manipulation of credit to avoid buying back expired stock.
    Inaccurate invoicing.
    Supplying nearly expired merchandise but charging full price.
    Partial delivery of merchandise.
    Fiddling with merchandise to be credited.

The Supply Chain Dilemma

The benchmark of success for most retail internal distribution systems is product flow rather than loss prevention or shrinkage management. The basic logic behind this approach is twofold: first and foremost, to prevent the expiration of goods in the warehouse.

Secondly, the books of the organization as a whole need to remain balanced, despite overage or shortage within individual store locations.

Tesco is a prime example of this scenario. When goods are received in a Tesco store, there is either a shortage or an overage for the particular store. The company's perception is that as long as the products exist within Tesco's supply chain network, they are not counted as shrinkage. There are two major problems with this arrangement; it encourages dishonesty within the supply chain network and it also causes significant shrinkage. Additionally, if there is constant overage in stores, this will clearly result in stores receiving products they do not require.

Another principle omitted from most retail supply chain relationships is the fundamental principle that states: "If the customer has not bought, no one has sold". (Goldratt, E. 2005) Goods sitting in the regional or shop warehouse are a monetary liability until they are moved to the shop floor or placed in the customers' shopping baskets.

In order for a supply chain system to be effective, mechanisms must be employed for performance measurement. The key performance indicator should be the reliability of the supplier; if a supplier delivers an order late it can cause shortage, ultimately causing customer service problems for the store.

Reliability is measured by assessing the price of the system that is affected as a result of the delayed delivery, multiplied by the numbers of days or hours it is late. Applying a monetary value to this situation enables the supplier to see the cost implications their actions have on the company, thereby forcing him to take corrective action to ensure deliveries arrive on time.

When goods arrive at the store, receivers must record any discrepancies discovered between the goods delivered and those stated on the delivery note.

If any item is found as part of the stock, yet are not recorded in the delivery notes, the following actions are advisable:

1. Isolate those items from the rest of the delivery.
2. Inform the distribution centre immediately.
3. The receiver must either log in the items in his store or forward it to another store.
4. Ensure all records are adjusted to reflect the new inventory status.

How to Train Receiving Employees

Receiving is the first line of defence in any retail environment. Backdoor receivers literally hold the cheque book of that organization. Therefore it is crucial to a retail business that these individuals receive a high level of training.

Receiver training must include the following areas:

1. Merchandise/products knowledge.
2. Basic mathematics to enable them to properly calculate.
3. The use of automated systems.
4. Store credit monitoring.

How to Prevent Receiving Losses

Effective prevention and/or reduction of receiving shrinkage requires the implementation of the following strategies:

1. Authorised Key Control

It goes without saying that leaving the receiving bay open and unattended is an invitation for shrinkage. Unattended receiving areas must be secured; organizations must ensure only authorized staff are made responsible for keys.

Well written, adequate policies and procedures are vital to ensure strict control of the receiving process. Any personnel failing to adhere to these must not be allowed access to this area.

2. Receiver Training

Many retailers have been unable to make the correlation between the quality of staff allowed to receive goods and receiving shrinkage. Numerous organizations do not have a dedicated, trained receiver; thus, any employee can receive and sign for deliveries.

Every error a receiver makes directly impacts the organization's bottom line. For this reason, it is crucial to provide receivers with extensive training, supported by expert levels of product knowledge. Supplier fraud primarily occurs because dishonest suppliers realize that receivers lack the prerequisite training and product knowledge.

3. Clearly Written Policies and Procedures

An informed and motivated workforce implementing formally written policies and procedures form the fundamentals of an efficient receiving shrinkage management system. Creating a standardized system of receiving sends a message to dishonest employees and suppliers alike that the organization considers shrinkage reduction a very high priority.

Include the following in your receiving policies and procedures:

> All items received must be counted and verified.
> Receiving must be conducted through a single entrance.
> Secure the entrance when unattended.

Periodically re-train receivers to ensure they are aware of the latest products and technology.

Permit only one active supplier in the receiving area at any time.

4. Effective Use of Technology

The use of advanced technologies has aided the receiving process for most retailers. Technologies such as RFID merchandise security tagging have revolutionized the receiving process, making it easier for retailers to track incoming products and increase inventory accuracy.

However, the use of technology can only be effective when those using it are properly trained in the functionalities of the devices they are using.

Technologies used to their fullest potential can provide enormous benefit to the retail receiving process. Those retailers who harness technology to its maximum have succeeded in reducing their shrinkage level by as much as 9.23%, reducing their accounts payable by 65% and increasing overall store profit by up to 3%. (Marquis, K. 2001).

5. Warehouse Stock Control

Excess stock in the warehouse is a sure-fire recipe for stock loss. Stock kept in the backroom or warehouse should never exceed 8-10% of total stock holding.

Always record and report any losses due to damage, expiration, over-ordering or theft.

6. Random and Periodic Auditing

Regular audits should always be performed on the receiving process to ensure integrity and compliance of the organization's operating policies and procedures.

Conduct routine audits, performed by both internal and external auditors, at least once a quarter.

Ultimate Receiving Shrinkage Prevention Formula

CORE PROBLEM:
- Receiving Shrinkage accounts for x% of retail shrinkage

OBSTACLES PREVENTING OVERCOMING THE PROBLEM:
+ Lack of & ineffective use of technology
+ Lack of proper training
+ Lack of proper policies and procedures
+ Lack of security measures
+ Poor auditing
+ Lack of mechanism for monitoring & compliance

SOLUTIONS TO THE PROBLEM:
+ Policies & Procedures:
    + Clear job description
    + Counting
    + Verification of delivery note
+ Proper Training:
    + Train assigned receivers to properly receive goods
    + Train staff to use technology effectively
+ Investing in appropriate technology
+ Proper mechanism for monitoring & compliance
+ Select appropriate people

+ Periodic & random auditing
  + Security Measures:
    + Access control
    + Key control

= Reduce Receiving Shrinkage by 2% in 90 Days

Ultimate Receiving Shrinkage Prevention Formula Explanation

Step one for solving any problem is to first identify the root cause of the problem. The retail profit protection formula diagram was developed to help retailers identify the core constraint(s) that might be serving as a hindrance towards them achievement of their goal of making profit.

Identify the Goal:

The first step in the diagram (from the top) is to identify the goal, as this is the ultimate target that they are aiming to achieve. In the above diagram specifically, the goal is to reduce receiving shrinkage by 2% in 90 days.

Identify the core problem

The second step is to identify the core constraint… what are the obstacles that are preventing us from reaching our goal of reducing receiving shrinkage by the target date?

What are the critical success factors we need to incorporate in order to achieve our goal?

Receiving shrinkage might be symptomatic of a deeper structural issue within our organization – the core constraint may be limited or non-existence policies and procedures, untrained receivers, unstructured receiving process, etc. Any of the above could be identified as the core constraint.

List all of what you consider obstacles and ask yourselves why they exist by answering the following questions:

Question: Why are there untrained receivers in our organization?
Answer: Because the receiving process is not perceived as essential by senior management, and therefore does not warrant special attention.

Question: Why doesn't senior management perceive receiving as a pivotal part of the store operations?
Answer: Because they do not understand the impact of receiving shrinkage on overall store profit margin.

Question: Why have they not linked receiving shrinkage with overall store profitability?
Answer: Because the store managers have not pointed it out to them.

Question: Why has the store manager not pointed it out to senior management?
Answer: Because the store manager has not conducted a comprehensive shrinkage analysis of their store to know the impact of each department's shrinkage.

Question: Why hasn't the store manager conducted a comprehensive analysis of the impact of shrinkage of each department of the store?
Answer: Because the store manager does not have the prerequisite expertise to conduct the analysis.

By following this method and repeatedly asking "why" over and over again, you will soon be able to identify your core issues. It is usually a single constraint or a few constraints that, once removed from the organization, will enable it to function smoothly.

Identify the Critical Success Factors

In this section, we need to identify the critical success factors that are required to be in place to allow us to move to the solution stage. For example, one of the critical success factors required to reduce receiving shrinkage would be for store managers to acquire the prerequisite expertise in order to conduct a comprehensive shrinkage analysis of their stores.

In order for store managers to acquire the prerequisite expertise, they need to be trained properly.

In order for store managers to receive this training, senior management needs to accept the correlation between receiving shrinkage and store manager's inability to conduct comprehensive shrinkage assessment of their store.

In order for senior management to be able to link conducting a comprehensive shrinkage analysis and manager training, they need to view shrinkage reduction as an integral part of their overall profit protection strategy.

By completing this exercise, retailers are able to determine the sequences of events or steps required before reaching the solution stage.

Identify the Solution

The final step in the process is the solution stage. At this stage, we arrive at the solution to the problem based upon the findings from the first two stages. Here, we identify the best solutions to address the core problem. In most cases identifying the solution is very easy if you have been honest with yourselves during the first two processes. If you have identified the core problem and critical success factors, all that is required is to put those conditions in place; then you can easily solve the problem.

We have identified lack of expertise as the main culprit hindering store managers from being able to conduct a comprehensive shrinkage analysis of their store. We have identified training for store managers as the critical success factor needed in order for managers to gain the prerequisite expertise. What we need to do is implement the necessary mechanism(s) to ensure store managers are provided with the appropriate training they require to gain the expertise.

We need to obtain senior management buy-in by providing them with the evidence required to convince them of the correlation between store manager's inability to conduct a shrinkage analysis of their store and the store's profit margin.

Please Note:
We have created a template that will assist retailers identify the core constraint that is preventing them from reaching their objectives in relation to receiving shrinkage.

We are aware that the dynamic in every organisation can be different. Therefore, the formula should only be used as a template to guide them in finding solutions to their own core constraints.

How to Apply the Lessons from This Part to Your Business

STEP 1
- Use The Ultimate Receiving Shrinkage Reduction Formula to identify the core problems with regards to receiving shrinkage in your business

STEP 2

- Provide receivers with extensive training; incorporating systems, technology and product knowledge.

STEP 3

- Ensure strict key control. Monitoring keys and access control might seem basic however it is the most fundamental aspect of preventing receiving shrinkage.

STEP 4

- Write policies and procedures with clarity ensuring there is a mechanism for compliance.

STEP 5

- Maintain strict backroom inventory control. Keeping the backroom tidy will make it easy for stock to be located.

STEP 6

- Conduct random and periodic audits. Auditing will identify any inconsistencies within the receiving process.

STEP 7

- Ensure credit for expired or damaged merchadise is reclaimed from vendor.

STEP 8

- Make effective use of technology. Ensure the technologies are fit for the purpose for which they were installed.

Chapter Five

Shrinkage the Profit Killer

Introduction

When I first started working for Tesco, I was provided with the standard company training. I was assigned to work in fresh food stock control. Danny*, who was my mentor and trainer, taught me all the things I needed to know about stock control. However, he also taught me things I did not need to know.

For an example:

In fresh food control, we were only to count the stock that was located in the front of the chiller. The items in the back were items left for expiration. This did not leave a great deal to do, so we would manoeuvre around the department, pretending to be busy and we'd "cook" the figures of available stock to present to our stock control manager.

He, in turn, took our figures at face value and ordered more stock, even though there was plenty of stock being left to decay in the chiller. Danny did not think anything of this practice, as everyone did the same thing!

Looking back on this, I wondered why or how we were able to get away with those practices. I came to the conclusion that shrinkage management (whether Tesco or other retailers) was never seen as a priority by top management. Instead it was seen as an inconvenience to the goal of increasing sales.

Most retailers continue to struggle with the connection between profit and shrinkage. In an industry where margins are low, you would think that management would want to do everything in their power to eliminate all profit draining activities. Shrinkage is the chief profit draining activity in any retail store.

There are many factors that contribute to shrinkage, including theft, damage, error or procedural malfunction.

This part will discuss shrinkage, both perishable and non-perishable. I will discuss the cost implications of shrinkage in the industry and the causes. I will suggest ways of tackling these issues and turning it around. By the end of this part, you will be able to understand the fundamentals of retail shrinkage. You will understand how and why these things occur. You will, also, have a step-by-step guide on how to apply these lessons to your business.

* Name changed to protect identity.

Chapter Five (a)

Perishable Shrinkage

Introduction

Visit any large supermarket in the morning the aroma in the air is always that of freshly baked bread. The reason for this; customers will frequent a particular supermarket over others for its perishable department. Therefore it is vital that freshness becomes the operating philosophy of any retail organisation that wants to remain profitable. A produce department accurately merchandised is a sight to behold; it is a symbol of beauty and magnificence. It conveys a message of freshness to customers which in turn creates customer loyalty and develops a satisfying perception about the supermarket.

The perishable department distinguishes one supermarket from another. Product availability, freshness and quality all contribute to the competitive edge one supermarket has over another. It is estimated that customers will spend 8% of their grocery outgoings in a store they perceive to have fresh produce (Crosett Company Newsletter. 2010).

Four essential facts about the perishable department:

1. It drives sales and profit.
2. Stores lose 20% of available perishable profit to shrinkage.
3. Reducing perishable shrinkage by 20% will increase total store profit by 33%.
4. Perishable department contributes the highest income; ironically it is also responsible for the highest level of shrinkage

Breakdown of Perishable Shrinkage

- Meat & Seafood: 39%
- Produce: 26%
- Deli: 19%
- Bakery 9%
- Floral: 4%
- Dairy: 3%

Causes of Perishable Shrinkage

- **Cashier Mistakes (15%):** 15% of store shrinkage is due to cashier errors. You can sort this by compliance testing, policies & procedures, and auditing.
- **Incorrect Handling (21%):** Train your staff in correct handling procedures and you can significantly reduce this aspect of your shrinkage.
- **Insufficient Ordering (27%):** By following 'smart ordering' and ordering for three days, your ordering process can become efficient.
- **Spoilage (21%):** You will inevitably have far less spoilage and discarded products if proper ordering and handling practices are adhered to.
- **Delivery Distress (4%):** This is slightly more difficult to control as sometimes products in transit unavoidably get damages.
- **Inadequate Admin (12%):** Adhering to proper file management policies and procedures will reduce your shrink.

56% of Total Store Shrinkage:

- Comes from that of meat, produce, deli, seafood, floral, bakery.

- These same departments contribute 30% of total store sales.

15% of Total Store Shrinkage

- Comes from the produce department.
- 9.1% of a typical supermarket sales are from the produce department & produce department shrinkage rate is at 5.40% of retail sales.

The Perishable Shrinkage Causal Quad

- Product receiving and handling practices
- Spoilage due to over stacking products
- Mistakes allowing stock to overstay in the backroom
- Theft by customers and employees

The Ultimate Challenge is to determine the amount required for maximum sales and minimum waste. This is a delicate balance to strike at all times.

How to Prevent Perishable Shrinkage

Correct Handling

- The vast majority of shrinkage in a perishable department is the result of incorrect product handling. The following are strategies for improving handling procedures:
- Goods receiving policies & procedures
- Strict chiller and display rotation policy
- Reduce price as soon as practically possible
- Control controllable shrinkage

Order for 3 days

- Retailers should ideally ensure they order perishables within a three day interval in anticipation of busy periods. Achieving this requires store managers to use information on customer buying habits, seasonality and supply availability.

Smart Display Space Allocation

- Managers need to be able to strike the balance between wanting to entice customers whilst maximising their products' shelf life. Creating an illusion of full shelf space requires managers to create an illusion of full boxes when in effect they're not.
- Replenishing often but in small amounts is the way to minimise deterioration in product quality whilst still creating an effective display.

Customer Demand

- Conduct research into or acquire transactional data to better understand customer demand for the perishable department.

Refrigeration & Storage

- Majority of perishable goods should be stored in a temperature controlled environment. Refrigeration must be checked on a daily basis to ensure that temperatures are maintained at an acceptable level.
- Clean and sanitise refrigerators regularly to kill any bacteria and to prevent cross contamination.

Sell Rather Than Lose

- To minimise your losses it is better to apply the adage *"Your first loss is your best loss"* and sell products at a discount rather than allow the products to perish.

Cashier Awareness

- Ensure cashiers:

- Are given adequate product knowledge training to enable them to identify and distinguish products.
- Are informed of the latest product prices especially high value items such as meat.

Code Storage Chiller

- A coded storage chiller ensures products are displayed on a first in first out basis. Departmental supervisors and managers must ensure codes are adhered to on a daily basis
- The turnover time has to be: 2 days for fresh seafood, 3 days for produce & 7 days for fresh meat & deli.

Order Smart

- Ordering smart is the key to reducing perishable shrinkage.
- Departmental or store managers need to understand their own customers buying habits, stock on hand, order in progress and projected sales as a guide to the amount of stock they will need to order.

Refrigeration Blinds

- These blinds assist in prolonging the shelf life of perishable items by reducing their exposure to direct sunlight.
- It is advisable to use them at the close of day.

Deli Product Opening and Resealing

- Ensure store staff are properly trained in opening and resealing deli products to increase the products shelf life:
- Use sterile blades to open products. Box cutters, pens, or used knives are inappropriate and unsanitary.

- Keep as much of the original packaging intact on deli meats and cheeses as possible to avoid exposing products to air and to associates' hands.
- Cover open products thoroughly with food-grade plastic wrap.

Open Products At The Right Time

- Opening products at the wrong time can cause shrinkage just as opening products incorrectly can.
- Avoid opening new packets of deli meat, cheeses or new containers of deli salad shortly before closing unless absolutely necessary.
- Do not pre-slice meat and cheeses late in the day. Slicing meats and cheeses reduces their shelf lives
- Do not bake more than necessary in the day. Many bakery products have shorter shelf lives than deli products. Fresh crusty bread baked immediately before closing will be day old bread the next morning.

Ultimate Perishable Shrinkage Reduction Formula

CORE PROBLEM:

- Perishable Shrinkage accounts for x% of retail shrinkage

OBSTACLES PREVENTING OVERCOMING THE PROBLEM:

+ Lack of inventory control

+ Lack of proper training

+ Lack of proper stock rotation policies and procedures

+ Lack of & ineffective use of technology

+ Lack of security measures

+ Lack of mechanism for monitoring & compliance

SOLUTIONS TO THE PROBLEM:

+ Policies & Procedures:
  + Clear job description
  + Markdown policy
  + Rule of 3 ordering
  + Sanitation
  + Date checking
  + Temperature Control
+ Proper mechanism for monitoring & compliance
+ Proper training:
  + Train assigned replenishment staff to properly rotate goods
  + Train staff to use technology effectively
+ Security Measures:
  + Secure high value items
+ Select appropriate people
+ Periodic & random auditing
+ Investing in the appropriate technology

= Reduce Perishable Shrinkage by 2% in 90 Days

Ultimate Perishable Shrinkage Reduction Formula Explanation

Step one for solving any problem is to first identify the root cause of the problem. The retail profit protection formula diagram was developed to help retailers identify the core constraint that are serving as a hindrance towards the achievement of their goal of making profit.

Identify the Goal:

The first step in the diagram (from the top) is to identify the goal this is the ultimate target that they are aiming for. In the above diagram the goal is to perishable shrinkage by 2% in 90 days.

Identify the Core Problem

The second step is to identify the core constraint... what are the obstacles that are preventing us from reaching our goal of reducing employee theft by the target date.

What are the critical success factors we need to install to be able to achieve our goal?

Perishable shrinkage might be symptomatic of a deeper structural issue within our organisation – the core constraint might be poor product handling practices, poor sanitation, inadequate merchandising practices etc. Any of the above could be the core constraint.

List all of what you consider obstacles and ask yourselves why they exist by answering the following questions:

Question: Why do poor product handling practices exist in our organisation?
Answer: Because receivers have received no training on how to best handle perishable goods when been received.

Question: Why have they not been trained in proper product handling technique?
Answer: Because the store manager has not requested resources for training from senior management.

Question: Why has the store manager not requested resources for training?
Answer: Because they have not made the correlation between poor product handling practices and perishable shrinkage.

Question: Why have they not made the correlation between poor product handling practices and perishable shrinkage?
Answer: Because the store managers do not know the causes of perishable shrinkage.

Question: Why don't the store managers know the causes of perishable shrinkage?
Answer: Because they have not been adequately trained on that themselves.

By following this method and repeatedly asking "why", you will be able to identify your core issues. It is always a single constraint or a few constraints that when removed from the organisation will enable it to function smoothly.

Identify the Critical Success Factors

In this section, we need to identify the critical success factors that are required to be in place to allow us to move to the solution stage. For example, one of the critical success factor required to reduce perishable shrinkage would be to improve on product handling practices.

In order to improve on product handling practices, receivers have to be trained in good product handling practices.

In order for receivers to gain good product handling practice training, store managers need to request resources for training.

In order for store managers to request resources they need to be able to make the correlation between perishable shrinkage and poor product handling practices.

In order for store managers to be able to make the correlation between perishable shrinkage and poor product handing practices, they have to receive training themselves.

By completing this exercise, retailers are able to determine the sequences of events or steps required before reaching the solution stage.

Identify the Solution

The final step in the process is the solution stage. It is at this stage that we arrive at the solution to the problem based upon the findings from the first two stages. At this stage we come up with the best solutions to address the core problem. In most cases identifying the solution is very easy if we have being honest with ourselves during the first two process. If we know the core problem and know the necessary conditions to be in place, all we need now is put those conditions in place and we can easily solve the problem.

We have identified poor products handling practices as the core problem in relation to perishable shrinkage and we have also identified training deficiencies as the critical success factors that needs to be in place in order to us to deal with the issue of poor products handling practices.

All we need now is to put in place the necessary mechanism to ensure both store managers and receivers are provided with the appropriate training they require to conduct their duties efficiently.

We need to get senior management buy-in by explaining to them the current problem, specify how it affects store operations and how the proposed solution would affect store operations and the company's overall profitability.

Please Note:

We have created a template that will assist retailers identify the core constraint that is preventing them from reaching their objectives in relation to perishable shrinkage.

We are aware that the dynamic in every organisation can be different. Therefore, the formula should only be used as a template to guide them in finding solutions to their own core constraints.

Chapter Five (b)

Non-Perishable Shrinkage

Introduction

Non-perishable goods, such as groceries, health & beauty items and general merchandise, make up about 60% of a store's sales. (Marquis, K.L. 2001) Damage, theft and accidents are the most notable causes of non-perishable shrinkage. Non-perishable shrinkage can be classified as known and unknown. Non-perishable shrinkage is easier to control than perishable shrinkage, with the implementation of a number of policies and procedures.

Classification of Non-Perishable Shrinkage

Known Shrinkage

The source for known shrinkage can be easily pinpointed. It's the result of damaged goods, administrative errors or fraud.

Unknown Shrinkage

Unknown shrinkage is a loss that cannot be pinpointed at the time of occurrence. Incidents of theft, whether customer or employee related, can cause unknown shrinkage. The reason for unknown shrinkage is the amount of time it takes to detect. It can take weeks or even months before the problem is discovered. This is especially true in stores that do not have a good inventory management system.

Non-Perishable shrinkage occurs in the following departments:

- Grocery
- General Merchandise

Health & Beauty

Examples of causes of such shrinkage are

Damage

Accident

Theft

Breakdown of Non-Perishable Shrinkage

- Grocery: 56%
- General Merchandise: 19%
- Health & Beauty: 13%
- Beer, Wine, and Spirit: 4%
- Frozen Food: 3%
- Other: 4%

Strategies for Preventing Non-Perishable Shrinkage

Preventing non-perishable shrinkage is a straight-forward task in comparison to perishable shrinkage. What is required is the introduction of the correct policies and procedures, the training of staff to implement those policies and procedures and the installation of mechanisms for monitoring compliance.

The process needs to take the following format:

1. Controlling Known Loss

Controlling known loss requires establishing mechanisms to ensure proper records are kept of all customer returns, damaged, distressed or expired goods. Damaged products can be discounted, returned to the supplier for credit or disposed off. When markdowns are conducted, or products are disposed of, accurate records must be kept to ensure the overall store inventory records are adjusted. Any area with excessive shrinkage must be thoroughly checked for systematic or procedural failure. It is essential employees are adequately trained and informed of the above processes.

2. Backdoor Receiving

A majority of store deliveries come from their own warehouses and the remainder are delivered to the store by suppliers.

Since "receiving" shrinkage accounts for approximately 10% of retail shrinkage, it is imperative that the receiving process is diligently over-seen. Policies and Procedures for the receiving of goods must be well written and communicated to all appropriate employees. This will ensure that everyone understands and is in compliance with these rules.

Depending on the size of retailer, the receiving process can be conducted either manually or automatically.

The most common method for receiving goods is using the manual system. This requires the receiving employee to physically count all the goods being delivered. If the receiver discovers a shortage, it is up to this employee to write up this information and pass it on to their supervisors or line managers.

The receiving employee must ensure the person delivering the goods is present during counting and writing up the report. The delivery person must sign the receiver's report, accepting the comments and findings that have been written up.

If the receiving process is automated, it is imperative that the system is working properly and being used to its fullest potential. The receivers must be trained to understand the operation of these systems and that the systems are being used to their fullest capacity. For these systems to function at their fullest capacity requires continual updating of software and constant contact with the system's supplier for up-to-date new features.

Due to the sheer volume of goods being received in many large retail stores, it is virtually impossible to count items individually. This is especially true for supermarkets. Therefore, retailers will scan cages of items instead of individual items.

While this method might seem easy, it increases the potential for shrinkage. In large stores like Tesco, there is an acceptance that on every delivery there is a shortage or an overage of goods.

In these situations, the retailer has a system whereby the store manager uses a credit and debit system. This means when a cage contains an overage of goods, there is a credit applied and when the cage has a shortage of goods there is a debit applied. While this system might seem pretty straight forward on the surface, in reality it is a recipe for the creation of shrinkage.

Dishonest employees within the supply chain may exploit this system and short change the store. Dishonest staff can also have a field day, as there will be no detection that the items disappeared within the store. If deliveries are not check upon arrival, it is impossible to determine where the shortage occurred, whether en route or within the store itself.

This will also create an unnecessary waste of human resources that will be assigned to find the missing items. Tesco's executive stated that it is easier to maintain the status quo than going through the expense of changing the system.

It is false economy to believe leaving a system broken is easier than the cost of repairing it. Ignoring the problem will become even more costly in the long run. In order for Tesco to solve this issue, they would firstly need to establish a policy of "spot checking" cages at random. With each delivery, choosing cages to be thoroughly checked and recording all discrepancies. When the supply chain and dishonest employees get drift that cages will be randomly checked, they will think twice about stealing as they will most likely get caught.

Secondly, the burden of proof must be placed on the supply chain. If too many discrepancies are recorded, they will be forced into necessary action to increase their order accuracy. Another avenue is using source tagging for high value products. Although these measures will not completely eliminate discrepancies, it will help in reducing the problem to a minimum.

Furthermore, conducting periodic inventory count and auditing the process will reduce the possibility for shrinkage.

3. Pricing Management

When addressing pricing discrepancies in the store, take the following into consideration:

- Procedures for pricing change
- Management of pricing/scan information
- Auditing of direct supplier pricing

4. Warehouse Inventory Control

Retailers have one thing in common, irrespective of size, the issue of forecasting. Retailers have yet to find a fail-safe way to forecast customer's behaviour. Software is available to help retailers make an educated guess although it is not 100% accurate.

The inability to forecast has been responsible for either over-ordering or out-of-stock scenarios in many retail stores. One way to limit this problem is to organise your warehouse.

When the warehouse is well organised, it becomes easy to locate missing products. Secondly it sends a message to employees and suppliers alike that the organisation is serious about shrinkage.

Furthermore, products poorly arranged or rotated can result in damage, or expiration. It is therefore important that measures are taken to conduct regular inventory control.

Ultimate Non-Perishable Shrinkage Reduction Formula

CORE PROBLEM:
- Non-perishable Shrinkage accounts for x% of retail shrinkage

OBSTACLES PREVENTING OVERCOMING THE PROBLEM:
+ Lack of inventory control
+ Lack of proper training
+ Lack of proper stock rotation policies and procedures
+ Poor Auditing
+ Lack of & ineffective use of technology
+ Lack of security measures
+ Lack of mechanism for monitoring & compliance

SOLUTIONS TO THE PROBLEM:
+ Policies & Procedures:
    + Clear job description
    + Markdown policy
+ Select appropriate people
+ Proper mechanism for monitoring & compliance
+ Proper training:
    + Train assigned replenishment staff to properly merchandise goods
    + Train staff to use technology effectively
+ Security Measures:
    + Secure high value items
    + Loss prevention must be involved in the merchandising strategy

+ Periodic & random auditing

+ Store design

+ Investing in the appropriate technology

= Reduce Non-Perishable Shrinkage by 2% in 90 Days

Ultimate Non-Perishable Shrinkage Reduction Formula Explanation

Step one for solving any problem is to first identify the root cause of the problem. The retail profit protection formula diagram was developed to help retailers identify the core constraint that are serving as a hindrance towards the achievement of their goal of making profit.

Identify the Goal:

The first step in the diagram (from the top) is to identify the goal this is the ultimate target that they are aiming for. In the above diagram the goal is to reduce non-perishable shrinkage by 2% in 90 days.

Identify the Core Problem

The second step is to identify the core constraint… what are the obstacles that are preventing us from reaching our goal of reducing non-perishable shrinkage by the target date.

What are the critical success factors we need to install to be able to achieve our goal?

Non-perishable might be symptomatic of a deeper structural issue within our organisation – the core constraint might be lack inventory control, lack of security measure, poor auditing, etc. Any of the above could be the core constraint.

List all of what you consider obstacles and ask yourselves why they exist by answering the following questions:

Question: Why is there a lack of proper security measures in your organisation?
Answer: Because the loss prevention department is isolated from the rest of the retail operations.

Question: Why is loss prevention department isolated from the rest of retail operations?
Answer: Because loss prevention is not intertwined with the rest of the operations.

Question: Why can't loss prevention be intertwined with the rest of the operations?
Answer: Because loss prevention is outsourced.

Question: Why is loss prevention outsourced in many retail organisations?
Answer: Because they do not possess the expertise to properly conduct loss prevention internally.

By following this method and repeatedly asking "why", you will be able to identify your core issues. It is always a single constraint or a few constraints that when removed from the organisation will enable it to function smoothly.

Identify the Critical Success Factors

In this section, we need to identify the critical success factors that are required be in place to allow us to move to the solution stage. For example, one of the critical success factors required to reduce non-perishable shrinkage would be to make loss prevention an integral part of the retail operation.

In order to make loss prevention an integral part of the retail operation, we need to create an internal loss prevention department and a position of director of profit protection.

In order to create an internal loss prevention department, we either need to work with our current loss prevention service provider to assist us or hire an external consultant.

In order to create an internal loss prevention department senior management needs to be convinced of the added value of the creation of such department.

By completing this exercise, retailers are able to determine the sequences of events or steps required before reaching the solution stage.

Identify the Solution

The final step in the process is the solution stage. It is at this stage that you arrive at the solution to the problem based upon the findings from the first two stages. At this stage you come up with the best solutions to address the core problem. In most cases identifying the solution is very easy if you have been honest with yourselves during the first two processes. If you know the core problem and know the necessary conditions to be in place, all you need now is to put those conditions in place and you can easily solve the problem.

You have identified lack of proper security measures as your core problem and making loss prevention an integral part of your retail operations as the necessary conditions that need to be in place. What you need to do is to put in place the necessary mechanism to help in the creation of your own loss prevention department.

You need to get senior management buy-in by providing them with the evidence required to convince them that making loss prevention in integral part of retail operation is essential for helping the smooth running of retail operation and store profit margin.

Make arrangements to hire a consultancy firm to help create a loss prevention department for the store.

Please Note:

We have created a template that will assist retailers identify the core constraint that is preventing them from reaching their objectives in relation to non-perishable shrinkage.

We are aware that the dynamic in every organisation can be different. Therefore, the formula should only be used as a template to guide them in finding solutions to their own core constraints.

How to Apply the Lessons from This Part to Your Business

STEP 1
- Use The Ultimate Perishabe and Non-Perishable Shrinkage Reduction Formulas to identify the core problems with regards to non-perishable and perishable shrinkage in your business

STEP 2
- Conduct random and periodic auditing of both departments to ensure compliance with company's policies and procedures.

STEP 3
- Provide receivers with extensive training; encorporating systems, technology and product knowledge.

STEP 4
- Ensure employees receive a clearly written job description. This will enable them to have clarity of expectations and accountability.

STEP 5
- Write policies and procedures with clarity ensuring there is a mechanism for compliance.

Chapter Six

Shoplifting

Introduction

Today's retail world is one of intense competition, driven by the ever-changing needs and wants of consumers. Retailers all around the world are challenged to present a low key, relaxed shopping atmosphere, allowing their customers ease of access to their goods while simultaneously ensuring their protection from theft.

This requirement is pretty challenging in today's age, where shoplifting is no longer about the simplistic and petty teenage criminal acts. Nor is it about the needs of the homeless and addicts alike. Instead, shoplifting has evolved to the more professional level of Organized Retail Crime (ORC). Presently, it is a well-known fact that the ORC is directly responsible for the majority of items stolen from retailers worldwide. Thus, it is also no surprise that the sophistication involved in the act of shoplifting is on the rise to levels the retail industry never thought conceivable. These mastermind groups consist of highly trained individuals performing acts of thievery with an air of professionalism that is downright amazing. While you can still point to transients, teenagers and young adults as common culprits behind shoplifting, the reality is that the ORC nets a far bigger piece of the pie.

The internet has produced some great websites for trading and selling in the 21st century, including sites like eBay and Craigs List. Such websites have introduced a whole new dynamic to the shopping industry – and a whole new dynamic to retail crime. ORC criminal gangs love to target retail organizations whom they view as easy or soft targets. These are the stores who prefer to focus on quality customer service, displaying their merchandise in manners that are vulnerable to theft – making it easy to remove from the store.

With the exception of the US, Canada, and Australia, shoplifting continues to be the number1 cause of retail shrinkage in all corners of the world. The 2010 Global Retail Theft Barometer Report confirms this, reporting that shoplifting accounted for approximately $45.5 billion, or 42.4%, of retail shrinkage.

In this part, you will learn the precise steps that are required to prevent or reduce shoplifting inside your store. The first portion will address the root causes and costs of shoplifting, while the second portion will detail step-by-step instruction for shoplifting prevention. By the end of this part, you should never suffer the ill effects of shoplifting in your store again – and more importantly, you will be able to watch your profits sky rocket.

Why Does Shoplifting Take Place?

The simple answer to the question why does shoplifting take place is: because shoplifters can get away with it. *Shoplifting is a crime of opportunity, when you remove the opportunity you remove the possibility.*

Picture this scenario for a moment the US president visits Afghanistan and decides to walk the streets of Kabul to greet the Afghan people or the Israeli Prime Minister decides to walk the streets of Gaza to interact with the Palestinian people. It would only happen in a Hollywood movie. The US president is the most powerful man in the world with the most sophisticated security apparatus yet he does not chance it. I realise these are extreme examples that might not seem relevant to our subject of discussion here. But on a daily basis many retailers enact similar scenarios in their store in a different form.

Let me return to the story I briefly told in the introduction to further stress this point. A few years back, I was employed as a store detective for a leading retailer in the UK. On my very first day of work, as I was in the middle of a briefing with the office I was to relieve, I noticed a couple walk into the store and headed to the coat section. I stood there perplexed as I witnessed the lady remove one of the coats from the hanger, try it on, and then casually walk to the exit with her partner and scurry into the waiting getaway car. £900 walked out the door with such incredible ease, making me think "Holy cow! How can this sort of thing happen in broad daylight??"

The answer was actually quite apparent: The coats were prominently displayed right near the exit.

Keeping this experience as a vivid memory, any time I was assigned to a different store, I took great care to walk around and look for high value items that were not securely displayed. I would call the store manager over and advise that the items needed to be relocated to more secure locations within the store. To my disbelief, most managers failed to take my advice – in their eyes, I am merely a store detective. What the heck did I know about proper merchandising?

Then, there was the time I worked at a store in London Colney. Immediately upon entering the store, I noticed coats worth £250 prominently displayed near the store entrance. Without hesitation, I located the store manager and expressed my concern to him. I even joked with him how even the CIA Director at the time, George Tenant, could not possibly protect those coats where they were positioned. This manager chose to ignore my warning – and a few hours later, some of the coats were stolen, just as I had predicted.

When I approached the manager again, I figured he would pay more attention to me now that my gloomy prediction came true. Once again, he failed to heed my warning – only paying attention to me once 20 of those 25 coats were stolen.

At this same location, there are two big retailers who shared a single toilet facility located outside of both stores. Shoplifters knew this and would steal from one store, head to the direction of the toilet, pass through the other store and escape. When they were stopped and questioned by our store security, they would always mention they were on their way to the toilet. There was no stopping them – they were correct about heading that direction, given the location of the toilet. The mere location of the toilet led to thousands lost to shoplifting. Yet neither store's management could pinpoint the location of the toilet as one of the primary causes to their shrinkage.

I share these two stories with you to emphasize a very important point: Shoplifting occurs in most retail stores simply because it is allowed to take place. This is a crime of opportunity; eliminate the opportunity and you reduce its possibility.

Two things continue to hinder retailers' effort to fight shoplifting:

1. Their obsession with increased sales at the expense of security.
2. Their unwillingness to create and implement the necessary policies and procedures required to prevent shoplifting in their stores.

Retailers worldwide spend billions on loss prevention technology, yet never examine the needed changes to policies and procedures to prevent shoplifting from flourishing. Spending billions on security makes little sense when you are displaying a £900 coat at the entrance of your store or have a £1000 electronic device improperly secured when displayed.

Proper staff training in shoplifting awareness is the single most effective tool against shoplifting. To illustrate this point, consider the results of a research study by the National Retail Research Group (NRRG) (USA). This study revealed that employees trained in shoplifting awareness reduced shoplifting by 33%, while security officers who were also trained reduced it by only 2%. For retail stores to secure goods on the sales floor, the first step should be to alter the widespread thought process in the retail corporate offices to realize that putting a £900 coat by the entrance or a £1000 camera in an open and unsecure location is NOT good customer service.

Remember! The US president has the finest security apparatus in the world but he does not go on a stroll in the streets of Kabul.

How Does Shoplifting Affect the Retail Industry?

Society's perception of shoplifting contributes to the difficulties of stopping it. Last December, a Catholic priest, in a sermon to his congregation, informed them how it is permissible to shoplift only if they were facing difficulties. This remark exemplifies the attitude many have in society – a Robin Hood-like mentality of stealing from the rich to give to the poor. Society perceives shoplifting as a victimless crime, not fully understanding the larger impact of the crime on everyone. 89% of young people confessed to being an acquaintance of a shoplifter and 66% of them socialise with a shoplifter, according to the National Association for Shoplifting Prevention.

To put this in perspective, shoplifting presents an incredible challenge for retailers and customers alike. The consequences can be catastrophic to retailers, forcing many out of business completely.

Consumers feel the effect as well, paying higher prices for products due to overhead pertaining to the costs of loss prevention: personnel, equipment, additional staff wages and direct consequences such as lost sales and profit.

The economic impact is equally catastrophic – retailers who are seeking to cut costs in an attempt to save their business implement staff redundancies leading to lost jobs and higher unemployment figures.

Organised Retail Crime (ORC): The New Dynamic In Shoplifting

The emergence of Organized Retail Crime (ORC) into the world of shoplifting has introduced a completely new dynamic to the retail industry. Traditionally, shoplifting has been committed by individuals seeking survival, personal gain, or support of their habits. Interestingly enough, members of these organized criminal gangs do not match this description. Rather, they are gangs of well-organized, professional thieves who exhibit a level of sophistication never before witnessed in the retail industry. ORC costs retailers millions annually with no signs of slowing down.

For example, a BBC report on ORC published on 11 January 2010 (Crime gangs 'dominate shop theft') illustrates just how much damage the ORC is capable of doing to retail: they are capable of stealing up to £7,500 worth of products within 4 minutes and almost £100,000 worth of spoils daily. When you consider their operational sophistication, meticulous planning, and capability of walking away with thousands of pounds in merchandise, the ORC is truly a very real force to be reckoned with.

What law enforcement is most afraid of is how easily ORC gangs can be used as a source of funding for more serious and complex crime or even terrorist attacks. As long as retail organizations are perceived as soft targets for criminal gangs, and as long as the court system treats organized retail theft as shoplifting, the problem is destined to get worse.

Let's be clear here: ORC is not shoplifting. There is a very distinct difference between shoplifting for personal gain or survival versus activities by an organized criminal gang for the sole purpose of raising money for more serious crimes or even to fund a lavish lifestyle. Law enforcement and courts alike have yet to realize this fact, making it increasingly challenging for retail loss prevention staff to effectively handle the situation.

The primary gang active in the UK is the 150 member strong Glasgow-based McGovern team. This gang has terrorized Scotland for many years, and is now branching out all over the UK. It is conceivable that they are even spreading their reach into Europe. The most lethal ORC gangs can be found in the former eastern blocks as well as in the Republics that comprised the former Yugoslavia.

Thousands of members strong, these gangs routinely hit retailers all around Europe they perceive to be easy targets. Due to the ease of international travel in the EU, these individuals can very quickly and easily migrate from country to country perpetrating their crimes. What's more, these gangs make use of fake and stolen credit/debit cards that they are able to use for ordering thousands of pounds of merchandise to false addresses, taking the merchandise and disappearing into thin air.

Hot Spots

The figure below shows the most frequently target departments: Health & beauty followed by meat, baby products, cigarettes, beer, wine & spirit.

- Health & Beauty: 32%
- Meat: 24%
- Cigarettes: 13%
- Baby Products: 13%
- Beer, Wine, and Spirits: 10%
- Other: 8%

Hot Products

- Health, Beauty, and Cosmetic Items: 22%
- Meat: 14%
- Cigarettes: 14%
- Baby Milk: 8%
- Analgesics: 8%
- Razor Blades: 8%
- Batteries: 7%
- Alcohol: 5%
- Other: 14% (represents CD's, DVD's, and electronic devices)

The above figure shows the most frequently targeted products: Health, beauty & cosmetics, followed by meat & cigarettes, razor blades, analgesics, batteries etc. DVDs, CDs and electronic devices are the products most at risk in department stores and superstores.

Times Shoplifting Incidents Are Most Likely to Occur

Psychologists say that 90% of the things we do are habitual. Starting with the time we get out of bed, the way we wash, dress or eat –

these can be the same daily. Shoplifting is also a habit, therefore, not an exception to this rule.

Individual shoplifters tend to steal at a particular time of the day / week. In general, shoplifters do not like being noticed; therefore they tend to carry out their acts primarily when the store is full of shoppers; this tends to be at lunch time, between 3:00pm and 6.00pm and on weekends.

For stores that operate a 24/7 service, shoplifters steal late at night or early in the morning. They see these as times when there will be fewer loss prevention personnel and those on duty tend not to be as vigilant as they would be at other times.

The pie chart below displays the times of shoplifting occurrences:

Shoplifting Triggers

A variety of significant triggers for shoplifting are often attributed to the following:

Shoplifting Triggers

- Individual Gain
- The Desire To Belong

- Financial Pressures
- Psychosomatic Challenges

Who Are Shoplifters?

It is difficult to piece together a comprehensive profile of a shoplifter as they hail from diverse societal backgrounds. There are times when loss prevention personnel are able to spot a shoplifter based upon his/her demeanours, appearance or activities in the store. For instance, consider someone who is wearing a winter jacket in the middle of summer; someone taking an empty bag into a retail store; or someone stepping into an exclusive store who is not attired like the kind of clientele that might typically visit that shop – these are all common indicators of a shoplifter.

However, professional shoplifters are acutely aware of this and they are much more likely to blend in with the crowd. The current rise in so-called middle class shoplifters and ORC has infused a totally new dynamic, making it difficult for loss prevention personnel to easily distinguish between a legitimate shopper and a shoplifter.

Adolescent Shoplifter
- Adolescent shoplifters are usually youths from under privileged backgrounds who, out of the desire to show off to their peers, usually steal expensive items. It can also include youths from privileged upbringings who, despite their wealth, feel disenchanted and isolated from society. Shoplifting for them is a way of rebelling against society and getting back at their parents. They usually steal in groups to distract loss prevention personnel.

Experienced Shoplifter

- Experienced shoplifters can be well trained and a nightmare for loss prevention personnel, being versatile they are able to easily avoid detection. Members of organised retail theft syndicates are typical examples of experienced shoplifters. They are made up of a criminal gang who do not steal for pleasure. They are often intelligent and well educated people who have accepted shoplifting as a profession as they use proceeds from it to support luxurious lifestyles. They understand that shoplifting is an easy but lucrative crime and the punishment for being caught for shoplifting is far less than other offences.

Inexperienced Shoplifter

- In most instances, an inexperienced shoplifter steals without any preplanning. They might respond to an opportune moment, instant rush of adrenaline or a desire to demonstrate loyalty to members of their group. Sometimes they are forced or coerced into shoplifting by adults or so-called mentors whom they look up to. With the passage of time, inexperienced shoplifters gain experience and continue to strike on their own.

Homeless Person & Addicts

- Out of the desire to survive or feed their habits, the homeless and addicts are prolific shoplifters, who see shoplifting as their only safe option. Other than burglary or outright theft (which they may get imprisoned for), shoplifting for them is a safer bet. For one, it is easy and secondly, even if they got caught, chances are they will only be banned from the particular store, in which case they can just go into another store and continue unabated.

Kleptomaniac

- Kleptomaniac shoplifters do not steal for any particular economic need or pressure, but for the adrenaline rush and excitement it brings them. Shoplifting for them is a challenge that if they overcame would bring a rush of excitement to their lives. They can be compulsive thieves, stealing repeatedly even if they are caught. The condition often requires medical intervention to enable them to quit.

Organised Retail Crime

- ORC gangs are made up of well-organized and well trained individuals who consider shoplifting a profession. They do not steal for pleasure or personal use, the merchandise they steal is either sold onto the black market or to smaller retail operations, which see them as a cheap source of supply. Their professionalism makes them very difficult to spot and even when spotted they can easily get themselves out of the situation.

Shoplifting Techniques

- Pushchairs or car seats contained in shopping trolley's are often used to conceal stolen goods
- Shoplifters may snatch goods making a run for a waiting getaway vehicle.
- Some shoplifters wrap clothes around their legs, or tuck stolen items into socks.
- Female shoplifters may carry items between bras, hidden under long dresses, tights, or overcoats.
- In fitting rooms – they put on stolen clothes or shoes. They either abandon their own garments or put them back on to cover the stolen attire.

- They conceal stolen products in bags, newspapers, shopping bags, purses, clothes fitted with large pockets, inner lining of coats, or under clothing.
- Shoplifters operate solo or in a group. If functioning as a group, one individual is commonly employed to distract loss prevention personnel. When loss prevention personnel target the person who seems to behave suspiciously, the accomplice fulfill his/her act unnoticed.

Tell-Tale Signs of a Shoplifter

- A group of teenagers entering a store at the same time, few of them will cause disturbance to draw attention away from the main person carrying on the stealing.
- Out of place outfits i.e. overcoat on a hot day or a raincoat when it is sunny
- Somebody carrying empty bags, boxes or umbrellas which they can use to cover stolen items
- A worried-looking person who constantly touches the rear of his/her head, tugging at sleeves, or altering socks, breaks into cold sweat and blushing
- Incredibly picky individuals who are unable to decide on a purchase decision.
- Someone visiting the store repeatedly without buying anything.
- Someone placing his/her personal items in trolley
- Repeatedly looking around rather than at merchandise on the shelf or in their hands
- An empty shelf or hole in the shelf
- An early morning or late night shopper

Shoplifting and the Law

On many occasions during my time as a store detective, we had to let shoplifters get away with their loot for fear of not adhering to the letter of the law. The law states clearly that before making an arrest as loss prevention personnel, you must ensure that: 1) you have seen the person select the item; 2) conceal it; and 3) leave the store without making any attempt to pay for it. It sounds simple in theory; yet not always that simple in practice, especially in situations when one is working in a massive store.

Picture this: On a Saturday you are working at a 40,000 square foot store with over 1,000 shoppers in the store. When you spot a shoplifter, you are expected to follow that person for the duration of the time they are in the store with an uninterrupted view before you can legally stop or arrest them. This is one of the biggest obstacles to preventing shoplifting. Even though the law is there to regulate the activities of loss prevention and ensure fairness, the impracticality of implementing the law makes it a hindrance to the process.

When I worked as a store detective in Slough, I once noticed a lady who would walk around the store for about an hour and then leave without buying anything. This would happen every week without fail. I pursued her around the store, attempting to catch her red handed, yet I was never able to. She was either acting as a diversion for someone else or she noticed who I was and decided against taking any action, despite my plain-clothes. However, whatever was going on with her was just not right; I could not get my head around it. Also, I was the only security officer in the store at the time when she came in; therefore, I could not leave and go into the camera room to keep surveillance on her. Even if I did see her take an item, by the time I left the camera room to make an arrest, I would have interrupted my vigil. This is the type of difficult situation many loss prevention personnel encounter on a daily basis.

Knowing full well that the law is not going to be changed anytime soon to prevent this (my type of situation in Slough) from occurring, retailers should devise their own loss prevention strategy around the law. For instance, they should not placing loss prevention personnel in the position I was – alone in the shop, making it impossible for me to catch the lady red handed.

I faced similar situations when working on Sundays at the store in Camberley. The store opened officially at 11 am; however, customers were allowed to enter the store from around 10:30 am. When we started work at 11 am, upon arrival at around 11:01 am we would notice someone walking away with a trolley full of goods. The till opens at 11:00 am, even the fastest cashier would not have been able to scan a full trolley of goods that fast. The fact remains that because we did not see them select the goods we were not in a position to stop them. Even if the goods are tagged, half an hour is enough time for professional shoplifters to go into the changing rooms and remove the tags.

If loss prevention personnel or retail staff should attempt an arrest they must ensure they adhere to the following procedures:

STEP 1
- Ensure they see the individual enter the store and pick up an item.

STEP 2
- They must see the individual conceal the item.

STEP 3
- They must keep an uninterrupted view of the individual.

STEP 4

- They must see the individual leave the store without making an attempt to pay for the item.

Before the decision is made to actually stop the person, there must be two loss prevention personnel present. Under no circumstances should a single loss prevention personnel attempt to institute an arrest on his or her own. If it must be done, they must call for back up and request that CCTV be positioned in the location the arrest is to take place. A seemingly simple arrest could get out of hand unexpectedly.

One day I was at work in a town somewhere near London called Cheshunt. While I stood at the entrance, I noticed a female entering the store. Within minutes I saw her leaving. My instinct told me that something wasn't right, it was just not possible for her to have entered the store, chosen the items she wanted, gone to the till, pay and be out that fast. I was certain that the whole time she had stood very close to me; I had my eyes on her. However, since I was not totally sure, I decided to employ another tactic. As she walked out I said 'security can I have a word with you', I did not finish the sentence and she started running. I chased her into the car park, all the while calling for back up. I was running so fast, I could not give my exact location to my colleagues. I managed to catch up with her at the end of the car park where I took the goods from her and was walking her back to the store, when out of the blue came a guy walking towards me with a knife. He kept saying 'I swear to god if you don't leave her now I am going to stab you'. I stood there thinking to myself 'if someone is going to get hurt here tonight then god it should not be me'. The first thing that came to my mind was to use the radio as a weapon to defend myself, yet I still questioned myself if I could justify this in a court of law? I have been trained to deal with situations such as these, therefore I did not panic.

I knew I could take the guy but what about the girl? What if she hit me with something behind my neck? I managed to entangle myself from the situation without anyone getting hurt.

I learned two lessons that night. One was to never, under any circumstances, chase after a shoplifter on my own without a backup – especially in the dark in areas I did not know well. Secondly, training does pay off. If I was not trained well enough before that night, I would have panicked and used the radio or done something really stupid that would have caused either me or one of them to get injured.

The moral of this story is that no loss prevention personnel should ever put themselves in that sort of position; it might end tragically for either them or the person involved. They should only attempt to institute an arrest when they are sure that it is safe to do so.

How to Calculate the Cost of Shoplifting

Total Sales = £10,000,000
Percent of Shrinkage = 2%
Total Shrinkage = £200,000
Percent of Shoplifting = 21%
Total Shoplifting = £42,000
Amount of Stores = 15
Shoplifting Shrinkage For All Stores = £630,000

[Figure 18]

The above calculation provides an example of a retailer with a turnover of ten million pounds. A shrinkage level of two percent, will amount to two hundred thousand pounds. Shoplifting accounts for twenty-one percent of total retail shrinkage. Twenty-one percent of two hundred thousand pounds is forty-two thousand pounds. Therefore, a retailer with a turnover of ten million pounds would be losing forty-two thousand pounds annually to shoplifting. Multiply that by the number of stores you have and will be able to determine how much profit your business is losing to shoplifting.

How to Prevent Shoplifting

Shoplifting, like any crime, is impossible to eliminate. For some people, shoplifting is a profession; this is how they make their living. The perceived danger or difficulties they may encounter at a particular time are not enough to dissuade them from committing the crime. There are also some who see shoplifting as literally their only means of survival. For drug addicts wanting to feed their habits, shoplifting provides the only means of obtaining the necessary cash.

With this in mind; how can retailers prevent their store from being used by a professional shoplifter who sees it as a job or from drug addicts who consider it their cash dispenser?

***The first step is to understand that shoplifters will operate in an environment they perceive as* EASY.**

Therefore, it is essential to ensure that your store is not perceived as an easy target. In many instances, when a shoplifter takes up residency in your store, they never leave until the final curtain is brought down.

These are some of the measures that can be used to help combat shoplifting:

Change of Policies and Procedures:

Changing the present policies and procedures in most retail organisations will dramatically cut shoplifting by as much as 60%. What I mean is this, take the example of the situation I gave in the introduction about two big retailers sharing one toilet facility located outside both of their stores. Changing that alone can save both retailers thousands in lost profit. All they need to do is relocate their toilets.

The legal opening hours on Sunday for retailers in the UK is 11 am. Many retailers, such as the one I used to work for, open their doors at 10:30 am to allow customers to start browsing. In itself this is not a bad idea, except for the fact that loss prevention personnel started work at 11:00 am. So between 10:30 am and 11:00 am the shop is left completely at the mercy of shoplifters. And the smart ones do take advantage of it. Again by changing the starting time of loss prevention to 10:30 am, this retailer could be saving thousands.

There is the situation of scheduling. You have these 40-50,000 square feet shops with multiple entrances and on many occasions I would be the only officer on duty. For a start, being on my own, it was dangerous to attempt to stop anyone. Secondly, there were multiple exits; therefore, a shoplifter does not necessarily need to pass by where I was stood. Thirdly, I was not in uniform, which means I was not even serving as a deterrent. Someone in the head office, in their infinite wisdom, decided it was more cost effective to have a solitary loss prevention personnel working in a 50,000 square feet store, without thinking of the implications. Who said that I was the only one who knew that I was alone? Shoplifters perform reconnaissance on the store they want to steal from before they commit the crime. They assess security and they even know store detectives. A store detective can easily catch a newbie shoplifter but not a seasoned one. They study our movement and they know how we walk and behave.

Dishonest employees also knew when I was alone in a store. Most retail employees live within a 6-7 mile radius of the store. Where do you think the people who shoplift from your store live? Answer: within a 6-7 mile radius of your store! So if the employees and shoplifters live in the same neighbourhood, swim in the same pool, eat in the same restaurant, do you not think that they sometimes collaborate? I am sure that the moment some dishonest staff noticed that I was alone in the store; they quickly phoned their mates to inform them.

Almost every morning on my way to work, I stop at an ASDA store to buy my lunch. About 9 out of 10 times that I visit the store, there will be no security officer on duty. Sometimes when I work late, I go to the same store for my late night shopping. I noticed at night, there is usually a security officer on duty; yet in the day security is scarcely visible. The reason for this is ASDA uses both in-house and contract security. While the contract security ensure they are there on time and they try to do their job because as a contractor the other staff are watching them. On the other hand, in-house security staff are mates with the other staff; therefore they can show up late and will leave their post while on duty to chat with the other staff. I am not saying this to defend contract security; after all most of the contract security themselves are not loss prevention professionals. But the difference is this: the contract security officer understands that his company might lose the contract if he does not at least pretend to be working. In-house security staff are not trained to the same standard as contract security and feel they are not required to show the same level of professionalism that contract security has to demonstrate. I am certain this arrangement is responsible for a large percentage of ASDA's shoplifting problems. Changing this policy alone would significantly reduce ASDA's shoplifting challenges.

I have a friend who is a manager at Tesco. He always complains about being in the 'red', which means he is struggling to bring his shrinkage level down. However, whenever I visit his store, the security officer is busy stacking shelves. This does not only occur in his store, it happens in many Tesco stores; especially in Tesco Express. When I speak to security officers and ask them why they are stacking shelves instead of performing their duties, they say it is to make the 'manager happy'.

For my friend to come out of the red, the first thing he needs to do is ensure that his security officer starts performing his official duties.

In the PC World store where I buy my computer accessories, the security officer is mostly at the till serving customers instead of performing his security duties.

Retailers in the UK always complain that the authorities do not take shoplifting seriously. Yet how can the authorities take this serious when retailers themselves do not take the issue serious? With just a few policy changes I can guarantee that retailers can reduce their shoplifting problems by as much as 60-70%.

Tesco and PC World need to ensure that their security officers are performing their official duties and not stacking shelves or serving customers at the till. ASDA must change that arrangement that causes the interval between the time contact security leave and in-house security takes over. Those few hours could make the difference in their shoplifting level, which also impacts their profit margin. As for my former employers, they really need to reconsider their Sunday scheduling for loss prevention – the half hour between when loss prevention starts and when the tills are open could make a huge difference in their profit margin. Furthermore having a single security officer in a massive store is false economy.

Trained Employees:

This fact would shock you but an employee trained in shoplifting awareness is the most effective tool against shoplifting. For example, an employee notices a shoplifter and approaches the person politely to greet them asking if there was anything they could do to make their shopping experience pleasant. That question alone could be enough to deter a potential shoplifter. Shoplifters do not like being noticed – therefore the fact that someone has walked up to them, in their mind, means that they have been noticed and they will sprint out of your store in a second. Employees need to be taught the basics about shoplifting; how shoplifters look, how they normally behave etc. Though expenditure is attached to training employees, an educated workforce will in the end pay better dividends in contrast to an uneducated one.

The following chart illustrates this point.

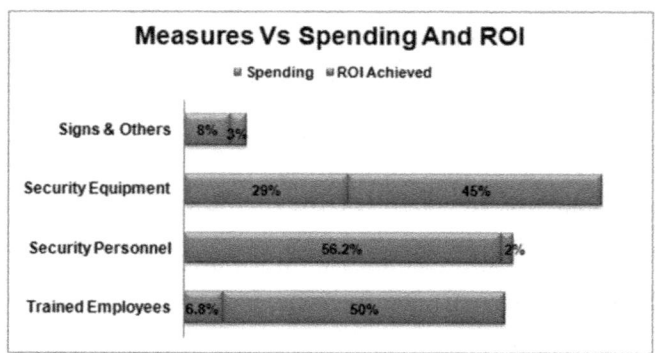

Strategic Merchandising for Security:

I relayed the accounts of two incidents in London Colney and Camberley when coats worth £250 and £900 were displayed at the entrance of a store. The company thought displaying the coats at the entrance would entice customers as they entered the store. While in theory this is good thinking, the practicalities and cost implications associated with such thinking is enormously expensive. Curry's Digital is one example of this sort of theoretical logic, where expensive electronic items are displayed without a secure merchandising protection system. Today, there are lots of merchandising technologies available that allow customers to have the same experience of touching the items without being able to remove the items from the store. They could use source tagging or discreet tags that do not cause customer discomfort.

Retailers need to be able to strike the balance between the desire to increase sales by enticing customers and the need to secure their products. Creative merchandising for security is an art that should be employed and mastered. Construction of shop displays need to be conducted in consultation with loss prevention personnel to ensure that product protection is incorporated into the design and installation.

Preventative Store Design:

Store design remains another effective tool in the battle against shoplifting. It is imperative that the concept of loss prevention is incorporated into the overall design of the store.

How to Implement Preventative Store Design:

- The amount of entrances and exits must be sufficient enough to make it comfortable for customers and staff to enter and exit the store.
- The entrances must be designed in such a way that they do not allow anyone to quickly rush into the store and run out into a waiting vehicle.

- If possible the car park must be as far away as possible from the entrance of the store and there must be enough "white space" between the entrance and the road. When you enter an ASDA or a Tesco there is this gap between the entrance and the road, this is a brilliant idea of a "white space". It would be difficult for anyone to carry out a bulk-snatch in an ADSA or Tesco store because they have to go through that "white space" by which time the person would have been caught by loss prevention personnel.
- The roads leading in and out of the store must have speed bumps to limit the possibility of people speeding off.
- Goods must be merchandised in such a way that they are difficult to steal in order to discourage anyone from even making an attempt.
- There needs to be a 'busy motorway' system where high value goods are displayed securely in areas that are frequented and visible to staff. All staff members need to be encouraged to frequent that specific route. They need to walk those routes whenever they move around the shop.
- Never stack goods to the point where they obscure the view of staff. We see this mainly during promotions or bank holidays when goods are stacked one on top of the other making it difficult for staff to see over to the other side.
- Small-sized high value items, such as Gillette blades, must be displayed close to or behind the till.
- And most importantly, the store must be kept neat at all times of the day.
- An untidy store sends a signal to shoplifters that no one cares. Conversely, a tidy store with an organized manner says something like – we are watching you.
- The right lighting system has to be in place to limit blind spot.

- Do not forget the signs; signs telling shoplifters that they will be prosecuted are enough to put off some shoplifters.

Excellent Customer Service Strategy:

Implementing an excellent customer service strategy can be another indispensable tool against shoplifting. You can never go wrong with extraordinary customer service. When approached by a member of staff, a legitimate customer feels valued and appreciated. On the other hand a shoplifter may feel nervous and appear uneasy. The last thing a shoplifter wants is to be noticed. Therefore instead of appreciating exceptional customer service; they will run away from it.

Make sure there are a sufficient number of visible employees in busy periods. Staff must be taught to greet every customer and offer assistance. If they notice someone standing and looking lost, they need to approach the individual and offer assistance by saying 'I will be standing there if ever you need me'. Any would-be shoplifter will immediately feel uneasy because they know they have been noticed, ruining their plan.

Train Loss Prevention Personnel

The idea of saying 'train loss prevention personnel' might sound ludicrous to some people as they naturally assume that loss prevention personnel are supposed to be trained. Let me give you a shocker, most loss prevention personnel are not trained well enough to perform the task assigned to them.

One day whilst on duty in Camberley, I noticed two females in the jewellery aisle. The fact that I was standing there did not bother them, they just started filling their bags right in front of me. I could not believe what I was seeing. Whether they thought that I was a shoplifter myself, I will never know. After they had taken enough to their satisfaction, they casually walked towards the entrance and exited the store. I radioed for back up, when my two colleagues arrived, we proceeded to intercept and arrest them.

We spoke to them, introduced ourselves and asked them to accompany us back to the store. They attempted to run but we quickly grabbed hold of them and walked them towards the store. At the entrance of the store, one of them dropped to the floor. We tried to raise her from the floor but we were unable to. For the ensuing 45 minutes, three big loss prevention officers could not restrain a tiny lady. It became so embarrassing with customers coming into the store, staring at three hefty looking loss prevention officers having trouble restraining a tiny lady.

What was the reason for this? Lack of training. None of us had received any training in physical intervention.

Like us on that day, many loss prevention officers are inadequately trained to perform their duties effectively. I had never heard of the word 'shrinkage' until I became a consultant. I'm sure 9 out of 10 loss prevention officers have never heard of the word "shrinkage."

You cannot shoot a target you can't see. If loss prevention personnel do not understand the meaning of the word shrinkage how can they prevent it?

Maybe if my Tesco manager friend took the time to teach his security officer the meaning of shrinkage he will realize that his job in the store is to prevent shrinkage *not* to stack shelves.

Stopping Organised Retail Crime:

Stopping an Organised Retail Crime gang might seem a tall order for a single retailer, and it is indeed a difficult one. However, it can be done. Retailers first and foremost must recognize the fact that a new dynamic has been introduced into their terrain. Consequently, their loss prevention strategies must be updated to match this new reality. Their staff must be trained differently from the traditional shoplifting prevention training and preventative policies and procedures must be created to reflect the new situation.

Law enforcement agencies and the law must be updated to reflect that ORC is not the same as shoplifting. This is not to excuse shoplifting or to say it is less of a crime than ORC. However, the current reality is shoplifters are treated with kids' gloves by the law – one of many reasons why many people perceive it as less of a crime. But ORC is in a league of its own. Not only are the ORC gangs costing retailers significantly more, they are bad for the economy. Most importantly, ORC is a threat to our security; therefore they must be seen in that context.

How Technology Can Help Prevent Shoplifting

The best shoplifting technologies are known to reduce shoplifting by as much as 25% in the first 6 months of implementation. However, as with any technology, the key phrase is; used effectively. For example, some retailers install expensive CCTV without having it monitored or they have a single person monitoring multiple cameras. The most interesting aspect is having CCTV installed without first consulting loss prevention. This may result in having an insufficient amount of cameras or cameras being incorrectly positioned.

Technology is only beneficial if it removes a constraint. The big question each retailer needs to ask before investing in shoplifting technology is this:

'Is shoplifting the core constraint or is it a symptom of deeper structural challenges within their organisation?'

Let me elaborate on this point with an example. In the retail industry the key performance indicator (KPI) is increased sales. As a result of this KPI, store managers and sales directors will bend over backwards to do everything within their powers to entice customers – including placing high value items in unsecured locations of the store. Without changing this mind-set, the possibilities of any loss prevention technology being effective are pretty slim. No amount of technology can prevent a £1000 camera from being stolen if it is located in a vulnerable location in a store or without the appropriate security tag.

Ultimate Shoplifting Prevention Formula

CORE PROBLEM:
- Shoplifting accounts for x% of retail shrinkage

OBSTACLES PREVENTING OVERCOMING THE PROBLEM:
+ Poor merchandising
+ Poor store design
+ Poor security measures

SOLUTIONS TO THE PROBLEM:
+ Store Design:
    + Consider shrinkage management when designing store
    + Consult loss prevention professionals when designing store
    + Involve loss prevention personnel when installing technology in store
+ Proper Merchandising:
    + Involve loss prevention in decisions regarding merchandising
    + Make effective use of appropriate tags
    + Place small high value items behind the till or in glass cabinets

+ Display high value items in visible locations most frequented by store employees
 + Train Staff:
   + Train employees in shoplifting awareness
 + Proper Security Measures:
   + Ensure adequate number of loss prevention personnel
   + Make effective use of loss prevention technology

= Reduce Shoplifting by 2% in 90 Days

Ultimate Shoplifting Prevention Formula Explanation

To solve any problem, one must first identify the root cause. The retail profit protection formula diagram was developed to help retailers identify the core constraint that might be preventing them from reaching their profit-making goals.

Identify The Goal:

The first step in the diagram (from the top) is to identify the goal – this is the ultimate target that they are aiming for. Let's say the goal is to reduce shoplifting by 2% in 90 days; we would put that at the top of the diagram.

Identify The Core Problem:

The second step is to identify the core problem: What are the obstacles preventing a retailer from reaching their goal by the target date? While a retailer might consider shoplifting to be the problem, it might be symptomatic of a deeper structural issue – perhaps location of merchandise, lapse in policies and procedures, untrained staff etc.

In this section the aim will be to ask the necessary "whys" – for once a retailer has been able to answer the "whys", they can move on to contemplate asking the "how" question.

List all of what you consider obstacles and ask yourselves why they exist by answering the following questions:

Question: Why does my merchandising problem exist?
Answer: Because those responsible for merchandising do not have sufficient knowledge regarding loss prevention.

Question: Why do they lack this knowledge?
Answer: Because they haven't received any loss prevention training.

Question: Why haven't they received any loss prevention training?
Answer: Because the organization has reduced its training budget.

Question: Why did it reduce its training budget?
Answer: Because it received an inadequate return on investment for previous training programmes.

Question: Why didn't it achieve a return on investment for previous training?
Answer: Because the training provider failed to provide an adequate standard of training.

By following this method and repeatedly asking "why", you will be able to identify your core issues. Typically, it is always a single constraint or a few constraints; once these are removed from the organization, smooth functionality results.

Identify the Critical Success Factors:

In this section, we should identify the critical success factors required to be in place to allow us to move on to the solution stage. For example, one of the critical success factors required to reduce shoplifting would be to make the right merchandising decisions.

In order to make the right merchandising decisions, those in charge of merchandising must receive loss prevention training.

In order for them to receive loss prevention training you will need to get senior management buy-in.

In order for senior management to buy-in, they must be convinced that shoplifting prevents them from reaching their overall objective of making profit.

In order to get senior management to view shoplifting as a hindrance; store managers must be able to demonstrate the monetary value of shoplifting to senior management.

Identify the Solution:

The final step in the process is the solution stage. This is the stage where we arrive at the solution to the problem based upon the findings from the first two stages. At this stage we can identify the best solutions to address the core problem. In most cases, pinpointing the solution can be very easy assuming we were being honest with ourselves during the first two processes. Once we know the core problem and know the required conditions that need to be in place, all we need is to do is put those conditions in place. Thus, we can easily solve the problem.

Let's say we have identified merchandising as the core problem that is making shoplifting possible in our store. All we need are simple changes in policies and procedures for merchandising. What should be done to solve merchandising problems?

We need to place goods in more secure locations in the store.

Use the appropriate tags for high value goods.

Provide merchandising managers with loss prevention training.

Ensure coherent communication between store managers and head office with regards to merchandising.

Please Note:

We have created a template that will assist retailers identify the core constraint that is preventing them from reaching their objectives in relation to shoplifting.

We are aware that the dynamic in every organisation can be different. Therefore, the formula should only be used as a template to guide them in finding solutions to their own core constraints.

How to Apply the Lessons from This Part to Your Business

STEP 1
- Use the Ultimate Shoplifting Prevention Formula to identify the core problems with regards to shoplifting in your business

STEP 2
- Analyse your current policies and procedures to identify which ones facilitates shoplifting in your store.
- Modify or replace any policy or procedure that facilitates shoplifting.

STEP 3
- Provide your employees with comprehensive training in shoplifting prevention techniques.
- Remember they are your most effective arsenal against shoplifting.

STEP 4
- Strategically merchandise your goods; placing high value merchandise in more secure locations and smaller sized high value goods must be placed next to the cashier.
- Remember placing goods in locations that facilitate their easy removal from the store is basically putting them into the shoplifters hands.

STEP 5
- Make appropriate use of electronic tags.
- Use source tags whenever possible.

STEP 6
- Store design must take preventative measures into account such as ensuring exits and entrances are sufficient enough to serve the purpose of convenience for both customers and staff.

STEP 7
- Employ an excellent customer service strategy that makes legitimate customers feel welcome and shoplifters uncomfortable.
- Remember a shoplifter will always run away from an extra friendly retail employee.

STEP 8
- Train loss prevention personnel ensuring they are adequately trained to perform their duties.

STEP 9
- Improve your current loss prevention training and your capacity taking into account the new dynamic of organised retail crime.
- Remember organised retail crime is currently the main source of retail theft.

STEP 10
- Make effective use of technology.
- The current shoplifting technology used effectively can reduce your shoplifting problems significantly.

Chapter Seven

The Most Effective Retail Loss Prevention Technologies

Introduction

The effective use of the best retail technologies can increase a retailer's profit by 9.7% within 90 days. The return on investment (ROI) for any retail loss prevention technology can be easily calculated and benefits demonstrated right down to the last cent.

The origin of this part can be traced to an experience I had in my search for retail loss prevention technology for one of our clients. We had a client from the Middle East who came to us for retail loss prevention training. As a part of the training process, we were asked to provide advice to them regarding the latest loss prevention technologies currently being used in the UK.

I contacted several retail loss prevention technology merchants, setting up appointments to discuss their products. I noticed those companies did one of two things: 1) they sent out technicians, who were able to explain the functionality of their products in confusing 'techie' language, yet were unable to explain the ROI or 2) salesmen who lack the technical knowledge necessary to explain the functionality of the products. The final straw was a visit to a company in London that provides software support to the likes of Tesco, Marks & Spencer and many of the big retailers in the UK. Their sales rep gave us the mother of all boring and confusing presentations; when we left the meeting we were more confused than when we entered!

My client made their request very clear to them: at the time they had multiple supermarkets and hypermarkets that use three different systems, what they needed was a single system that would either combine the three systems or a new system that would perform the tasks of their current systems. They needed a receiving system that automatically indicated replenishment requirements with a direct link to their supply chain and a POS system that has CCTV integrated to enable them to detect exceptions and send a report directly to their head office.

Such systems and even some that perform more complex tasks do exist. However, finding a company with a good salesman who is able to clearly articulate the benefit of their products in addition to demonstrating its functionality proved remarkably difficult. Leaving the final meeting, it dawned on me that many retailers such as my client are clamouring for the right information to be able to make an informed decision before investing in loss prevention technology.

I thought to myself "I wish there was a guide that would list all the current retail technologies on the market, their functionalities, their ROI and where they can be sourced."

My aim here is not to endorse any specific technology over another, as I do not work for any technology company nor am I sponsored by any of them. This is a completely independent, objective, and non-biased retail loss prevention technology guide that has the simple goal of answering the following questions for retailers:

- What are the types of retail loss prevention technologies available?
- What are their functionalities including features and benefits
- What constraint do they diminish?
- Where can they be sourced?

- What policies and procedures helped retailers to operate without that technology?
- What policies and procedures should they put in place now to adapt to the new technology?
- Is the technology future-proof?

We have all at one time or another purchased technologies that have found their place amongst the junk in our cellar. We cannot even muster up the courage to get rid of them, even though we know that in a few months' time they will become obsolete. In a business environment, we cannot afford to allow a technological device to sit in our storeroom. The reason why we purchased it in the first place was for convenience; ease of production or to increase productivity. Redundant technology is not performing those functions; they simply create unnecessary expense by sitting in the office or storeroom.

This part will show you how to avoid making that sort of costly mistake and give you the steps to follow when considering investing in loss prevention technology.

Technologies That Prevent Employee Theft

The 2010 Global Retail Theft Barometer Report revealed that employee theft accounted for 43.7% ($17.2 billion) of retail shrinkage in the US. This figure far exceeded shoplifting, which accounted for 34.9% of their shrinkage. Employees taking advantage of their position of trust are capable of inflicting more damage on retailers than shoplifters. The average customer-related theft amounts to £66, while the average employee theft results in £1,318 of losses for a retailer. (Global Retail Theft Barometer Report 2010).

Given that employees have access to insider privileges, such as keys, security codes and most importantly the trust of their employers, it can be incredibly difficult to detect employee theft.

Except in situations where employees are blatantly dishonest, their actions can go undetected for months or even years on end. However, effective use of loss prevention technologies has resulted in a tremendous decrease in cases of employee theft.

Below are some of the most effective retail technologies, currently available, which can assist in reducing employee theft in the retail industry.

Exception-Based Reporting (EBR)

Exception based reporting (EBR) helps to identify instances of fraudulent activities that are likely to occur. EBR has increased retailers ability to identify suspicious activities without having to examine mountains of sales records.

EBR also analyses and encompasses all areas of the operation from the point of sale, to purchasing, receiving to merchandising.

How Does It Work?

STEP 1

- An employee commits fraud at the point of sale.

STEP 2

- The data is transmitted to loss prevention.

STEP 3

- Loss prevention checks the data to detect evidence of inconsistency or fraud.

STEP 4

- An investigation ensues with evidence from CCTV and reports. The evidence is precise to the time the incident occurred.

STEP 5

- The suspected employee is apprehended and disciplined.

Where Can EBR Technologies Be Sourced?

Aspect Loss Prevention

- Contact: Cheryl Blake
- 5735 W. Old Shakopee Road, Bloomington, MN 55437
- Telephone: 952-936-9280 or Fax: 952-936-9701
- Email: cblake@aspectlp.com
- Website: www.aspectlp.com

Lp Innovations

- 37 Birch Street, Milford, MA 01757
- Tel: 877-574-6682
- Email: solutions@lpinnovations.com

Gulfcoast Software Soultions

- Contact: Tim Lindblom
- 912 Drew St, Clearwater, FL 33755
- Telephone: 727-441-2131 or Fax: 813-436-5256
- Email: sales@gulfcoastsoftware.com
- Website: www.gulfcoastsoftware.com

Micros-retail

- 1800 W. Park Dr., Ste 250, Westboro, MA 01581
- Telephone: 888-328-2826 or Fax: 508-647-9495

- Email: info@micros-retail.com
- Website: www.micros-retail.com

Stoplift Checkout Vision Systems

- StopLift, Incorporated, Cambridge, Massachusetts.
- Telephone – 1.877.258.6424
- Call 866-426-2479 x703
- Email info@stoplift.com

Point of Sale Systems

Point of sale systems (POS) use complicated algorithms to track people and merchandise. These systems pick up items on the counter and determine whether someone is actually stood by or standing next to the counter. It allows loss prevention personnel to witness a transaction in real time as the system is shown on a computer screen or monitor that is connected to the CCTV system.

The data collected is stored and used to identify correlations between POS transaction reports and exception reports.

The data and video analytics give loss prevention personnel the ability to detect fraudulent cashier behaviours. It has proven to be very effective in cases involving void manipulation, merchandise passing and discount fraud.

How Does It Work?

STEP 1

- A cashier commits theft or fraudulent activity.

STEP 2

- Point of sale video analysis detects and records the fraudulent behaviour.

STEP 3

- Loss prevention personnel are alerted, they view the video analytics data, POS transaction reports and exception reports and make comparison for correlations.

STEP 4

- If there is evidence of wrong doing, an investigation is launched and employee responsible is disciplined.

Where Can POS Technologies Be Sourced?

Intelliq Professional

- UK Head Office: 2nd Floor, 36 Harbour Exchange Square, London, E14 9GE
- Telephone UK +44 (0)20 7517 1000
- USA Head Office: Waltham – Bay Colony Center, 2nd Floor, 1050 Winter Street, Suite 1000, Waltham, Massachusetts 02451
- Telephone USA +1-847-341-4893 / +1-312-622-2151
- Email: website@intelliq.com

Auto-star's POS Solutions

- Head Office: 147 Sixth Street SE, Medicine Hat, AB T1A 1G7, Canada
- North America: (888) 460-6963 or (403) 529-5595
- Australia: 1800 686 705
- Fax: (403) 528-2540
- Email: info@auto-star.com

Revionics

- Head Office: 2998 Douglas Blvd, Suite 350, Roseville, CA 95661
- Phone: (916) 797-6051 or (866) 580-RAPS (7277)

- Fax: (916) 797-6081

Protech Systems Co. Ltd

- Protech Building: No. 24, Lane 365, Yang Goang Street, Nei Hu Distric, Taipei 114, Taiwan
- Tel: +886-2-8751-1111
- Fax: +886-2-8751-1199

Electronic Journals

Electronic Journals record information of all transactions in a retail store. They collect information regarding credit card, gift card, refunds and void transactions at the point-of-sale.

How Does It Work?

STEP 1

- Customer enters the store and makes a purchase with their credit card.

STEP 2

- The electronic journal records the customer's credit card number.

STEP 3

- The store can then retrieve the information when they print receipts for the customer.

STEP 4

- The customer will then be able to link the purchase with their credit card information when they receive the receipt of the purchase.

Where Can Electronic Journals Be Sourced?

Se-kure Controls® Security Systems

- Email: jmang@se-kure.com
- USA: (847) 288-1111
- Fax: (847) 288-9999

Sir Solutions Inc

- 650-3565 East Jarry street, Montreal (QC) H1Z 4K6
- Toll free:1 800 264-9554
- Fax: 514 593-4810
- Email: info@sirsolutions.com

Access Pos

- Access POS, LLC, 990 Lone Oak Road, Ste.102, Eagan, MN 55121
- Tel USA: Toll Free: 800-521-3757 Or 651-209-3140
- Tel Outside USA: 011 +1-651-209-3140
- Email: customerservice@accesspos.com

Checkpoint Systems Inc.

- 101 Wolf Drive, Thorofare, NJ, USA
- Tel: 1-800-257-5540 or 1-800-257-5540

Technologies That Prevent Shoplifting

In the 2010 Global Retail Theft Barometer Report, shoplifting was revealed to be one of the biggest causes of retail shrinkage, except in the US. (Global Retail Theft Barometer Report 2010)

Shoplifting is a crime of opportunity; remove the opportunity and you reduce the possibility.

Modern anti-shoplifting technologies have proven to be very effective in reducing shoplifting when used effectively.

The best shoplifting technologies are known to reduce shoplifting by as much as 25% within the first 6 months after implementation.

However, as with any technology, the key phrase is: used effectively.

For example, some retailers install expensive CCTV, yet don't have it monitored; they may also have a single person monitoring multiple cameras. In some instances, CCTV is installed without consulting the loss prevention department. This can result in having an insufficient number of cameras and/or cameras being incorrectly positioned; engineers may not know all of the blind spots in the store.

To repeat this very significant point: *technology is beneficial only if it removes a constraint*. The main question each retailer needs to ask before investing in shoplifting technology is this:

Is shoplifting the core constraint or is it a symptom of deeper structural challenges within their organization?'

Facial Recognition

Facial recognition technology operates by scanning an individual's face as they enter the store and saving the data. This ensures that known shoplifters are immediately noticed as they enter the store before they have the opportunity to steal. If they are already banned from the store, they can be immediately escorted out by loss prevention personnel. The technology can also help in spotting unknown shoplifters. If an individual enters a store multiple times in a day without purchasing any item, that immediately raises suspicion. Facial recognition technology also helps loss prevention personnel maintain surveillance on any individual they deem suspicious.

How Does It Work?

STEP 1
- A shoplifter enters a shop

STEP 2
- The facial recognition system compares his/her face to known shoplifters

STEP 3
- If tile face matches a known shoplifter, or sane suspicious person

STEP 4
- The system alerts loss prevention personnel who either promptly escort the individual out of the store or keep an eye on him/her

STEP 5
- If the individual tries to steal something, being unaware that there is extra surveillance on him/her, loss prevention apprehends him/her.

Where Can Facial Recognition Technology Be Sourced?

Intellio
- Szerb Antal u.3, Budapest, H-1021, Hungary
- Tel: +36-1-220-4279
- Fax: +36-1-221-9216

Bottom of Basket

Bottom of basket technology detects items that are concealed at the bottom of shopping trolleys. Cashiers may not check shopping trolleys to ensure that all items were placed on the conveyor belt – many shoppers with sinister motives are aware of that. With this technology, items left in the trolley at the bottom will trigger a sound that alerts the cashier. At this point it is dependent on the cashier to act on the warning or choose to ignore it.

Sometimes, retailers mount mirrors on the checkout lane, or focus cameras on the bottom of trolleys with monitors placed at cashiers' desk. These systems are effective when cashiers are attentive. There are times when cashiers are distracted or simply too busy to pay attention to the monitor or mirror. In these instances, bottom of basket technology becomes increasingly useful, since it alerts cashiers of items left at the bottom of the trolley.

How Does It Work?

STEP 1
- A customer leaves some items at the bottom of the trolley

STEP 2
- As the cashier processes their order, an alarm sounds alerting the cashier that items are in the trolley that also need to be scanned.

STEP 3
- The cashier reacts based on the alarm, retrieves the items from the trolley and scans them

STEP 4
- There was no loss as customer pays for all their items

Where Can Bottom of Basket Technology Be Sourced?

Evolution Robotics Inc.

- USA Head Office: 433 N. Fair Oaks Avenue, Pasadena, CA 91103
- Phone: +1 (626) 773-7500
- Fax: +1 (626) 773-7540
- Germany Head Office: An der Maikammer 31, 42533 Velbert, Germany
- Phone: +49-2053-4913719
- Fax: +49-2053-50796
- Email: sales@evoretail.com

IBM Retail Store Solutions

- For customers with fewer than 1000 employees 877-IBM-ACCESS (877-426-2223)
- For large enterprise, government and education customers 888-839-9289
- Email: ews@us.ibm.com

Ceiling Mirrors

Ceiling mirrors perform two important functions in a retail store:

1. Complement electronic systems
2. Expose blind spots in the shop

This allows loss prevention personnel or store associates to keep watch on high value items. They are primarily used in convenience stores.

How Does It Work?

STEP 1
- A shoplifter conceals an item without knowing that loss prevention personnel or store staff are watching them through the mirror

STEP 2
- They attempt to leave the store.

STEP 3
- Loss prevention personnel approaches him/her at the store exit and confront them about the item that they have taken.

STEP 4
- The shoplifter is ultimately forced to hand over the item to the loss prevention personnel.

STEP 5
- The individual is either banned from the store or detained until Police arrives

Ink Tags

Ink tags are most commonly used by clothing retailers. When tags are attached to clothes, they need to be removed with special tag removers (which are kept at the till) before a shopper can leave the store with the clothes. If a shoplifter or anyone else attempts to force the tags off the clothing, the ink inside the tag spills out, staining the clothes, essentially damaging them.

However, shoplifters have managed to find a loophole that can bypass the system. Occasionally they use tape to seal off the holes of the tag, to prevent the ink from spilling out and staining the clothes. This only works with the tags in which the holes are actually visible, which is why it is advisable to invest in tags with tiny holes.

Another way to get around the ink tag technology is by freezing the clothes and the tag before attempting to remove the tag. In this way, the ink cannot spill since it is frozen.

How Does It Work?

STEP 1

- A shoplifter attempts to steal clothes.

STEP 2

- They notice that it has an ink tag attached.

STEP 3

- They try to forcibly remove the tag.

STEP 4

- The vials of ink inside the tag break, releasing ink that stains the clothes.

STEP 5

- The clothes are stained and no good to the shoplifter.

Where Can Ink Tags Be Sourced?

Sensortags Inc

- 5660 Roberts Rd, Terre Haute, IN 47805, USA
- Toll free USA & Canada: 800-934-7080 or 812-877-9930

Invotech UK Ltd

- Unit 19 Kepler, Lichfield Road Industrial Estate, Tamworth, Staffordshire B79 7XE, United Kingdom
- Tel: 01827 312136
- Fax: 01827 312137

- Email: info@invotech.co.uk

Theft Control Inc

- 31 Misty Meadow Drive, Boynton Beach, FL 33436
- Phone Toll Free: 1-877-757-7639
- Email: info@inktagpro.com

Unisen

- 512 NW 77th Street, Boca Industrial Park, Boca Raton, Florida 33487 USA
- Phone Toll Free: US+Canada 1-888 998 2299 or 561-998-9983
- Fax: +561-998-4897

Vitag Security And Technology

- Phone: Local: 1300 551 662
- International: +61 3 9894 8051
- Email: info@vitag.com.au

Electronic Article Surveillance (EAS)

The main function of an Electronic Article Surveillance system is to serve as a deterrent. This system involves using electronic security towers and electronic security tags. If a shoplifter attempts to steal a tagged item, as he approaches the exit, an alarm is triggered which alerts store staff and loss prevention personnel.

The tags that are attached to items are meant to be removed or deactivated at the till. However, when the tag is not removed, it triggers an alarm at the exit. Shoplifters are finding creative ways of removing the tags but the system still remains an effective one, especially against amateur shoplifters.

Dual Resonator EAS stickers placed on smaller items such as Gillette razor blades and Beecham's cold medicines can also act as an effective deterrent. They are more effective because they are difficult to remove, therefore making it difficult for shoplifters to steal.

How Does It Work?

STEP 1

- A shoplifter enters a store and conceals an item

STEP 2

- This item is fitted with an EAS tag.

STEP 3

- They proceed towards the exit where there is electronic security towers

STEP 4

- As they pass the security towers, an alarm sounds alerting store staff and loss prevention personnel

STEP 5

- Store security apprehend them and they are taken to custody.

Where Can EAS Be Sourced?

Aim Inc.

- Contact: Diana Bowser
- 125 Warrendale-Bayne Road, Suite 100, Warrendale, PA 15086
- Tel: +1 724-934-4470
- Fax: +1 724-934-4495
- Email: diana@aimglobal.org

Unisen

- 512 NW 77th Street, Boca Industrial Park, Boca Raton, Florida 33487 USA

- Phone Toll Free: US+Canada 1-888 998 2299 or 561-998-9983
- Fax: +561-998-4897

Checkpoint Systems, Inc.

- 101 Wolf Drive, Thorofare, NJ, USA
- Tel: +1-800-257-55

Receiving Technologies

The core function of an inventory control system is to reduce out-of-stock or unavailability. The latest inventory control systems use barcode scanning technology to track the movement of stock from the warehouse to the point-of-sale in order to prevent shortage and shrinkage.

The system uses hardware and software-based tools to automate the tracking of inventory within the system and request replenishment as needed. The systems work on live data through the use of wireless technologies which transmit information to a central computer system as transactions take place at the point-of-sale.

How Does It Work?

STEP 1
- A barcode is applied to an item.

STEP 2
- When the barcode is scanned, the data is read and stored.

STEP 3
- The data is transmitted to a central computer system which tells the system the item's status; still in stock or it sold therefore requiring replenishment.

STEP 4

- The appropriate department now takes the request based upon the information received.

Where Can Inventory Control Systems Be Sourced?

Manhattan Associates

- Telephone: +1 770-955-7070
- Email: info@manh.com

Check Point Systems Inc.

- 101 Wolf Drive, Thorofare, NJ, USA
- Tel: +1-800-257-55

Windward Software Inc.

- Suite 200 – 3547 Skaha Lake Road, Penticton, BC V2A 7K2
- Toll Free: (800) 663-5750
- Phone: (250) 492-8888
- Fax: (250) 492-8886
- Email: sales@wws5.com

Barcodes Inc

- Phone 1-800-351-9962
- Fax 1-312-212-1800
- Email: customerservice@barcodesinc.com

Multi-Purpose Technologies

The below technologies can be used as dual and multi-use technologies – as a result of their functionalities they can be effective in preventing any of the above shrinkage related challenges:

Credit Card Technology

Credit card theft is rampant both online as well as offline. This can be the result of a lack of proper control mechanisms to ensure cards are checked properly or the sheer sophistication of the individuals involved in the crime.

The increase in online shopping has also seen a simultaneous increase in credit card fraud. Furthermore, criminal elements are now using their own sophisticated technologies which enable them to easily place fake magnetic chips on cards to read or change card details.

Loss prevention technology companies have developed technologies that enable retailers to track credit card transactions and foil fraudulent ones before they occur. The ability to place a 'red flag' on a card that shows up when they are presented for transactions have somewhat reduced incidents of credit card fraud.

How Does It Work?

STEP 1
- An individual presents a card for payment at a till.

STEP 2
- An alert shows on the screen that the card is lost or stolen

STEP 3
- Cashier requests permission to call for authorisation

STEP 4
- The Individual either makes an excuse and leaves or is apprehended

Where Can Credit Card Technologies Be Sourced?

Cardsave

- Parkway Offices, Acorn Business Park, Moss Road, Grimsby, Lincolnshire, UK DN32 0LW
- Tel: 0800 5244 539
- Fax:0844 209 1510
- Email: info@cardsave.net

Retail Merchant Services Ltd

- Matrix House, North Fourth Street, Milton Keynes, MK9 1NJ
- Telephone: 0845 241 9960
- Email: sales@retailmerchantsservices.co.uk

123 Send Ltd

- Contact: 123 Hire Sales Team
- 120 Leman Street, London, E1 8EU
- Telephone: 0800 54 23 123
- Fax: 0800 54 27 123

Mobile Terminals

- Sales:
- Tel: 0845 459 4601
- Email: sales@mobile-terminals.co.uk
- Technical:
- Tel: 0845 459 4603
- Email: support@mobile-terminals.co.uk

CCTV

The integration of closed circuit television (CCTV) into other loss prevention technologies has dramatically improved the functionality and effectiveness of the device. Presently CCTV can be integrated into different types of loss prevention technologies allowing loss prevention personnel to have a birds-eye view of incidents as they occur. For example most sophisticated POS systems are now fitted with CCTV; enabling loss prevention personnel to either view fraud in real time or view them minutes after the incident occurs.

Furthermore, the technology has developed to the point that loss prevention personnel do not need to view hours of tape to find a specific incident. For example, when an exception occurs at a till a report is generated and sent straight to loss prevention providing details of the time the incident took place along with the images associated to that incident. CCTV can be utilized in all areas of store operations, whether in receiving, on the shop floor or in the warehouse.

How Does It Work?

STEP 1

- An exception occurs at the till

STEP 2

- A report is generated and automatically sent to the loss prevention department with the associated images

STEP 3

- Loss prevention personnel view the images and approach the individual concerned with evidence

STEP 4

- As a result of photographic evidence, the individual is apprehended without wasting loss prevention resources on hours of investigation.

Where Can CCTV Be Sourced?

Se-kure Controls® Security Systems

- Email: jmang@se-kure.com
- USA: (847) 288-1111
- Fax: (847) 288-9999

Quick Response CCTV

- 129 Streatham High Road, Streatham, London, SW16 1HJ
- www.qrcctv.co.uk

2020 Vision Systems Ltd

- 28 Northumberland Square, North Shields, NE30 1PW
- www.2020cctv.com

Merchandising Technologies

Another effective tool against shoplifting is the use of creative merchandising technologies. There are numerous types available depending on the level of protection required and the type of item to be protected.

Merchandising technologies are required to protect high value items such as Gillette razor blades, DVD's, electronic items, expensive alcohol and health and beauty products.

How Does It Work?

STEP 1

- Merchandise are either placed in sale boxes, glass displays, or other forms of merchandising security are attached to them

STEP 2

- When the items are forcefully removed from its position, an alarm is triggered notifying loss prevention personnel or the store manager.

STEP 3

- Loss prevention personnel move towards the spot the alarm was triggered and CCTV is immediately deployed to view everyone leaving the area.

STEP 4

- The culprit is apprehended and detained.

Where Can Merchandising Technologies Be Sourced?

Secure Merchandise Displays Ltd.

- 6 Westerman Close, Sawtry, Cambridgeshire, PE28 5PJ, UK
- Phone: 01480 210 908
- Fax: 01487 834 692
- Email: info@smd-l.com

Intelligent Loss Prevention

- 1400 Eddy Avenue, Rockford, IL 61103
- Phone: 800.747.4384
- Fax: 815.877.6563

FFR-DSI

- 8181 Darrow Road, Twinsburg, OH 44087
- Tel: (330) 998-7800 or (800) 422-2547
- Fax: (330) 998-7801 or (800) 422-2502
- Email: info@ffr-dsi.com

RFID Technology

Radio frequency Identification Device is arguably the most effective multi-purpose technology presently on the market. It has a variety of applications including: inventory control, product replenishment capability, receiving, product rotation, manifesting and product traceability. The beauty of this technology is its ability to track goods from the factory all the way through to the point-of-sale; greatly reducing the possibility of shrinkage, out-of-stock or products going missing in the store.

1. RFID shelf level monitoring technology ensures retailers do not lose sales due to out-of-stock or miscplacement
2. RFID customer loyalty card recognise customers and prompts promotions options based upon data from previous purchases
3. RFID technology enables swift inventory control resulting in counting reduction, minimising stock shortage and provides information on the amount of actual inventory on hand
4. RFID POS fosters faster checkout, resulting in queue reduction at checkout; increasing customer satisfaction

How Does It Work?

STEP 1
- A product is source tagged with RFID technology from the factory

STEP 2
- It is traced all through it journey from factory to supply chain all the way to store warehouse

STEP 3
- When received by store it immediately enters store inventory system

STEP 4

- Customer brings the item to the point-of-sale

STEP 5

- It immediately orders a replacement

Where Can RFID Technology Be Sourced?

Checkpoint Systems

- 101 Wolf Drive, Thorofare, NJ, USA
- Tel: +1-800-257-55

Hitachi Rfid Solutions

- RFID Solutions, System Solutions Division, Hitachi Europe Ltd, Whitebrook Park Lower Cookham Road, Maidenhead, Berkshire, SL6 8YA, United Kingdom
- Email: mu.solution@hitachi-eu.com

Barcode Technologies

- 9, Canalside, Northbridge Road, Berkhamsted, Hertfordshire, HP4 1EG
- Tel: 01442 872 232
- Fax: 01442 871 178
- Email: info@barcode-uk.com

Technology Summary

Technologies have historically been introduced by companies with the objective of creating convenience, increased productivity, automating processes, reducing overheads, capture events and information. Loss prevention technologies have brought tremendous benefit in term of waste reduction, increase efficiency, reduction in both internal and external fraud and theft.

Retailers who have integrated technologies into their loss prevention strategies continue to receive a rewarding ROI. The most successful retailers are those who have harnessed the power of technology effectively in combination with the appropriate policies and procedures.

Finally before investing in any loss prevention technology retailers must answer the following 7 fundamental questions:

- What are the types of retail loss prevention technologies available?
- What are their functionalities including features and benefits
- What constraint do they diminish?
- Where can they be sourced?
- What policies and procedures helped retailers to operate without that technology?
- What policies and procedures should they put in place now to adapt to the new technology?
- Is the technology future-proof?

Summary

Since 2007, twenty-four thousand four hundred and forty-six (24, 446) large and medium size retail stores close down resulting in two hundred and nineteen thousand five hundred and two thousand (219,502) retail staff losing their jobs.

These days, one can almost walk around the High Street and take a bet with hundred per cent accuracy on which High Street retailer will be out of business the next week, month or year.

If someone was to place a gun to my head and force me to choose the top five High Street retailers who will cease to exist five years from today, my pick will be the following:

- PC World
- Staples
- WH Smith
- HMV
- Dixons

When they eventually close shop, they will blame the recession and difficult trading conditions.

However, what I have proved in this books is, success or failure in retail has little to do with external factors.

Retailers fail because they do not give thought to the things we have discussed in this book. It is my hope that you immediately put the information you have learnt into action in your business.

I have tried to make the information as practical as possible in order for them to be easily implemented. I have done my part, it is your turn.

Good luck!

Great Books by Romeo

Book Romeo now!
+44(0)78 650 49508
romeo@theprofitexperts.co.uk

27.9% The Most Effective Retail Shrinkage Reduction Technologies

Prior to investing in any technology, there are vital questions that need to answered; those questions along with their answers can be found in this e-book.

This e-book was conceived out of our own desperate efforts to answer those questions.

What you will learn:
- Technologies That Prevent Employee Theft
- Technologies That Prevent Shoplifting

- Receiving Technologies
- Multi-purpose Technologies

12.24% The Most Effective Retail Employee Error Reduction Strategies

Employee errors in pricing, accounting and receiving contribute approximately 18% of retail shrinkage; this equates to £18,623 in losses to an average supermarket or store and almost £49,679 in losses to a superstore. This means that a store or supermarket that operates with a 1% net profit will need to make an additional £3million in annual sales in order to recover profit lost due to employee errors. By the same measure a typical hyper store will need to increase its sales by £8million.

You will learn:

- Constitutes as Retail Employee Error
- to Calculate the Cost of Employee Error
- to Calculate Additional Sales Required to Recover Losses Caused by Employee Error
- of Employee Error
- to Reduce Employee Error
- Ultimate Employee Error Prevention Formula
- to Apply the Lessons from This E-Book to Your Business

43.5% The Most Effective Retail Profit Protection Strategies

The retail landscape is changing rapidly with the constant increase in internet shopping. From 2005 to 2009, the online shopping population grew to 1.6 billion.

It is predicted to rise to 2.3 billion by 2014 with gross revenue totalling $778.6 billion. This is bad news for traditional brick and mortar retail businesses.

The question is: are you prepared? You will find your answer in this eBook.

What you will learn:
- The Conventional Approach to Loss prevention
- Why Loss Prevention is Critical to Retail
- Loss Prevention Spending vs Return on Investment
- What You Are Losing
- Profit vs Sales Calculation
- How to Create a Culture of Loss Prevention
- Effective Shrinkage Management Strategies
- The Ultimate Profit Protection Formula

24.5% The Most Effective Perishable And Non-Perishable Shrinkage Reduction Strategies

This e-book is jam packed with information on the causes of retail shrinkage, types of retail shrinkage, the cost of shrinkage to the retail industry and how shrinkage can be prevented. It is a comprehensive e-book on how and why shrinkage occurs and it provides a step-by-step guide on how to prevent shrinkage.

You will learn:

- An Introduction to Perishable Shrinkage
- Breakdown of Perishable Shrinkage
- Causes of Perishable Shrinkage
- How to Prevent Perishable Shrinkage
- The Ultimate Perishable Shrinkage Prevention Formula
- An Introduction to Non-Perishable Shrinkage
- Classification of Non-Perishable Shrinkage
- Breakdown of Non-Perishable Shrinkage
- Strategies for Preventing Non-Perishable Shrinkage
- The Ultimate Non-Perishable Shrinkage Prevention Formula
- How to Apply The Lessons From This E-Book to Your Business

27.8% The Most Effective Retail Employee Theft Reduction Strategies

The majority of retail employees are decent people who go to work each day to serve their customers and make their living.

However, there are the rotten apples that contaminate the good names of the rest.

This e-book is an instructional guide to retailers to show them how to minimise and prevent employee theft in their stores. Like shoplifting most incidents of employee theft occur because the opportunity exists. When retailers remove the opportunity, they can reduce the possibilities. This e-book will show retailers how to remove the opportunities that allow employee theft in their stores.

You will learn:

- Why Employees Steal
- The Process of Employee Theft
- Signs of Employee Theft
- How to Calculate the Cost of Employee Theft
- How to Prevent Employee Theft
- How Technology Can Help Prevent Employee Theft
- The Ultimate Employee Theft Prevention Formula

84%: The Most Effective Strategies for Increasing Retail Profit

The formula for increasing profit in retail is to increase sales and reduce shrinkage. How can retailers increase sales and reduce shrinkage? The answer is in this book.

You will learn everything you need to know about:

- Creating a Culture of Loss Prevention
- Employee Error
- Employee Theft
- Shoplifting
- Perishable and Non-Perishable Shrinkage
- Receiving Shrinkage
- Technologies that Help to Reduce Retail Shrinkage

Visual Merchandise: How to Create a Beautiful Yet Profitable Display

Merchandise display is the most effective form of advertising for a retail store. The more attractive a display, the higher the possibility of increasing sales. This book will show retailers how to create a display that is so attractive that it would increase their footfall tenfold.

You will learn:

- The psychology behind visual merchandising
- How to use visual merchandising to increase retail sales
- Challenges facing visual merchandisers
- How to burst the price myth with creative merchandise display
- The best merchandise display strategies
- How to maximise display space allocation with creative fixtures
- The pros and cons of using a planogram
- The pros and cons of hiring visual merchandising companies
- Most effective visual merchandise technologies
- How to display merchandise for maximum profit

Store Design Blueprint: How to Design an Attractive But Profitable Store

There are three fundamental principles that underpin a retail store design:

1. Attract customers as they pass by the store
2. Entice them to enter the store
3. Persuade them to buy

The aim of this book is to show retailers how to apply these principles to this store design.

You will learn:

- Store design psychology – what you must know to succeed
- Store design – Image selling
- How to use store design to increase sales
- Store design for increased customer flow
- Choosing your store colour and layout
- The best retail store lighting system
- How to wow customers with creative storefront design
- How to choose the right materials for store design
- Designing store for profit – design security
- Store design technologies

How to Market and Manage A Professional Firm Series: How to make 7 Figure annually as a doctor, dentist, accountant, lawyer, consultant and private security firm owner.

There are four elements essential for the success of any business:

1. Visionary leadership
2. Great people
3. Good system
4. Good marketing system

In the How to Market and Manage A Professional Firm Series, we teach professional entrepreneurs how to effectively utilize these four elements for the development of their businesses.

Many professionals are good technicians. They are good at their professions, however, when it comes to running business they are challenged.

The aim of the 7 Figure Code Books Series is to show professionals how to enhance their technical skills and apply similar levels of structural thinking into building a 7 Figure business.

There is no reason why a doctor or lawyer should not be able to easily make 7 Figure per annum. We show them how to achieve this in the How to Market and Manage A Professional Firm Series.

You will learn:

- How to create an effective business system that runs on auto-pilot
- How to recruit and retain only top talents
- How to develop an effective marketing system
- How to create new market for a product or service
- How the attract new clients and retain existing ones

Book Romeo

Book Romeo now by calling:
+44(0)78 650 49508
Or email: romeo@theprofitexperts.co.uk

www.ingramcontent.com/pod-product-compliance
Lightning Source LLC
Chambersburg PA
CBHW051621170526
45167CB00001B/21